A TEXTBOOK OF ENGINEERING MATHEMATICS

A TEXTBOOK OF

ENGINEERING MATHEMATICS

For

B.TECH. (5th *Semester*)

Computer Science and Information Technology
FOR MAHATMA GANDHI UNIVERSITY, KOTTAYAM, KERALA
(Strictly According to the Latest Syllabus)

By

N.P. BALI
Former Principal
S.B. College, Gurgaon
Haryana

JAYASREE. T.G.
Asst. Professor in Mathematics
Adishankara Institute of
Engineering and Technology Kalady,
Kerala

UNIVERSITY SCIENCE PRESS

(An Imprint of Laxmi Publications Pvt. Ltd.)

BANGALORE • CHENNAI • COCHIN • GUWAHATI • HYDERABAD
JALANDHAR • KOLKATA • LUCKNOW • MUMBAI • RANCHI
NEW DELHI • BOSTON, USA

Published by :

UNIVERSITY SCIENCE PRESS

(*An Imprint of Laxmi Publications Pvt. Ltd.*)

113, Golden House, Daryaganj,
New Delhi-110002

Phone : 011-43 53 25 00
Fax : 011-43 53 25 28

www.laxmipublications.com
info@laxmipublications.com

First Edition : 2013

OFFICES

India

✆ **Bangalore**	080-26 61 15 61	✆ **Jalandhar**	0181-222 12 72
✆ **Chennai**	044-24 34 47 26	✆ **Kolkata**	033-22 27 43 84
✆ **Cochin**	0484-237 70 04, 405 13 03	✆ **Lucknow**	0522-220 95 78
✆ **Guwahati**	0361-254 36 69, 251 38 81	✆ **Mumbai**	022-24 91 54 15, 24 92 78 69
✆ **Hyderabad**	040-24 65 23 33	✆ **Ranchi**	0651-221 47 64

UEM-9681-125-ENGG MATH V MGU (KE)-JAY C—

Typeset at : Goswami Associates, Delhi. *Printed at* : Repro Knowledgecast Limited, Thane

CONTENTS

PREFACE

The objective of this book is to provide the readers with the thorough understanding of the topics included in the courses of Computer Science in an easy and simple way. The topics which are very relevant with respect to university syllabus are fully covered by this book and will support in self study. Each module of this book covers the latest syllabus prescribed by Mahatma Gandhi University (MGU) for the fifth semester of B.Tech. Courses in Computer Science.

Almost all problems are worked out and additional problems are incorporated from latest Mahatma Gandhi University Question papers to increase the flavor of the book.

All efforts have been made to keep the book free from errors. Although suggestions and recommendations for the improvement of the book, are invited.

We wish our readers good luck for brilliant success in life.

—Authors

SYLLABUS

EN010501 B ENGINEERING MATHEMATICS–IV

(CS, IT)

Teaching sheme **Credits 4**

2 hours lecture and 2 hour tutorial per week

Objective: *To use basic numerical techniques for solving problems and to know the importance of learning theories in mathematics and in queueing system.*

Module 1 : Finite differences (12 hours)

Finite difference operators Δ, ∇, E, μ, δ-interpolation using Newtons forward and backward formula—Newton's divided difference formula—Numerical differentiation using Newtons forward and backward formula—Numerical integration—Trapezoidal rule—Simpsons $1/3^{rd}$ and $3/8^{th}$ rule.

Module 2 : Z transforms (12 hours)

Definition of Z transforms—transform of polynomial function and trignometric functions—shifting property, convolution property-inverse transformation—solution of 1st and 2nd order difference equations with constant coefficients using Z transforms.

Module 3 : Discrete numeric functions (12 hours)

Discrete numeric functions—Manipulations of numeric functions-generating functions—Recurrence relations—Linear recurrence relations with constant coefficients—Homogeneous solutions—Particular solutions—Total solution—solution by the method of generating functions.

Module 4 : Complex integration (12 hours)

Functions of complex variable—analytic function—Line integral—Cauchy's integral theorem—Cauchy's integral formula—Taylor's series, Laurent's series—Zeros and singularities—types of singularities—Residues—Residue theorem—evaluation of real integrals in unit circle—Contour integral in semi circle when poles lie on imaginary axis.

Module 5 : Queueing Theory (12 hours)

General concepts—Arrival pattern—service pattern—Queue disciplines—The Markovian model $M/M/1/\infty$, M/M/1/N—steady state solutions—Little's formula.

MODULE 1
Finite Differences

1.1. THE FORWARD DIFFERENCE OPERATOR Δ

Let $y = f(x)$.

The values, which the independent variable x takes, are called *arguments* and the corresponding values of $f(x)$ are called *entries*. The difference between consecutive values of x is called the *interval of differencing*.

If the interval of differencing be h and the first argument be a, then

Arguments x	:	a,	$a + h$,	$a + 2h$,	$a + 3h$,	......
Entries f(x)	:	$f(a)$,	$f(a + h)$,	$f(a + 2h)$,	$f(a + 3h)$,	......

For brevity, these entries are denoted by

$$y_0, \quad y_1, \quad y_2, \quad y_3, \ \ldots\ldots$$

$y_1 - y_0 = f(a + h) - f(a)$ is called the *first forward difference* of y_0 and is denoted by Δy_0 or $\Delta f(a)$. Thus

$$\Delta y_0 = y_1 - y_0 \quad \text{or} \quad \Delta f(a) = f(a + h) - f(a)$$

Similarly, $\Delta y_1 = y_2 - y_1, \quad \Delta y_2 = y_3 - y_2$

In general, $\Delta y_n = y_{n+1} - y_n \quad \text{or} \quad \Delta f(x) = f(x + h) - f(x)$

The differences of the first forward differences are called second forward differences. Thus

$\Delta (\Delta y_0) = \Delta (y_1 - y_0)$ or $\Delta^2 y_0 = \Delta y_1 - \Delta y_0$ is called the second forward difference of y_0.

Similarly,

$$\Delta^2 y_1 = \Delta y_2 - \Delta y_1, \quad \Delta^2 y_2 = \Delta y_3 - \Delta y_2$$

In general, $\Delta^2 y_n = \Delta y_{n+1} - \Delta y_n$

Similarly, we can define differences of higher order.

The table showing the various forward differences is called forward *differences table* and is given below.

Argument x	*Entry* y	*First Diff.* Δy	*Second Diff.* $\Delta^2 y$	*Third Diff.* $\Delta^3 y$
a	y_0			
		$y_1 - y_0 = \Delta \mathbf{y_0}$		
$a + h$	y_1		$\Delta y_1 - \Delta y_0 = \Delta^2 \mathbf{y_0}$	
		$y_2 - y_1 = \Delta y_1$		$\Delta^2 y_1 - \Delta^2 y_0 = \Delta^3 \mathbf{y_0}$
$a + 2h$	y_2		$\Delta y_2 - \Delta y_1 = \Delta^2 y_1$	
		$y_3 - y_2 = \Delta y_2$		
$a + 3h$	y_3			

y_0 is called the leading term and $\Delta y_0, \Delta^2 y_0, \Delta^3 y_0, \ldots\ldots$ are called the leading differences.

The operator Δ has the following properties :

(*i*) $\Delta c = 0$, c being a constant.

(*ii*) $\Delta cf(x) = c\,\Delta f(x)$

(*iii*) $\Delta\,[a\,f(x) + bg(x)] = a\,\Delta f(x) + b\,\Delta g(x)$

(*iv*) The nth difference of an nth degree polynomial is a constant = (co-eff. of x^n) $n\,!\,.\,h^n$ and hence higher order differences are zero.

ILLUSTRATIVE EXAMPLES

Example 1. *Prove that :*

(*i*) $\Delta\,[f(x)\,g(x)] = f(x+h)\,\Delta g(x) + g(x)\,\Delta f(x)$ (*ii*) $\Delta\left[\dfrac{f(x)}{g(x)}\right] = \dfrac{g(x)\,\Delta f(x) - f(x)\,\Delta g(x)}{g(x+h)\,g(x)}$.

Sol. (*i*)
$$\begin{aligned}\Delta\,[f(x)\,g(x)] &= f(x+h)\,g(x+h) - f(x)\,g(x)\\ &= f(x+h)\,g(x+h) - f(x+h)\,g(x) + f(x+h)\,g(x) - f(x)\,g(x)\\ &= f(x+h)\,[g(x+h) - g(x)] + g(x)\,[f(x+h) - f(x)]\\ &= f(x+h)\,\Delta g(x) + g(x)\,\Delta f(x).\end{aligned}$$

(*ii*)
$$\Delta\left[\frac{f(x)}{g(x)}\right] = \frac{f(x+h)}{g(x+h)} - \frac{f(x)}{g(x)} = \frac{f(x+h)\,g(x) - f(x)\,g(x+h)}{g(x+h)\,g(x)}$$
$$= \frac{f(x+h)\,g(x) - f(x)\,g(x) + f(x)\,g(x) - f(x)\,g(x+h)}{g(x+h)\,g(x)}$$
$$= \frac{g(x)\,[f(x+h) - f(x)] - f(x)[g(x+h) - g(x)]}{g(x+h)\,g(x)} = \frac{g(x)\,\Delta f(x) - f(x)\,\Delta g(x)}{g(x+h)\,g(x)}.$$

Example 2. *Evaluate the following, interval of differencing being unity.*

(*i*) $\Delta\,tan^{-1}\,ax$ (*ii*) $\Delta\left(\dfrac{2^x}{(x+1)\,!}\right)$ (*iii*) $\Delta\left(\dfrac{e^x}{e^x + e^{-x}}\right)$ (*iv*) $\Delta\,(e^{2x}\,log\,3x)$.

Sol. (*i*) $\Delta\,\tan^{-1} ax = \tan^{-1} a(x+1) - \tan^{-1} ax$
$$= \tan^{-1}\frac{a(x+1) - ax}{1 + a(x+1)\,.\,ax} = \tan^{-1}\frac{a}{1 + a^2x + a^2x^2}.$$

(*ii*)
$$\Delta\left(\frac{2^x}{(x+1)\,!}\right) = \frac{2^{x+1}}{(x+2)\,!} - \frac{2^x}{(x+1)\,!} = \frac{2^{x+1} - 2^x(x+2)}{(x+2)\,!} = \frac{2^{x+1} - x\,.\,2^x - 2^{x+1}}{(x+2)\,!} = -\frac{x\,.\,2^x}{(x+2)\,!}.$$

(*iii*)
$$\Delta\left(\frac{e^x}{e^x + e^{-x}}\right) = \frac{e^{x+1}}{e^{x+1} + e^{-(x+1)}} - \frac{e^x}{e^x + e^{-x}}$$
$$= \frac{e^{2x+1} + e - e^{2x+1} - e^{-1}}{[e^{x+1} + e^{-(x+1)}]\,(e^x + e^{-x})} = \frac{e - e^{-1}}{(e^{x+1} + e^{-x-1})\,(e^x + e^{-x})}.$$

(*iv*)
$$\begin{aligned}\Delta\,(e^{2x}\log 3x) &= e^{2(x+1)}\log 3(x+1) - e^{2x}\log 3x\\ &= e^{2(x+1)}\log 3(x+1) - e^{2(x+1)}\log 3x + e^{2(x+1)}\log 3x - e^{2x}\log 3x\\ &= e^{2(x+1)}\,[\log 3(x+1) - \log 3x] + [e^{2(x+1)} - e^{2x}]\log 3x\end{aligned}$$

$$= e^{2x+2} \log \frac{3(x+1)}{3x} + e^{2x}(e^2 - 1) \log 3x$$

$$= e^{2x}\left[e^2 \log\left(1+\frac{1}{x}\right) + (e^2 - 1)\log 3x\right].$$

Example 3. *Evaluate the following, interval of differencing being h:*

(*i*) $\Delta\,(x^2 + \sin x)$ (*ii*) $\Delta\,(\sin 2x \cos 4x)$ (*iii*) $\Delta \cot a^x$ (*iv*) $\Delta\left(\frac{x^2}{\sin 2x}\right)$.

Sol. (*i*) $\Delta\,(x^2 + \sin x) = \Delta x^2 + \Delta \sin x$

$$= [(x+h)^2 - x^2] + [\sin(x+h) - \sin x]$$

$$= 2hx + h^2 + 2\cos\left(x+\frac{h}{2}\right)\sin\frac{h}{2}$$

$$= h(h+2x) + 2\sin\frac{h}{2}\cos\left(x+\frac{h}{2}\right)$$

(*ii*) $\Delta(\sin 2x \cos 4x) = \Delta\,(\tfrac{1}{2}\,.\,2\cos 4x \sin 2x)$

$$= \tfrac{1}{2}\,\Delta\,(\sin 6x - \sin 2x) = \tfrac{1}{2}\,(\Delta \sin 6x - \Delta \sin 2x)$$

$$= \tfrac{1}{2}\,[\{\sin 6(x+h) - \sin 6x\} - \{\sin 2(x+h) - \sin 2x\}]$$

$$= \tfrac{1}{2}\,[2\cos(6x+3h)\sin 3h - 2\cos(2x+h)\sin h]$$

$$= \sin 3h \cos 3(2x+h) - \sin h \cos(2x+h)$$

(*iii*) $$\Delta \cot a^x = \cot a^{x+h} - \cot a^x = \frac{\cos a^{x+h}}{\sin a^{x+h}} - \frac{\cos a^x}{\sin a^x}$$

$$= \frac{\sin a^x \cos a^{x+h} - \cos a^x \sin a^{x+h}}{\sin a^{x+h} \sin a^x} = \frac{\sin(a^x - a^{x+h})}{\sin a^{x+h} \sin a^x} = \frac{\sin a^x(1-a^h)}{\sin a^{x+h} \sin a^x}$$

(*iv*) $$\Delta\left(\frac{x^2}{\sin 2x}\right) = \frac{(x+h)^2}{\sin 2(x+h)} - \frac{x^2}{\sin 2x} = \frac{(x+h)^2 \sin 2x - x^2 \sin 2(x+h)}{\sin 2(x+h)\sin 2x}$$

$$= \frac{(x+h)^2 \sin 2x - x^2 \sin 2x + x^2 \sin 2x - x^2 \sin 2(x+h)}{\sin 2(x+h)\sin 2x}$$

$$= \frac{[(x+h)^2 - x^2]\sin 2x - x^2\,[\sin 2(x+h) - \sin 2x]}{\sin 2(x+h)\sin 2x}$$

$$= \frac{h(h+2x)\sin 2x - 2x^2 \sin h \cos(2x+h)}{\sin 2(x+h)\sin 2x}.$$

Example 4. *Evaluate the following, the interval of differencing being h:*

(*i*) $\Delta^2\,(\cos 2x)$ (*ii*) $\Delta^2\,(ab^x)$

(*iii*) $\Delta^n\,a^{cx+d}$ (*iv*) $\Delta^n \cos\,(cx+d)$.

Sol. (*i*) $\Delta \cos 2x = \cos 2(x+h) - \cos 2x$

$$= -\,2\sin(2x+h)\sin h = -\,2\sin h \sin(2x+h)$$

$$\Delta^2 \cos 2x = \Delta(\Delta \cos 2x)$$
$$= \Delta(-2 \sin h \sin (2x + h)) = -2 \sin h \, \Delta \sin (2x + h)$$
$$= -2 \sin h [\sin \{2(x + h) + h\} - \sin (2x + h)]$$
$$= -2 \sin h \,.\, 2 \cos (2x + 2h) \sin h = -h \sin^2 h \cos (2x + 2h).$$

(ii) $$\Delta(a\, b^x) = a\, \Delta(b^x) = a\,(b^{x+h} - b^x) = a\, b^x (b^h - 1) = a\,(b^h - 1)\, b^x$$
$$\Delta^2 (ab^x) = \Delta(\Delta\, ab^x) = \Delta[a(b^h - 1)\, b^x]$$
$$= a\,(b^h - 1)\,\Delta b^x = a\,(b^h - 1)\,.\, b^x (b^h - 1) = a\,(b^h - 1)^2 \,.\, b^x.$$

(iii) $$\Delta\, a^{cx+d} = a^{c(x+h)+d} - a^{cx+d} = a^{cx+d} \,.\, (a^{ch} - 1) = (a^{ch} - 1)\, a^{cx+d}$$
$$\Delta^2 a^{cx+d} = \Delta(\Delta\, a^{cx+d}) = \Delta\,(a^{ch} - 1)\, a^{cx+d}$$
$$= (a^{ch} - 1)\,\Delta\, a^{cx+d} = (a^{ch} - 1)(a^{ch} - 1)\, a^{cx+d} = (a^{ch} - 1)^2\, a^{cx+d}$$

Similarly, $\Delta^3 a^{cx+d} = (a^{ch} - 1)^3 \,.\, a^{cx+d}$ and so on

Generalising, $\Delta^n a^{cx+d} = (a^{ch} - 1)^n \,.\, a^{cx+d}$.

(iv) $$\Delta \cos (cx + d) = \cos [c(x + h) + d] - \cos (cx + d)$$
$$= -2 \sin \left(cx + d + \frac{ch}{2}\right) \sin \frac{ch}{2}$$
$$= 2 \sin \frac{ch}{2} \cos \left[cx + d + \frac{ch}{2} + \frac{\pi}{2}\right] \qquad \left[\because\ -\sin\theta = \cos\left(\frac{\pi}{2} + \theta\right)\right]$$
$$= 2 \sin \frac{ch}{2} \cos \left[cx + d + \frac{ch + \pi}{2}\right]$$

Thus the first difference of $\cos (cx + d)$ is obtained by multiplying by the constant factor $2 \sin \frac{ch}{2}$ and increasing the angle by $\frac{ch + \pi}{2}$.

$$\Delta^2 \cos (cx + d) = \Delta[\Delta \cos (cx + d)]$$
$$= \Delta\left[2 \sin \frac{ch}{2} \cos \left(cx + d + \frac{ch + \pi}{2}\right)\right]$$
$$= 2 \sin \frac{ch}{2}\, \Delta \cos \left(cx + d + \frac{ch + \pi}{2}\right)$$
$$= 2 \sin \frac{ch}{2} \,.\, 2 \sin \frac{ch}{2} \cos \left[cx + d + 2\left(\frac{ch + \pi}{2}\right)\right]$$
$$= \left(2 \sin \frac{ch}{2}\right)^2 \cos \left[cx + d + 2\left(\frac{ch + \pi}{2}\right)\right]$$

Similarly, $\Delta^3 \cos (cx + d) = \left(2 \sin \frac{ch}{2}\right)^3 \cos \left[cx + d + 3\left(\frac{ch + \pi}{2}\right)\right]$

....

....

Generalising, $\Delta^n \cos (cx + d) = \left(2 \sin \frac{ch}{2}\right)^n \cos \left[cx + d + n\left(\frac{ch + \pi}{2}\right)\right]$.

1.2. DIFFERENCES OF FACTORIAL POLYNOMIAL

If n is a positive integer, then the expression

$$x(x-h)\,(x-2h)\,......(x-\overline{n-1}h)$$

involving n factors, beginning with x and decreasing by h every time, is called a factorial polynomial of degree n and is denoted by $x^{(n)}$.

For example, $x^{(1)} = x,\ x^{(2)} = x(x-h),\ x^{(3)} = x(x-h)\,(x-2h)$

$$\Delta\, x^{(n)} = (x+h)^{(n)} - x^{(n)}$$

$$= [(x+h)\,(x)\,(x-h)\ ......\ (x-\overline{n-2}\,h)]$$

$$- [x(x-h)\ ......\ (x-\overline{n-2}\,h)\,(x-\overline{n-1}\,h)]$$

$$= x(x-h)\ ......\ (x-\overline{n-2}\,h)\ [(x+h)-(x-\overline{n-1}h)]$$

$$= nh\,.\,x(x-h)\ ......\ (x-\overline{n-2}\,h) = nh\,.\,x^{(n-1)}$$

Similarly, $\Delta^2\, x^{(n)} = \Delta\,(x^{(n)}) = nh\ \Delta x^{(n-1)}$

$$= nh\,.\,(n-1)\,h\,x^{(n-2)} = n(n-1)\,h^2\,x^{(n-2)}$$

$$\Delta^3\, x^{(n)} = n(n-1)\,(n-2)\,h^3\,x^{(n-3)}$$

....

$$\Delta^n\ x^{(n)} = n(n-1)(n-2)\ ......\ 2\,.\,1\ h^n = n\,!\,.\,h^n = \text{constant}$$

$$\Delta^{n+1}\,x^{(n)} = 0$$

Note. If $h = 1,\ \Delta\,x^{(n)} = nx^{(n-1)}$.

⇒ Differencing is analogous to differentiation.

⇒ The process of getting the function whose first differences are given is analogous to integration.

Example 5. *Express the function $f(x) = 2x^3 + 3x^2 - 5x + 4$ and its successive differences in factorial notation. Also obtain a function whose first difference is $f(x)$.*

Sol. We first express $f(x)$ in factorial notation.

Let $f(x) = A_0\,x^{(3)} + A_1\,x^{(2)} + A_2\,x^{(1)} + A_3$

1	2	3	– 5	$4 = A_3$
		2	5	
2	2	5	$0 = A_2$	
		4		
	2	$9 = A_1$		
	$2 = A_0$			

[**Explanation.** Write the co-efficients of $f(x)$ in the first row. Divide $f(x)$ by x. The remainder is $4 = A_3$ and the quotient is $2x^2 + 3x - 5$. Separate the remainder from the quotient by drawing a vertical line. Divide $2x^2 + 3x - 5$ by $x - 1$. For this, draw a vertical line to the left of the leading co-efficient 2 and write 1 to its left. In the quotient, the leading co-efficients is 2. Multiply 2 by 1 and add the product to 3, thus getting 5. Multiply 5 by 1 and add the product to – 5, thus getting 0. The remainder is $0 = A_2$ and the quotient is $2x + 5$. Divide $(2x + 5)$ by $x - 2$. For this, write 2 to the left of the vertical line. In the quotient, the leading co-efficient is 2. Multiply 2 by 2 and add the product 4 to 5, thus getting 9. The remainder is $9 = A_1$ and the quotient is 2. This last quotient, which is a constant, is A_0.

Thus A_3, A_2, A_1, A_0 are the successive remainders in the division of $f(x)$ by x, $x-1$, $x-2$]

$\therefore \quad f(x) = 2x^{(3)} + 9x^{(2)} + 4 \; ; \qquad \Delta f(x) = 6x^{(2)} + 9x^{(1)}$

$\Delta^2 f(x) = 12x^{(1)} + 9 \; ; \qquad \Delta^3 f(x) = 12$

Differences of higher order are zero.

Now, let $F(x)$ be the function whose first difference is $f(x)$. Then,

$$\Delta F(x) = f(x)$$

$$\Rightarrow \quad F(x) = \frac{1}{\Delta} f(x) = \frac{1}{\Delta} [2x^{(3)} + 9x^{(2)} + 4] = 2 \,.\, \frac{x^{(4)}}{4} + 9 \,.\, \frac{x^{(3)}}{3} + 4 \,.\, x^{(1)} + c$$

$$= \frac{1}{2} \,.\, x(x-1)(x-2)(x-3) + 3x(x-1)(x-2) + 4x + c$$

$$= \frac{1}{2} [x(x^3 - 6x^2 + 11x - 6) + 6x(x^2 - 3x + 2) + 8x] + c$$

$$= \frac{1}{2} (x^4 - 7x^2 + 14x) + c.$$

1.3. BACKWARD DIFFERENCE OPERATOR ∇

The backward difference operator ∇ is defined by

$$\nabla y_n = y_n - y_{n-1} \quad \text{or} \quad \nabla f(a) = f(a) - f(a-h)$$

Thus $\quad \nabla y_0 = y_0 - y_{-1}, \qquad \nabla y_1 = y_1 - y_0 \; \nabla y_2 = y_2 - y_1$ etc.

$$\nabla^2 y_0 = \nabla(\nabla y_0) = \nabla(y_0 - y_{-1}) = \nabla y_0 - \nabla y_{-1}$$

$$\nabla^2 y_1 = \nabla y_1 - \nabla y_0, \; \nabla^2 y_2 = \nabla y_2 - \nabla y_1 \text{ etc.}$$

The table showing the various backward differences is called backward difference table given below.

x	y	∇y	$\nabla^2 y$	$\nabla^3 y$
$a-3h$	y_{-3}			
		$y_{-2} - y_{-3} = \nabla y_{-2}$		
$a-2h$	y_{-2}		$\nabla y_{-1} - \nabla y_{-2} = \nabla^2 y_{-1}$	
		$y_{-1} - y_{-2} = \nabla y_{-1}$		$\nabla^2 y_0 - \nabla^2 y_{-1} = \nabla^3 \mathbf{y}_0$
$a-h$	y_{-1}		$\nabla y_0 - \nabla y_{-1} = \nabla^2 \mathbf{y}_0$	
		$y_0 - y_{-1} = \nabla y_0$		
a	y_0			

1.4. THE DISPLACEMENT (OR SHIFT) OPERATOR E

The operator E increases the value of the argument by one interval.

If $\quad x : a, \; a+h, \; a+2h, \ldots\ldots$ and $y_0 = f(a)$, $y_1 = f(a+h)$, $y_2 = f(a+2h)$, ...

then $\quad Ef(a) = f(a+h)$ or $Ey_0 = y_1$; $Ef(a+h) = f(a+2h)$ or $Ey_1 = y_2$

When the operator E is applied twice, the value of the argument increases by two intervals.

$$E^2 y_0 = y_2, \quad E^2 y_1 = y_3, \quad E^2 y_n = y_{n+2} \quad \text{In general } E^r y_n = y_{n+r}, \; E^{-r} y_n = y_{n-r}$$

The operator E has the following properties :

(*i*) $Ecf(x) = cEf(x)$; (*ii*) $E[af(x) + bg(x)] = aEf(x) + bEg(x)$

(*iii*) $E^m[E^n f(x)] = E^{m+n} f(x)$; (*iv*) E and Δ are commutative, *i.e.*, $E\Delta f(x) = \Delta E f(x)$.

1.5. (a) Relations Between Δ, ∇ and E

(*i*) **E ≡ 1 + Δ and Δ ≡ E – 1**

$$\Delta y_n = y_{n+1} - y_n = Ey_n - y_n = (E-1)y_n$$

$$\Rightarrow \quad \Delta \equiv E - 1 \quad \text{and} \quad E \equiv 1 + \Delta$$

Note. In general $E^n \equiv (1+\Delta)^n$.

(*ii*) **$\nabla \equiv 1 - E^{-1}$**

$$\nabla y_n = y_n - y_{n-1} = y_n - E^{-1}y_n = (1 - E^{-1})y_n \quad \Rightarrow \quad \nabla \equiv 1 - E^{-1}.$$

(*iii*) **$\nabla \equiv \Delta E^{-1}$**

$$\nabla y_n = y_n - y_{n-1} = \Delta y_{n-1} = \Delta E^{-1} y_n \quad \Rightarrow \quad \nabla \equiv \Delta E^{-1}.$$

Example 6. *Prove that* $\nabla E = E\nabla = \Delta = E - 1$.

Sol.
$$\nabla E y_n = \nabla y_{n+1} = y_{n+1} - y_n = \Delta y_n$$
$$E\nabla y_n = E(y_n - y_{n-1}) = y_{n+1} - y_n = \Delta y_n$$
$$(E-1)y_n = y_{n+1} - y_n = \Delta y_n$$

Hence $\quad \nabla E = E\nabla = \Delta = E - 1.$

Example 7. *Evaluate* $(\nabla + \Delta)^2 (x^2 + x)$, $h = 1$.

Sol.
$$\begin{aligned}(\nabla + \Delta)^2 (x^2 + x) &= (1 - E^{-1} + E - 1)^2 (x^2 + x)\\ &= (E - E^{-1})^2 (x^2 + x) = (E^2 - 2 + E^{-2})(x^2 + x)\\ &= E^2(x^2 + x) - 2(x^2 + x) + E^{-2}(x^2 + x)\\ &= [(x+2)^2 + (x+2)] - 2(x^2 + x) + [(x-2)^2 + (x-2)]\\ &= (x^2 + 5x + 6) - (2x^2 + 2x) + (x^2 - 3x + 2) = 8.\end{aligned}$$

Example 8. *Explain the difference between* $\left(\dfrac{\Delta^2}{E}\right) u(x)$ *and* $\dfrac{\Delta^2 u(x)}{Eu(x)}$.

Sol.
$$\left(\frac{\Delta^2}{E}\right) u(x) = \left[\frac{(E-1)^2}{E}\right] u(x) = \left(\frac{E^2 - 2E + 1}{E}\right) u(x)$$
$$= (E - 2 + E^{-1})\, u(x) = u(x+1) - 2u(x) + u(x-1)$$

$$\frac{\Delta^2 u(x)}{Eu(x)} = \frac{(E-1)^2 u(x)}{u(x+1)} = \frac{(E^2 - 2E + 1)\, u(x)}{u(x+1)} = \frac{u(x+2) - 2u(x+1) + u(x)}{u(x+1)}$$

The difference is evident.

Example 9. *Prove that :*

(*i*) $\Delta \log f(x) = \log\left[1 + \dfrac{\Delta f(x)}{f(x)}\right]$

(*ii*) $\left(\dfrac{\Delta^2}{E}\right) x^3 = 6x$ *interval of differencing being unity.*

Sol. (*i*) $\quad \Delta \log f(x) = \log f(x+1) - \log f(x)$

$$= \log\left[\frac{f(x+1)}{f(x)}\right] = \log\left[\frac{E\, f(x)}{f(x)}\right]$$

$$= \log\left[\frac{(1+\Delta)\, f(x)}{f(x)}\right] = \log\left[\frac{f(x) + \Delta f(x)}{f(x)}\right] = \log\left[1 + \frac{\Delta f(x)}{f(x)}\right].$$

(ii) $\left(\frac{\Delta^2}{E}\right)x^3 = \frac{(E-1)^2}{E}x^3 = \frac{E^2-2E+1}{E}x^3$

$$= (E - 2 + E^{-1})\,x^3 = Ex^3 - 2x^3 + E^{-1}\,x^3 = (x+1)^3 - 2x^3 + (x-1)^3$$
$$= (x^3 + 3x^2 + 3x + 1) - 2x^3 + (x^3 - 3x^2 + 3x - 1) = 6x.$$

Example 10. *Find* $(\Delta - \nabla)\,x^2$, *where h is the interval of differencing.*

Sol. $(\Delta - \nabla)\,x^2 = [(E-1) - (1 - E^{-1})]\,x^2$

$$= (E - 2 + E^{-1})\,x^2 = Ex^2 - 2x^2 + E^{-1}\,x^2$$
$$= (x+h)^2 - 2x^2 + (x-h)^2 = 2h^2.$$

Example 11. *Evaluate* $\left(\frac{\Delta}{E}\right)^2 f(x)$, *where h is the interval of differencing.*

Sol. $\left(\frac{\Delta}{E}\right)^2 f(x) = \left(\frac{E-1}{E}\right)^2 f(x) = (1 - E^{-1})^2 f(x) = (1 - 2E^{-1} + E^{-2})\,f(x)$

$$= f(x) - 2E^{-1} f(x) + E^{-2} f(x) = f(x) - 2\,f(x-h) + f(x-2h).$$

Example 12. *Prove that* $\Delta\nabla \equiv \Delta - \nabla$.

Sol. $\Delta\nabla \equiv \Delta(1 - E^{-1}) \equiv \Delta - \Delta E^{-1} \equiv \Delta - \nabla.$

Example 13. *If D stands for the differential operator* $\frac{d}{dx}$, *prove that*

$$D = \frac{1}{h}\left[\Delta - \frac{1}{2}\Delta^2 + \frac{1}{3}\Delta^3 - \ldots\ldots\right].$$

Sol. We know that $E\,f(x) = f(x+h)$

$$= f(x) + h\,f'(x) + \frac{h^2}{2!}\,f''(x) + \frac{h^3}{3!}\,f'''(x) + \ldots\ldots \qquad \text{[Taylor's Expansion]}$$

$$= f(x) + hD\,f(x) + \frac{h^2}{2!}\,D^2 f(x) + \frac{h^3}{3!}\,D^3 f(x) + \ldots\ldots$$

$$= \left[1 + hD + \frac{(hD)^2}{2!} + \frac{(hD)^3}{3!} + \ldots\ldots\right] f(x) = e^{hD}\,f(x)$$

$\Rightarrow$ $\quad E = e^{hD} \;\Rightarrow\; 1 + \Delta = e^{hD} \;\Rightarrow\; \log(1+\Delta) = hD$

$\therefore$ $\quad D = \frac{1}{h}\log(1+\Delta) = \frac{1}{h}\left(\Delta - \frac{1}{2}\Delta^2 + \frac{1}{3}\Delta^3 \ldots\ldots\right).$

Example 14. *Prove that* $\nabla y_{n+1} = h\left[1 + \frac{1}{2}\nabla + \frac{5}{12}\nabla^2 + \ldots\ldots\right] y_n'.$

Sol. $\nabla y_{n+1} = y_{n+1} - y_n = (E-1)y_n = (e^{hD} - 1)\,y_n$

$$= \left[1 + hD + \frac{(hD)^2}{2!} + \frac{(hD)^3}{3!} + \ldots\ldots - 1\right] y_n = h\left[1 + \frac{1}{2!}hD + \frac{1}{3!}(hD)^2 + \ldots\ldots\right] Dy_n$$

$$= h[1 + \tfrac{1}{2}\,hD + \tfrac{1}{6}\,h^2D^2 + \ldots\ldots]\,y_n' \qquad \ldots(1)$$

Now $\quad E = e^{hD} \;\Rightarrow\; e^{-hD} = E^{-1} = 1 - (1 - E^{-1}) = 1 - \nabla$

$\Rightarrow \quad -hD = \log(1 - \nabla) = -\nabla - \frac{1}{2}\nabla^2 - \frac{1}{3}\nabla^3 \ldots\ldots \quad \Rightarrow \quad hD = \nabla + \frac{1}{2}\nabla^2 + \frac{1}{3}\nabla^3 + \ldots\ldots$

$\therefore$ From (1), we have

$$\nabla y_{n+1} = h[1 + \tfrac{1}{2}(\nabla + \tfrac{1}{2}\nabla^2 + \ldots\ldots) + \tfrac{1}{6}(\nabla + \tfrac{1}{2}\nabla^2 + \ldots\ldots)^2 + \ldots\ldots]\, y_n'$$

$$= h\,[1 + \tfrac{1}{2}\nabla + (\tfrac{1}{4} + \tfrac{1}{6})\nabla^2 + \ldots\ldots]\, y_n' = h\,[1 + \tfrac{1}{2}\nabla + \tfrac{5}{12}\nabla^2 + \ldots\ldots]\, y_n'.$$

Example 15. *Given that :*

x :	1	2	3	4	5
y :	2	5	10	17	26

Find the value of $\nabla^2 y_5$.

Sol. $\nabla^2 y_5 = (1 - E^{-1})^2 y_5 = (1 - 2E^{-1} + E^{-2})\, y_5$

$= y_5 - 2E^{-1} y_5 + E^{-2} y_5 = y_5 - 2y_4 + y_3 = 26 - 2(17) + 10 = 2.$

1.5. (b) Other Operators

(*i*) **Central Difference Operator δ**

The central difference operator δ is defined as

$$\delta f(x) = f\left(x + \frac{h}{2}\right) - f\left(x - \frac{h}{2}\right)$$

(*ii*) **Averaging Operator μ**

The averaging operator μ is defined as $\mu f(x) = \dfrac{1}{2}\left[f\left(x + \dfrac{h}{2}\right) + f\left(x - \dfrac{h}{2}\right)\right]$.

1.5. (c) Relations Between the Operators

(*i*) $\delta = E^{1/2} - E^{-1/2}$ (*ii*) $\mu = \dfrac{1}{2}(E^{1/2} + E^{-1/2})$

(*iii*) $\delta = \Delta E^{-1/2}$ (*iv*) $\delta = \nabla E^{1/2}$.

Proof. (*i*) $\delta f(x) = f\left(x + \frac{h}{2}\right) - f\left(x - \frac{h}{2}\right) = E^{1/2} f(x) - E^{-1/2} f(x) = (E^{1/2} - E^{-1/2}) f(x)$

$\therefore \quad \delta = E^{1/2} - E^{-1/2}$

(*ii*) $\mu f(x) = \dfrac{1}{2}\left[f\left(x + \dfrac{h}{2}\right) + f\left(x - \dfrac{h}{2}\right)\right] = \dfrac{1}{2}\,[E^{1/2} f(x) + E^{-1/2} f(x)]$

$= \dfrac{1}{2}(E^{1/2} + E^{-1/2}) f(x)$

$\therefore \quad \mu = \dfrac{1}{2}(E^{1/2} + E^{-1/2})$

(*iii*) $\delta f(x) = f\left(x + \frac{h}{2}\right) - f\left(x - \frac{h}{2}\right) = \Delta f\left(x - \frac{h}{2}\right) = \Delta E^{-1/2} f(x)$

$\therefore \quad \delta = \Delta E^{-1/2}$

(*iv*) $\delta f(x) = f\left(x + \frac{h}{2}\right) - f\left(x - \frac{h}{2}\right) = \nabla f\left(x + \frac{h}{2}\right) = \nabla E^{1/2} f(x)$

$\therefore \quad \delta = \nabla E^{1/2}$.

Example 16. *Prove that:*

(*i*) $hD = \log(1 + \Delta) = -\log(1 - \nabla) = \sinh^{-1}(\mu\delta)$

(*ii*) $\mu^2 = 1 + \frac{1}{4}\delta^2$ (*iii*) $\Delta = \frac{1}{2}\delta^2 + \delta\sqrt{1 + \frac{1}{4}\delta^2}$.

Sol. (*i*) We know that

$$e^{hD} = E = 1 + \Delta$$

$\therefore$ $hD = \log(1 + \Delta)$ ...(1)

Also $hD = \log E = -\log E^{-1} = -\log(1 - \nabla)$ ...(2)

and $\mu\delta = \frac{1}{2}(E^{1/2} + E^{-1/2})(E^{1/2} - E^{-1/2}) = \frac{1}{2}(E - E^{-1}) = \frac{1}{2}(e^{hD} - e^{-hD}) = \sinh(hD)$

$\Rightarrow$ $hD = \sinh^{-1}(\mu\delta)$ ...(3)

From (1), (2) and (3), we have

$$hD = \log(1 + \Delta) = -\log(1 - \nabla) = \sinh^{-1}(\mu\delta).$$

(*ii*) $1 + \frac{1}{4}\delta^2 = 1 + \frac{1}{4}(E^{1/2} - E^{-1/2})^2 = 1 + \frac{1}{4}[(E^{1/2} + E^{-1/2})^2 - 4] = 1 + \frac{1}{4}[(2\mu)^2 - 4] = \mu^2.$

(*iii*) $\frac{1}{2}\delta^2 + \delta\sqrt{1 + \frac{1}{4}\delta^2} = \frac{1}{2}(E^{1/2} - E^{-1/2})^2 + (E^{1/2} - E^{-1/2})\sqrt{1 + \frac{1}{4}(E^{1/2} - E^{-1/2})^2}$

$$= \frac{1}{2}(E + E^{-1} - 2) + (E^{1/2} - E^{-1/2})\sqrt{\frac{1}{4}(4 + E + E^{-1} - 2)}$$

$$= \frac{1}{2}(E + E^{-1} - 2) + \frac{1}{2}(E^{1/2} - E^{-1/2})(E^{1/2} + E^{-1/2})$$

$$= \frac{1}{2}[(E + E^{-1} - 2) + (E - E^{-1})] = \frac{1}{2}(2E - 2) = E - 1 = \Delta.$$

Example 17. *Prove that:*

(*i*) $\Delta x^m - \frac{1}{2}\Delta^2 x^m + \frac{1.3}{2.4}\Delta^3 x^m - \frac{1.3.5}{2.4.6}\Delta^4 x^m + ... = \left(x + \frac{1}{2}\right)^m - \left(x - \frac{1}{2}\right)^m$

(*ii*) $xy_1 + x^2y_2 + x^3y_3 + ... = \frac{x}{1-x}y_1 + \left(\frac{x}{1-x}\right)^2 \Delta y_1 + \left(\frac{x}{1-x}\right)^3 \Delta^2 y_1 + ...$

(*iii*) $u_0 + \frac{u_1 x}{1!} + \frac{u_2 x^2}{2!} + \frac{u_3 x^3}{3!} + ... = e^x\left(u_0 + x\Delta u_0 + \frac{x^2}{2!}\Delta^2 u_0 + \frac{x^3}{3!}\Delta^3 u_0 + ...\right)$.

Sol. (*i*) L.H.S. $= \Delta\left(1 - \frac{1}{2}\Delta + \frac{1.3}{2.4}\Delta^2 - \frac{1.3.5}{2.4.6}\Delta^3 + ...\right) x^m$

$$= \Delta(1 + \Delta)^{-1/2} x^m = \Delta E^{-1/2} x^m$$

$$= \Delta\left(x - \frac{1}{2}\right)^m = \left(x + \frac{1}{2}\right)^m - \left(x - \frac{1}{2}\right)^m = \text{R.H.S.}$$

(ii) $$\text{R.H.S.} = \frac{x}{1-x}\left[1+\frac{x}{1-x}\Delta+\left(\frac{x}{1-x}\right)^2\Delta^2+\ldots\ldots\right]y_1$$

$$= \frac{x}{1-x}\left[1-\frac{x}{1-x}\Delta\right]^{-1}y_1 = \frac{x}{1-x}\left[\frac{1-x(1+\Delta)}{1-x}\right]^{-1}y_1$$

$$= x\left[\frac{1}{1-x(1+\Delta)}\right]y_1 = x\left(\frac{1}{1-x\text{E}}\right)y_1$$

$$= x(1-x\text{E})^{-1}y_1 = x(1+x\text{E}+x^2\text{E}^2+\ldots\ldots)\,y_1 = xy_1+x^2y_2+x^3y_3+\ldots\ldots$$

$$= \text{L.H.S.}$$

(iii) $$\text{L.H.S.} = u_0+\frac{x}{1!}\text{E}u_0+\frac{x^2}{2!}\text{E}^2u_0+\frac{x^3}{3!}\text{E}^3u_0+\ldots\ldots$$

$$= \left(1+\frac{x\text{E}}{1!}+\frac{x^2\text{E}^2}{2!}+\frac{x^3\text{E}^3}{3!}+\ldots\ldots\right)u_0 = e^{x\text{E}}u_0 = e^{x(1+\Delta)}u_0 = e^x\,.\,e^{x\Delta}u_0$$

$$= e^x\left(1+x\Delta+\frac{x^2\Delta^2}{2!}+\frac{x^3\Delta^3}{3!}+\ldots\ldots\right)u_0$$

$$= e^x\left(u_0+x\Delta u_0+\frac{x^2}{2!}\Delta^2u_0+\frac{x^3}{3!}\Delta^3u_0+\ldots\ldots\right)$$

$$= \text{R.H.S.}$$

TEST YOUR KNOWLEDGE

1. Prove that $\Delta\left(\frac{u_x}{v_x}\right) = \frac{v_x\Delta u_x - u_x\Delta v_x}{v_x\,v_{x+1}}$.

2. Prove that :

(i) $\text{E}^{-1} = 1-\nabla$

(ii) $\nabla^2 = 1-2\text{E}^{-1}+\text{E}^{-2}$

(iii) $(1+\Delta)(1-\nabla) = 1$

(iv) $\Delta\nabla = \nabla\Delta = \Delta - \nabla = \delta^2$

(v) $\Delta + \nabla = \frac{\Delta}{\nabla} - \frac{\nabla}{\Delta}$

(vi) $\nabla\text{E} = \text{E}\nabla = \Delta = \text{E}-1$

(vii) $e^{-h\text{D}} = 1-\nabla$, where $\text{D} \equiv \frac{d}{dx}$.

3. Evaluate the following, the interval of differencing being unity:

(i) $\Delta \log x$

(ii) $(\text{E}^{-1}\,\Delta)x$

(iii) $\left(\frac{\Delta^2}{\text{E}}\right)x^2$

(iv) $\frac{\Delta^2\,x^3}{\text{E}x^3}$

(v) $\frac{\nabla^2x^2}{\text{E}[x+\log x]}$

(vi) $\Delta^2\text{E}^3x^2$

(*vii*) $(2\Delta + 1)^2 (x + 2)^2$ (*viii*) $(E + 2)(E - 1)(e^x + x)$ (*ix*) $(\nabla + \Delta)^2 (x^2 + x)$.

(*x*) $\Delta^3(1 - x)(1 - 2x)(1 - 3x)$.

4. Evaluate $\Delta x \log x$, the interval of differencing being h.

5. Prove that $e^x = \left(\frac{\Delta^2}{E}\right) e^x \cdot \frac{Ee^x}{\Delta^2 e^x}$; the interval of differencing being unity.

6. If $f(E)$ is a polynomial in E, prove that $f(E)\, e^x = e^x f(e)$.

7. Prove that $y_4 = y_3 + \Delta y_2 + \Delta^2 y_1 + \Delta^3 y_1$.

8. Prove that $\frac{\Delta^2}{E} \sin(x + h) + \frac{\Delta^2 \sin(x + h)}{E \sin(x + h)} = 2(\cos h - 1)[\sin(x + h) + 1]$.

9. If $u_0 = 3$, $u_1 = 12$, $u_2 = 81$, $u_3 = 200$, $u_4 = 100$, $u_5 = 8$, find the value of $\Delta^5 u_0$.

10. Express $u = x^4 - 12x^3 + 24x^2 - 30x + 9$ and its successive differences in factorial notation. Hence show that $\Delta^5 u = 0$.

11. Express $y = 3x^3 + x^2 + x + 1$ in factorial functions and hence show that $\Delta^3 y = 18$.

12. Express $f(u) = u^4 - 3u^2 + 2u + 6$ in terms of factorial polynomials. Hence show that $\Delta^4 f(u) = 24$.

13. Find the function whose first difference is

(*i*) e^x (*ii*) $9x^2 + 11x + 5$

(*iii*) $3x^2 + 9x + 4$ (*iv*) $x^3 + 3x^2 + 5x + 12$.

14. Prove that

(*i*) $E^{1/2} = \mu + \frac{1}{2}\delta$ (*ii*) $E^{-1/2} = \mu - \frac{1}{2}\delta$ (*iii*) $\delta = 2 \sinh\left(\frac{hD}{2}\right)$

(*iv*) $\mu\delta = \frac{1}{2}(\Delta + \nabla) = \frac{1}{2}(E^{-1} + \Delta)$ (*v*) $\delta = \Delta(1 + \Delta)^{-1/2} = \nabla(1 - \nabla)^{-1/2}$

(*vi*) $\delta(E^{1/2} + E^{-1/2}) = \Delta E^{-1} + \Delta$ (*vii*) $\sqrt{1 + \delta^2\mu^2} = 1 + \frac{\delta^2}{2}$ (*viii*) $E^r = \left(\mu + \frac{\delta}{2}\right)^{2r}$

(*ix*) $E^{1/2} = \left(1 + \frac{\delta^2}{4}\right)^{1/2} + \frac{\delta}{2}$

15. Given that :

x :	1	2	3	4	5
y :	2	5	10	17	26

show that $\delta^4 y_3 = 0$.

16. Prove that :

(*i*) $\frac{\nabla^2 x^3}{\delta x^2} = 3\left(1 - \frac{1}{x}\right)$ (*ii*) $\delta^2 y_0 = y_1 - 2y_0 + y_{-1}$

(*iii*) $\delta^3 y_{1/2} = y_2 - 3y_1 + 3y_0 - y_{-1}$

17. Prove that :

(*i*) $u_0 - u_1 + u_2 - u_3 + \ldots\ldots = \frac{1}{2} u_0 - \frac{1}{4}\Delta u_0 + \frac{1}{8}\Delta^2 u_0 - \frac{1}{16}\Delta^3 u_0 + \ldots\ldots$

(*ii*) $\Delta^n y_x = y_{x+n} - {}^nC_1\, y_{x+n-1} + {}^nC_2\, y_{x+n-2} - \ldots\ldots + (-1)^n y_x$

(*iii*) $\Delta^n y_{x-n} = y_x - {}^nC_1\, y_{x-1} + {}^nC_2\, y_{x-2} - {}^nC_3\, y_{x-3} + \ldots\ldots$

Answers

3. (*i*) $\log\left(1+\frac{1}{x}\right)$ (*ii*) 1 (*iii*) 2 (*iv*) $\frac{6}{(x+1)^2}$

(*v*) $\frac{2}{x+1+\log(x+1)}$ (*vi*) 2 (*vii*) $x^2 + 12x + 32$

(*viii*) $e^x(e^2 + e - 2) + 3$ (*ix*) 8 (*x*) -36

4. $(x+h)\log\left(1+\frac{h}{x}\right) + h\log x$ **9.** 755

10. $x^{(4)} - 6x^{(3)} - 5x^{(2)} - 17x^{(1)} + 9$; $4x^{(3)} - 18x^{(2)} - 10x^{(1)} - 17$; $12x^{(2)} - 36x^{(1)} - 10$; $24x^{(1)} - 36$; 24

11. $3x^{(3)} + 10x^{(2)} + 5x^{(1)} + 1$ **12.** $u^{(4)} + 6u^{(3)} + 4u^{(2)} + 6$

13. (*i*) $\frac{e^x}{e-1} + c$ (*ii*) $3x^3 + x^2 + x + c$ (*iii*) $x^3 + 3x^2 + c$

(*iv*) $\frac{1}{4}(x^4 + 2x^3 + 11x^2 + 40x) + c.$

1.6. INTERPOLATION AND EXTRAPOLATION

If the values of $f(x)$ are known for $x = x_0, x_1, x_2, \ldots\ldots, x_n$, then the process of finding the value of $f(x)$ for any other value of x in the interval (x_0, x_n) is called **interpolation** and the process of finding the value of $f(x)$ for a value of x outside the interval (x_0, x_n) is called **extrapolation**.

1.7. NEWTON-GREGORY FORMULAE FOR EQUAL INTERVALS

(*a*) Newton-Gregory Forward Interpolation Formula

$$f(a+nh) = E^n f(a) = (1+\Delta)^n f(a)$$

$$= \left[1 + n\Delta + \frac{n(n-1)}{2!}\Delta^2 + \frac{n(n-1)(n-2)}{3!}\Delta^3 + \ldots\ldots\right] f(a)$$

$$= f(a) + n\Delta f(a) + \frac{n(n-1)}{2!}\Delta^2 f(a) + \frac{n(n-1)(n-2)}{3!}\Delta^3 f(a) + \ldots\ldots$$

This is called Newton-Gregory forward interpolation formula.

(*b*) Newton-Gregory Backward Interpolation Formula

$$f(a-nh) = E^{-n} f(a) = (E^{-1})^n f(a)$$

$$= (1-\nabla)^n f(a) = \left[1 - n\nabla + \frac{n(n-1)}{2!}\nabla^2 - \frac{n(n-1)(n-2)}{3!}\nabla^3 + \ldots\ldots\right] f(a)$$

$$= f(a) - n\nabla f(a) + \frac{n(n-1)}{2!}\nabla^2 f(a) - \frac{n(n-1)(n-2)}{3!}\nabla^3 f(a) + \ldots\ldots$$

This is called Newton-Gregory backward interpolation formula.

Note 1. With usual notation, the above formulae can be written as

$$f(a+nh) = y_0 + n\Delta y_0 + \frac{n(n-1)}{2!}\Delta^2 y_0 + \ldots\ldots$$

$$f(a-nh) = y_0 - n\nabla y_0 + \frac{n(n-1)}{2!}\nabla^2 y_0 - \ldots\ldots$$

Note 2. If $a + nh$ is near the beginning, use forward interpolation formula. If $a - nh$ is near the end, use backward interpolation formula.

Note 3. As far as possible, a should be so chosen that n lies between –1 and +1.

ILLUSTRATIVE EXAMPLES

Example 1. *Using Newton's forward interpolation formula, find y at x = 8 from the following table :*

x :	0	5	10	15	20	25
y :	7	11	14	18	24	32.

Sol. Here $a = 0, \quad h = 5,$

$a + nh = 8$ is nearer the beginning than end.

$$0 + 5n = 8 \quad \Rightarrow \quad n = 1.6$$

The following is the forward difference table :

x	y	Δy	$\Delta^2 y$	$\Delta^3 y$	$\Delta^4 y$	$\Delta^5 y$
0	**$7 = y_0$**					
		$4 = \Delta y_0$				
5	11		**$-1 = \Delta^2 y_0$**			
		3		**$2 = \Delta^3 y_0$**		
			1		**$-1 = \Delta^4 y_0$**	
10	14			1		**$0 = \Delta^5 y_0$**
		4			–1	
			2			
15	18					
		6		0		
			2			
20	24					
		8				
25	32					

Using Newton's forward interpolation formula

$$f(a + nh) = y_0 + n\Delta y_0 + \frac{n(n-1)}{2!}\Delta^2 y_0 + \frac{n(n-1)(n-2)}{3!}\Delta^3 y_0 + \frac{n(n-1)(n-2)(n-3)}{4!}\Delta^4 y_0$$

we get $$f(8) = 7 + (1.6)(4) + \frac{(1.6)(.6)}{2}(-1) + \frac{(1.6)(.6)(-.4)}{6}(2) + \frac{(1.6)(.6)(-.4)(-1.4)}{24}(-1)$$

$$= 7 + 6.4 - .48 - .128 - .022 = 13.4 - .630 = 12.770$$

$$= 12.77, \text{ correct to 2 decimal places.}$$

Example 2. *Given : sin 45° = 0.7071, sin 50° = 0.7660, sin 55° = 0.8192, sin 60° = 0.8660 find sin 52°, using Newton's forward interpolation formula.*

Sol. Let x denote the angle in degrees and $y = f(x) = \sin x$.

Here $a = 45$, $h = 5$, $a + nh = 52$ is nearer the beginning than end.

$$\therefore \qquad 45 + 5n = 52 \quad \Rightarrow \quad n = \frac{7}{5} = 1.4$$

The following is the forward difference table :

x	y	Δy	$\Delta^2 y$	$\Delta^3 y$
45	**0.7071** $= y_0$			
		0.0589 $= \Delta y_0$		
50	0.7660		− **0.0057** $= \Delta^2 y_0$	
		0.0532		− **0.0007** $= \Delta^3 y_0$
55	0.8192		− 0.0064	
		0.0468		
60	0.8660			

Using Newton's forward interpolation formula,

$$f(a + nh) = y_0 + n\Delta y_0 + \frac{n(n-1)}{2!}\Delta^2 y_0 + \frac{n(n-1)(n-2)}{3!}\Delta^3 y_0$$

$$= 0.7071 + (1.4)(0.0589) + \frac{(1.4)(.4)}{2}(-0.0057) + \frac{(1.4)(.4)(-.6)}{6}(-0.0007)$$

$$= 0.7071 + 0.08246 - 0.00160 + 0.00004$$

∴ $\sin 52° = 0.7880$, correct to 4 decimal places.

Example 3. *The following data gives the melting point of an alloy of lead and zinc, where t is the temperature in °C and p is the percentage of lead in the alloy.*

p(%) :	*60*	*70*	*80*	*90*
t :	*226*	*250*	*276*	*304*

Find the melting point of the alloy containing 84% of lead, using Newton's interpolation formula.

Sol. Here $a = 90$, $h = 10$, $a - nh = 84$ is nearer the end than beginning.

∴ $$90 - 10n = 84 \Rightarrow n = \frac{6}{10} = .6.$$

The following is the backward difference table :

p	t	∇t	$\nabla^2 t$	$\nabla^3 t$
60	226			
		24		
70	250		2	
		26		**0** $= \nabla^3 t_0$
80	276		**2** $= \nabla^2 t_0$	
		28 $= \nabla t_0$		
90	**304** $= t_0$			

Using Newton's backward interpolation formula,

$$f(a - nh) = t_0 - n\nabla t_0 + \frac{n(n-1)}{2!}\nabla^2 t_0$$

we get $$f(84) = 304 - (.6)(28) + \frac{(.6)(-.4)}{2}(2) = 304 - 16.8 - .24 = 286.96.$$

Example 4. *Form the difference table of $f(x) = x^3 - 3x^2 + 5x + 7$ for the values of 0, 2, 4, 6, 8 and extend the table for the calculation of f(10).*

Sol. Here $f(x) = x^3 - 3x^2 + 5x + 7$

$\therefore$ $f(0) = 7$

$f(2) = 8 - 12 + 10 + 7 = 13$

$f(4) = 64 - 48 + 20 + 7 = 43$

$f(6) = 216 - 108 + 30 + 7 = 145$

$f(8) = 512 - 192 + 40 + 7 = 367$

The following is the backward difference table :

x	$f(x)$	∇f	$\nabla^2 f$	$\nabla^3 f$	$\nabla^4 f$
0	7				
		6			
2	13		24	48	
		30			
4	43		72		0
		102		48	
6	145		120		
		222			
8	367				

Here $a = 8,$ $h = 2$ $a - nh = 10$

$\therefore$ $8 - 2n = 10 \Rightarrow n = -1$

Using Newton's backward interpolation formula,

$$f(a - nh) = f(a) - n\,\nabla f(a) + \frac{n(n-1)}{2!}\,\nabla^2 f(a) - \frac{n(n-1)(n-2)}{3!}\,\nabla^3 f(a) + \ldots\ldots, \text{ we get}$$

$$f(10) = 367 - (-1)(222) + \frac{(-1)(-2)}{2}(120) - \frac{(-1)(-2)(-3)}{6}(48)$$

$$= 367 + 222 + 120 + 48 = 757.$$

Example 5. *The following table gives corresponding values of x and y. From the difference table, express y as a function of x :*

x :	0	1	2	3	4
y :	3	6	11	18	27

Sol. Here $a = 0$, $h = 1$

The forward difference table is :

x	y	Δy	$\Delta^2 y$	$\Delta^3 y$
0	**3**			
		3		
1	6		**2**	
		5		**0**
2	11		2	
		7		0
3	18		2	
		9		
4	27			

Using Newton's forward interpolation formula,

$$f(a + xh) = y_0 + x\Delta y_0 + \frac{x(x-1)}{2!}\Delta^2 y_0$$

we get
$$f(x) = 3 + x(3) + \frac{x(x-1)}{2}(2) = 3 + 3x + x^2 - x = x^2 + 2x + 3.$$

1.8. LAGRANGE'S FORMULA FOR UNEQUAL INTERVALS

Let $y = f(x)$ be a function which takes the values $y_0, y_1, y_2, \ldots, y_n$ when x assumes the values $x_0, x_1, x_2, \ldots, x_n$ respectively. If the values of x are at equal intervals, we use Newton's forward or backward formula. If the values of x are not at equal intervals, we use the following formula :

$$f(x) = y_0 \frac{(x-x_1)(x-x_2)(x-x_3)\ldots(x-x_n)}{(x_0-x_1)(x_0-x_2)(x_0-x_3)\ldots(x_0-x_n)}$$
$$+ y_1 \frac{(x-x_0)(x-x_2)(x-x_3)\ldots(x-x_n)}{(x_1-x_0)(x_1-x_2)(x_1-x_3)\ldots(x_1-x_n)}$$
$$+ y_2 \frac{(x-x_0)(x-x_1)(x-x_3)\ldots(x-x_n)}{(x_2-x_0)(x_2-x_1)(x_2-x_3)\ldots(x_2-x_n)} + \ldots\ldots$$
$$+ y_n \frac{(x-x_0)(x-x_1)(x-x_2)\ldots(x-x_{n-1})}{(x_n-x_0)(x_n-x_1)(x_n-x_2)\ldots(x_n-x_{n-1})}$$

This is called Lagrange's interpolation formula for unequal intervals.

Example 6. *Using Lagrange's interpolation formula, find the values of y when x = 10, from the following table* :

x :	5	6	9	11
y :	12	13	14	16

Sol. Here $x_0 = 5,\quad x_1 = 6,\quad x_2 = 9,\quad x_3 = 11$

$y_0 = 12,\quad y_1 = 13,\quad y_2 = 14,\quad y_3 = 16$

Lagrange's interpolation formula is

$$f(x) = y_0 \frac{(x-x_1)(x-x_2)(x-x_3)}{(x_0-x_1)(x_0-x_2)(x_0-x_3)} + y_1 \frac{(x-x_0)(x-x_2)(x-x_3)}{(x_1-x_0)(x_1-x_2)(x_1-x_3)}$$
$$+ y_2 \frac{(x-x_0)(x-x_2)(x-x_3)}{(x_2-x_0)(x_2-x_1)(x_2-x_3)} + y_3 \frac{(x-x_0)(x-x_1)(x-x_2)}{(x_3-x_0)(x_3-x_1)(x_3-x_2)}$$

$$\therefore \quad f(10) = (12)\frac{(10-6)(10-9)(10-11)}{(5-6)(5-9)(5-11)} + (13)\frac{(10-5)(10-9)(10-11)}{(6-5)(6-9)(6-11)}$$
$$+ (14)\frac{(10-5)(10-6)(10-11)}{(9-5)(9-6)(9-11)} + (16)\frac{(10-5)(10-6)(10-9)}{(11-5)(11-6)(11-9)}$$
$$= (12)\frac{(4)(1)(-1)}{(-1)(-4)(-6)} + 13\frac{(5)(1)(-1)}{(1)(-3)(-5)} + (14)\frac{(5)(4)(-1)}{(4)(3)(-2)} + (16)\frac{(5)(4)(1)}{(6)(5)(2)}$$
$$= 2 - \frac{13}{3} + \frac{35}{3} + \frac{16}{3} = 14\frac{2}{3}.$$

Example 7. *Using Lagrange's formula, find the form of the function f(x) given that :*

x	:	0	2	3	6
$f(x)$	:	659	705	729	804

Sol. Here $x_0 = 0,\ x_1 = 2,\ x_2 = 3,\ x_3 = 6;\ y_0 = 659,\ y_1 = 705,\ y_2 = 729,\ y_3 = 804$

Using Lagrange's formula,

$$f(x) = y_0 \frac{(x - x_1)(x - x_2)(x - x_3)}{(x_0 - x_1)(x_0 - x_2)(x_0 - x_3)} + y_1 \frac{(x - x_0)(x - x_2)(x - x_3)}{(x_1 - x_0)(x_1 - x_2)(x_1 - x_3)}$$

$$+ y_2 \frac{(x - x_0)(x - x_1)(x - x_3)}{(x_2 - x_0)(x_2 - x_1)(x_2 - x_3)} + y_3 \frac{(x - x_0)(x - x_1)(x - x_2)}{(x_3 - x_0)(x_3 - x_1)(x_3 - x_2)}$$

$$= (659) \frac{(x-2)(x-3)(x-6)}{(0-2)(0-3)(0-6)} + (705) \frac{(x-0)(x-3)(x-6)}{(2-0)(2-3)(2-6)}$$

$$+ (729) \frac{(x-0)(x-2)(x-6)}{(3-0)(3-2)(3-6)} + (804) \frac{(x-0)(x-2)(x-3)}{(6-0)(6-2)(6-3)}$$

$$= -\frac{659}{36}(x^3 - 11x^2 + 36x - 36) + \frac{705}{8}(x^3 - 9x^2 + 18x)$$

$$- 81(x^3 - 8x^2 + 12x) + \frac{67}{6}(x^3 - 5x^2 + 6x)$$

$$= \frac{1}{72}(-x^3 + 29x^2 + 1602x + 47448).$$ | on simplification.

TEST YOUR KNOWLEDGE

1. Using Newton's forward interpolation formula and the given table of values :

x	:	1.1	1.3	1.5	1.7	1.9
y	:	0.21	0.69	1.25	1.89	2.61

obtain the value of y when $x = 1.4$.

2. In a certain experiment, the values of x and y were found as follows :

x	:	0	1	2	3	4	5	6
y	:	0	1	16	81	256	625	1296

Find the value of y when $x = 2.5$, using Newton's forward interpolation formula.

3. A function $f(x)$ is given by the following table. Find $f(0.2)$ by a suitable formula :

x	:	0	1	2	3	4	5	6
$f(x)$	:	176	185	194	203	212	220	229

4. The following are data from the steam table :

Temperature °C	:	140	150	160	170	180
Pressure kgf/cm^2	:	3.685	4.854	6.302	8.076	10.225

Using Newton's formula, find the pressure of steam for a temperature 142°C.

5. Distance in nautical miles of the visible horizon for given heights in metres above the surface of the earth are given by the following table :

x (*heights*)	:	100	150	200	250	300	350	400
y (*distance*)	:	12	16	21	27	36	50	72

Find the value of y when $x = 225$ metres.

6. Using Newton's forward formula, find sin 0.1604 from the following table :

x	:	0.160	0.161	0.162
$\sin x$	:	0.1593182066	0.1603053541	0.1612923412

7. Using Newton's forward interpolation, find the value of $\log_{10} \pi$, given

log 3.141 = 0.4970679364 ; log 3.142 = 0.4972061807 ; log 3.143 = 0.4973443810;

log 3.144 = 0.4974825374 log 3.145 = 0.4976206498

[**Hint.** $\pi = 3.1416$]

8. The table gives the distance in kilometres of the visible horizon for the given heights in metres above the earth's surface :

x (= *height*)	:	100	150	200	250	300	350	400
d (= *distance*)	:	10.63	13.03	15.04	16.81	18.42	19.90	21.27

Find the value of d when $x = 218$ metres.

9. If $u_0 = 1, u_1 = 0, u_2 = 5, u_3 = 22, u_4 = 57$, find $u_{0.5}$ by Newton's formula.

10. The following table gives corresponding values of x and y. Prepare a forward difference table and express y as a function of x. Also obtain y where $x = 2.5$.

x	:	0	1	2	3	4
y	:	7	10	13	22	43

11. Applying Newton's forward interpolation formula, compute the value of $\sqrt{5.5}$, given that $\sqrt{5}$ = 2.236, $\sqrt{6}$ = 2.449, $\sqrt{7}$ = 2.646 and $\sqrt{8}$ = 2.828, correct upto three places of decimal.

12. From the following table find the number of students who obtained less than 45 marks :

Marks	*Number of students*
30–40	31
40–50	42
50–60	51
60–70	35
70–80	31

[**Hint.** Use the following table :

Marks less than	*Number of students*
40	31
50	73
60	124
70	159
80	190]

13. Find the value of an annuity at $5\frac{3}{8}\%$, given the following table

Rate per cent	*Annuity value*
4	17.29203
$4\frac{1}{2}$	16.28889
5	15.37245
$5\frac{1}{2}$	14.53375
6	13.76483

14. Given :

x	1	2	3	4	5	6	7	8
$f(x)$	1	8	27	64	125	216	343	512

Estimate $f(7.5)$.

15. Given the table :

x	0	.1	.2	.3	.4
e^x	1	1.1052	1.2214	1.3499	1.4918

Find the value of $y = e^x$ when $x = .38$.

16. From the given table, compute the value of sin 38°

$x°$	0	10	20	30	40
$\sin x°$	0	0.17365	0.34202	0.50000	0.64279

17. Given the values :

x	0	2	3	6
$f(x)$	– 4	2	14	158

Using Lagrange's formula for interpolation, find the value of $f(4)$.

18. State Lagrange's interpolation formula. Use this formula to find the value of y, when $x = 5$, if the following values of x and y are given :

x	1	2	3	4	7
y	2	4	8	16	128

19. From an experiment, we get the following values of a function $\phi(x)$:

x	1	2	– 4
$\phi(x)$	3	– 5	4

Represent the function $\phi(x)$ approximately by a polynomial of degree 2, using Lagrange's interpolation formula.

20. Find $f(x)$, given :

x	0	1	2	4
$f(x)$	1	1	2	5

$f(x)$ being a cubic polynomial.

21. Use Lagrange's interpolation formula to find the value of y when $x = 10$, if the following table of x and y is given :

x	5	6	9	11
y	12	13	14	16

22. Apply Lagrange's formula to find $f(x)$ from the following data :

x	0	1	4	5
$f(x)$	4	3	24	39

23. Use Lagrange's interpolation formula to find y when $x = 5$ from the following data :

x	0	1	3	8
y	1	3	13	123

24. Find by interpolation the missing values in the following data :

x	0	5	10	15	20	25
y	6	10	—	17	—	31

25. Use Lagrange's interpolation formula and find the value at $x = 3.5$ with the following data for y:

x	1	3	5
y	1.5708	1.5719	1.5738

26. The observed values of a function are respectively 168, 120, 72 and 63 at the four positions 3, 7, 9 and 10 of the independent variable. What is the best estimate you can give for the value of the function at the position 6 of the independent variable ?

27. Given $\sum_{1}^{10} f(x) = 500426$, $\sum_{4}^{10} f(x) = 329240$, $\sum_{7}^{10} f(x) = 175212$ and $f(10) = 40365$, find $f(1)$.

28. Given $\sum_{11}^{20} f(x) = 44060$, $\sum_{14}^{20} f(x) = 38220$, $\sum_{17}^{20} f(x) = 27178$ and $f(20) = 8450$, find the value of $f(11)$.

29. Find a polynomial of degree 2 which takes the values

x	:	0	1	2	3	4	5	6	7
y	:	1	2	4	7	11	16	22	29

Answers

1. 0.96 **2.** 39 **3.** 177.75 **4.** 3.899 kg/cm^2
5. 23.71 **6.** 0.1597130849 **7.** 0.4971508883 **8.** 15.70 km
9. 0.125 **10.** $y = x^3 - 3x^2 + 5x + 7$; 16.375 **11.** 2.345
12. 48 **13.** 14.73659 **14.** 421.875 **15.** 1.4625
16. 0.51533 **17.** 40 **18.** 33
19. $\phi(x) = -\frac{1}{10}(13x^2 + 41x - 84)$ **20.** $\frac{1}{12}(-x^3 + 9x^2 - 8x + 12)$
21. 14.67 **22.** $f(x) = 2x^2 - 3x + 4$ **23.** 38.14 **24.** 13.25, 22.5
25. 1.5723 **26.** 147 **27.** 58843.4 **28.** 1522
29. $1 + \frac{x}{2} + \frac{x^2}{2}$.

1.9. (a) Divided Differences

Let $f(x_0), f(x_1), f(x_2), \ldots\ldots, f(x_n)$ be the values of the function $f(x)$ corresponding to the arguments $x_0, x_1, x_2, \ldots\ldots, x_n$.

The first divided difference for the arguments x_0, x_1 is defined as $\frac{f(x_1) - f(x_0)}{x_1 - x_0}$

and is denoted by $f(x_0, x_1)$ or $\underset{x_1}{\Delta} f(x_0)$ or $[x_0, x_1]$.

Thus
$$f(x_0, x_1) = \underset{x_1}{\Delta} f(x_0) = \frac{f(x_1) - f(x_0)}{x_1 - x_0}$$

Similarly,
$$f(x_1, x_2) = \underset{x_2}{\Delta} f(x_1) = \frac{f(x_2) - f(x_1)}{x_2 - x_1}$$

and
$$f(x_2, x_3) = \underset{x_3}{\Delta} f(x_2) = \frac{f(x_3) - f(x_2)}{x_3 - x_2} \text{ etc.}$$

The second divided difference for the arguments x_0, x_1, x_2 is defined as

$$f(x_0, x_1, x_2) = \underset{x_1, x_2}{\Delta^2} f(x_0) = \frac{f(x_1, x_2) - f(x_0, x_1)}{x_2 - x_0}$$

The third divided difference for the arguments x_0, x_1, x_2, x_3 is defined as

$$f(x_0, x_1, x_2, x_3) = \underset{x_1, x_2, x_3}{\Delta^3} f(x_0) = \frac{f(x_1, x_2, x_3) - f(x_0, x_1, x_2)}{x_3 - x_0} \text{ and so on.}$$

1.9. (b) Newton's Divided Difference Formula Is

$$\mathbf{f(x) = f(x_0) + (x - x_0) \underset{x_1}{\Delta} f(x_0) + (x - x_0)(x - x_1) \underset{x_1, x_2}{\Delta^2} f(x_0)}$$

$$\mathbf{+ \ldots\ldots + (x - x_0)(x - x_1) \ldots\ldots (x - x_{n-1}) \underset{x_1, \ldots\ldots, x_n}{\Delta^n} f(x_0)}$$

Example. *Using Newton's divided difference formula, evaluate f(8) and f(15), given*

x :	4	5	7	10	11	13
$f(x)$:	48	100	294	900	1210	2028

Sol. The divided difference table is as follows :

x	$f(x)$	$\Delta f(x)$	$\Delta^2 f(x)$	$\Delta^3 f(x)$
4	**48**			
		$\underset{5}{\Delta} f(4) = \frac{100 - 48}{5 - 4} = \mathbf{52}$		
5	100		$\underset{5,7}{\Delta^2} f(4) = \frac{97 - 52}{7 - 4} = \mathbf{15}$	
		$\underset{7}{\Delta} f(5) = \frac{294 - 100}{7 - 5} = 97$		$\underset{5,7,10}{\Delta^3} f(4) = \frac{21 - 15}{10 - 4} = \mathbf{1}$
7	294		$\underset{7,10}{\Delta^2} f(5) = \frac{202 - 97}{10 - 5} = 21$	
		$\underset{10}{\Delta} f(7) = \frac{900 - 294}{10 - 7} = 202$		$\underset{7,10,11}{\Delta^3} f(5) = \frac{27 - 21}{11 - 5} = 1$
10	900		$\underset{10,11}{\Delta^2} f(7) = \frac{310 - 202}{11 - 7} = 27$	
		$\underset{11}{\Delta} f(10) = \frac{1210 - 900}{11 - 10} = 310$		$\underset{10,11,13}{\Delta^3} f(7) = \frac{33 - 27}{13 - 7} = 1$
11	1210		$\underset{11,13}{\Delta^2} f(10) = \frac{409 - 310}{13 - 10} = 33$	
		$\underset{13}{\Delta} f(11) = \frac{2028 - 1210}{13 - 11} = 409$		
13	2028			

Newton's divided difference formula is

$$f(x) = f(4) + (x - 4) \underset{5}{\Delta} f(4) + (x - 4)(x - 5) \underset{5,7}{\Delta^2} f(4)$$

$$+ (x - 4)(x - 5)(x - 7) \underset{5,7,10}{\Delta^3} f(4) + \ldots\ldots$$

Putting $x = 8$, we get $f(8) = 48 + (8 - 4) \times 52 + (8 - 4)(8 - 5) \times 15 + (8 - 4)(8 - 5)(8 - 7) \times 1$

$$= 48 + 208 + 180 + 12 = 448$$

Putting $x = 15$, we get

$$f(15) = 48 + (15 - 4) \times 52 + (15 - 4)(15 - 5) \times 15 + (15 - 4)(15 - 5)(15 - 7) \times 1$$
$$= 48 + 572 + 1650 + 880 = 3150.$$

TEST YOUR KNOWLEDGE

1. Use Newton's divided difference formula to find $f(7)$, if
$f(3) = 24, f(5) = 120, f(8) = 504, f(9) = 720$ and $f(12) = 1716$.

2. Use Newton's divided difference formula to find $f(x)$ from the following data :

x :	0	1	2	4	5	6
$f(x)$:	1	14	15	5	6	19

3. Given the following data, find $f(x)$ as a polynomial in powers of $(x - 5)$:

x :	0	2	3	4	7	9
$f(x)$:	4	26	58	112	466	922.

4. Determine $f(x)$ as a polynomial in x for the following data using Newton's divided difference formula

x :	– 4	– 1	0	2	5
y :	1245	33	5	9	1335.

Answers

1. 336 **2.** $x^3 - 9x^2 + 21x + 1$ **3.** $(x - 5)^3 + 17(x - 5)^2 + 98(x - 5) + 194$

4. $1245 - 404(x + 4) + 94(x + 4)(x + 1) - 14(x + 4)(x + 1)x + 23(x + 4)(x + 1)x(x - 2)$

DIFFERENCE CALCULUS

1.10. NUMERICAL DIFFERENTIATION

(a) Forward Differences. Newton's forward interpolation formula is

$$f(a + xh) = f(a) + x\Delta f(a) + \frac{x(x-1)}{2!}\Delta^2 f(a) + \frac{x(x-1)(x-2)}{3!}\Delta^3 f(a) + \frac{x(x-1)(x-2)(x-3)}{4!}\Delta^4 f(a) + \ldots\ldots$$

$$= f(a) + x\,\Delta\, f(a) + \frac{x^2 - x}{2}\Delta^2 f(a) + \frac{x^3 - 3x^2 + 2x}{6}\Delta^3 f(a) + \frac{x^4 - 6x^3 + 11x^2 - 6x}{24}\Delta^4 f(a) + \ldots.$$

Differentiating w.r.t. x, we get

$$hf'(a + xh) = \Delta f(a) + \frac{2x - 1}{2}\Delta^2 f(x) + \frac{3x^2 - 6x + 2}{6}\Delta^3 f(a) + \frac{4x^3 - 18x^2 + 22x - 6}{24}\Delta^4 f(a) + \ldots.$$

Differentiating again w.r.t. x, we get

$$h^2 f''(a + xh) = \frac{2}{2}\Delta^2 f(a) + \frac{6x-6}{6}\Delta^3 f(a) + \frac{12x^2 - 36x + 22}{24}\Delta^4 f(a) + ...$$

Differentiating again w.r.t. x,

$$h^3 f'''(a + xh) = \frac{6}{6}\Delta^3 f(a) + \frac{24x - 36}{24}\Delta^4 f(a) + ...$$

Putting $x = 0$ and simplifying

$$\mathbf{hf'(a) = \Delta f(a) - \tfrac{1}{2}\Delta^2 f(a) + \tfrac{1}{3}\Delta^3 f(a) - \frac{1}{4}\Delta^4 f(a) + ...}$$

$$\mathbf{h^2 f''(a) = \Delta^2 f(a) - \Delta^3 f(a) + \frac{11}{12}\Delta^4 f(a) - \frac{5}{6}\Delta^5 f(a) + ...}$$

$$\mathbf{h^3 f'''(a) = \Delta^3 f(a) - \frac{3}{2}\Delta^4 f(a) + ...}$$

Similarly, we can find formulae for higher order derivatives.

(*b*) **Backward Differences.** Newton's backward interpolation formula is

$$f(a - xh) = f(a) - x\nabla f(a) + \frac{x(x-1)}{2!}\nabla^2 f(a) - \frac{x(x-1)(x-2)}{3!}\nabla^3 f(a)$$
$$+ \frac{x(x-1)(x-2)(x-3)}{4!}\nabla^4 f(a) ....$$

$$= f(a) - x\nabla f(a) + \frac{x^2 - x}{2}\nabla^2 f(a) - \frac{x^3 - 3x^2 + 2x}{6}\nabla^3 f(a)$$
$$+ \frac{x^4 - 6x^3 + 11x^2 - 6x}{24}\nabla^4 f(a) ......$$

Differentiating w.r.t. x, we get

$$-hf'(a - xh) = -\nabla f(a) + \frac{2x-1}{2}\nabla^2 f(a) - \frac{3x^2 - 6x + 2}{6}\nabla^3 f(a)$$
$$+ \frac{4x^3 - 18x^2 + 22x - 6}{24}\nabla^4 f(a)$$

Differentiating again w.r.t. x, we get

$$h^2 f''(a - xh) = \frac{2}{2}\nabla^2 f(a) - \frac{6x-6}{6}\nabla^3 f(a) + \frac{12x^2 - 36x + 22}{24}\nabla^4 f(a) - ....$$

Putting $x = 0$ and simplifying

$$\mathbf{hf'(a) = \nabla f(a) + \tfrac{1}{2}\nabla^2 f(a) + \tfrac{1}{3}\nabla^3 f(a) + \tfrac{1}{4}\nabla^4 f(a) + ...}$$

$$\mathbf{h^2 f''(a) = \nabla^2 f(a) + \nabla^3 f(a) + \frac{11}{12}\nabla^4 f(a) + \frac{5}{6}\nabla^5 f(a) + ...}$$

Similarly, we can find formulae for higher order derivatives.

ILLUSTRATIVE EXAMPLES

Example 1. *Find the first, second and third derivatives of the function tabulated below, at the point x = 1.5.*

x :	1.5	2.0	2.5	3.0	3.5	4.0
$f(x)$:	3.375	7.0	13.625	24.0	38.875	59.0.

Sol. The forward difference table is

x	$f(x)$	$\Delta f(x)$	$\Delta^2 f(x)$	$\Delta^3 f(x)$	$\Delta^4 f(x)$
1.5	**3.375**				
		3.625			
2.0	7.000		**3.000**		
		6.625		**0.750**	
2.5	13.625		3.750		**0**
		10.375		0.750	
3.0	24.000		4.500		0
		14.875		0.750	
3.5	38.875		5.250		
		20.125			
4.0	59.000				

Here $a = 1.5$, $\quad h = 0.5$

The first derivative of $f(x)$ at $x = a$ is given by

$$hf'(a) = \Delta f(x) - \tfrac{1}{2}\Delta^2 f(a) + \tfrac{1}{3}\Delta^3 f(a) - \tfrac{1}{4}\Delta^4 f(a)$$

$\Rightarrow \quad (0.5)f'(1.5) = 3.625 - \tfrac{1}{2}(3.000) + \tfrac{1}{3}(0.750) = 3.625 - 1.500 + 0.250 = 2.375$

$\therefore \quad f'(1.5) = 2 \times 2.375 = 4.750$

The second derivative of $f(x)$ at $x = a$ is given by

$$h^2 f''(a) = \Delta^2 f(a) - \Delta^3 f(a) + \frac{11}{12}\Delta^4 f(a)$$

$\Rightarrow \quad (0.5)^2 f''(1.5) = 3.000 - 0.750 = 2.250$

$\therefore \quad f''(1.5) = 4 \times 2.250 = 9.000$

The third derivative of $f(x)$ at $x = a$ is given by

$$h^3 f'''(a) = \Delta^3 f(a) - \frac{3}{2}\Delta^4 f(a) \quad \Rightarrow \quad (0.5)^3 f'''(1.5) = 0.75$$

$\therefore \quad f'''(1.5) = 8 \times 0.750 = 6.000.$

Example 2. *A slider in a machine moves along a fixed straight rod. Its distance x cm along the rod is given below for various values of the time t sec. Find the velocity and acceleration of the slider when t = 0.3 sec.*

t :	0	0.1	0.2	0.3	0.4	0.5	0.6
x :	30.13	31.62	32.87	33.64	33.95	33.81	33.24

Sol. Velocity at $t = 0.3$ is $f'(0.3)$ and acceleration at $t = 0.3$ is $f''(0.3)$, where $x = f(t)$.

We use the values of x from $t = 0.2$ to $t = 0.6$.

The forward difference table is

t	x	Δx	$\Delta^2 x$	$\Delta^3 x$	$\Delta^4 x$
0.2	**32.87**				
		0.77			
0.3	33.64		**– 0.46**		
		0.31		**0.01**	
0.4	33.95		– 0.45		**0.01**
		– 0.41		0.02	
0.5	33.81		– 0.43		
		– 0.57			
0.6	33.24				

Here $a = 0.2, \quad h = 0.1, \quad a + th = 0.3$

$\therefore \quad 0.2 + 0.1, t = 0.3 \Rightarrow t = 1$

Newton's forward interpolation formula is

$$f(a + th) = f(a) + t\Delta f(a) + \frac{t(t-1)}{2!}\Delta^2 f(a) + \frac{t(t-1)(t-2)}{3!}\Delta^3 f(a) + \frac{t(t-1)(t-2)(t-3)}{4!}\Delta^4 f(a)$$

$$= f(a) + t\Delta f(a) + \frac{t^2 - t}{2}\Delta^2 f(a) + \frac{t^3 - 3t^2 + 2t}{6}\Delta^3 f(a) + \frac{t^4 - 6t^3 + 11t^2 - 6t}{24}\Delta^4 f(a)$$

Differentiating w.r.t. 't', we get

$$hf'(a + th) = \Delta f(a) + \frac{2t-1}{2}\Delta^2 f(a) + \frac{3t^2 - 6t + 2}{6}\Delta^3 f(a) + \frac{4t^3 - 18t^2 + 22t - 6}{24}\Delta^4 f(a)$$

Differentiating again w.r.t. 't', we get

$$h^2 f''(a + th) = \frac{2}{2}\Delta^2 f(a) + \frac{6t-6}{6}\Delta^3 f(a) + \frac{12t^2 - 36t + 22}{24}\Delta^4 f(a)$$

Substituting the values, we get

$$(0.1)\, f'(0.3) = 0.77 + \frac{1}{2}(-0.46) - \frac{1}{6}(0.01) + \frac{1}{12}(0.01)$$

$$\Rightarrow \quad f'(0.3) = 10[0.77 - 0.23 - 0.0017 + 0.0008] = 10 \times 0.5391 = 5.34$$

$\therefore$ Velocity when $t = 0.3$ is 5.34 cm/sec.

Also $$(0.1)^2 f''(0.3) = -0.46 + 0 - \frac{1}{12}(0.01)$$

$$\Rightarrow \quad f''(0.3) = 100[-0.46 - 0.0008] = -46.08$$

$\therefore$ Acceleration when $t = 0.3$ is -46.08 cm/sec^2.

Example 3. *A rod is rotating in a plane about one of its ends. If the following table gives the angle θ radians through which the rod has turned for different values of time t seconds, find its angular velocity and angular acceleration when t = 0.7 seconds.*

t seconds :	*0.0*	*0.2*	*0.4*	*0.6*	*0.8*	*1.0*
θ radians :	*0.0*	*0.12*	*0.48*	*1.10*	*2.0*	*3.20*

Sol. The backward difference table is

t	θ	$\nabla\theta$	$\nabla^2\theta$	$\nabla^3\theta$	$\nabla^4\theta$
0.0	0.0				
		0.12			
0.2	0.12		0.24		
		0.36		0.02	
0.4	0.48		0.26		0
		0.62		0.02	
0.6	1.10		0.28		**0**
		0.90		**0.02**	
0.8	2.0		**0.30**		
		1.20			
1.0	**3.20**				

Angular velocity at $t = 0.7$ is $f'(0.7)$ and angular acceleration at $t = 0.7$ is $f''(0.7)$, where $\theta = f(t)$.

Newton's backward interpolation formula is

$$f(a - th) = f(a) - t\nabla f(a) + \frac{t(t-1)}{2!}\nabla^2 f(a) - \frac{t(t-1)(t-2)}{3!}\nabla^3 f(a)$$

$$= f(a) - t\nabla f(a) + \frac{t^2 - t}{2}\nabla^2 f(a) - \frac{t^3 - 3t^2 + 2t}{6}\nabla^3 f(a)$$

Differentiating w.r.t. 't', we get

$$-hf'(a - th) = -\nabla f(a) + \frac{2t-1}{2}\nabla^2 f(a) - \frac{3t^2 - 6t + 2}{6}\nabla^3 f(a)$$

or $$hf'(a - th) = \nabla f(a) - \frac{2t-1}{2}\nabla^2 f(a) + \frac{3t^2 - 6t + 2}{2}\nabla^3 f(a) \qquad ...(1)$$

Differentiating again w.r.t. t, we get

$$-hf''(a - th) = -\frac{2}{2}\nabla^2 f(a) + \frac{6t-6}{6}\nabla^3 f(a)$$

or $$hf''(a - th) = \nabla^2 f(a) - (t-1)\nabla^3 f(a) \qquad ...(2)$$

Here $a = 1.0$, $h = 0.2$, $a - th = 0.7$

$\therefore$ $$1.0 - 0.2t = 0.7 \Rightarrow t = \frac{0.3}{0.2} = 1.5$$

From (1), $$(0.2)f'(0.7) = 1.20 - \frac{2(1.5)-1}{2}(0.30) + \frac{3(1.5)^2 - 6(1.5) - 2}{6}(0.02)$$

$\Rightarrow$ $$f'(0.7) = 5[1.20 - 0.30 - 0.0008] = 4.50$$

$\therefore$ Angular velocity when $t = 0.7$ is 4.50 radians/sec.

From (2), $(0.2)^2 f''(0.7) = 0.30 - (1.5 - 1)(0.02)$

$\Rightarrow$ $$f''(0.7) = 25[0.30 - 0.01] = 7.25$$

$\therefore$ Angular acceleration when $t = 0.7$ is 7.25 radian/sec^2.

TEST YOUR KNOWLEDGE

1. From the following data :

x :	0.00	0.05	0.10	0.15	0.20	0.25
y :	0.00000	0.10017	0.20134	0.30452	0.41075	0.52110

evaluate $\frac{dy}{dx}$ at $x = 0.00$.

2. Obtain the first and second derivatives of $\sqrt{x}$ at $x = 15$ from the table :

x :	15	17	19	21	23	25
$\sqrt{x}$:	3.873	4.123	4.359	4.583	4.796	5.000

3. From the following table, calculate $\frac{dy}{dx}$ and $\frac{d^2y}{dx^2}$ at $x = 1.35$

x :	1.1	1.2	1.3	1.4	1.5	1.6
y :	– 1.62628	0.15584	2.45256	5.39168	9.12500	13.83072

4. Obtain the first and second derivatives of the function tabulated below, at the point $x = 0.6$

x	y
0.4	1.5836494
0.5	1.7974426
0.6	2.0442376
0.7	2.3275054
0.8	2.6510818

5. A function is given according to the table given below :

x	0.35	0.40	0.45	0.50	0.55	0.60	0.65
y	1.52153	1.50594	1.48797	1.46746	1.44424	1.41808	1.38869

Find the derivative for $x = 0.40$.

6. The population of a certain town (as obtained from census data) is shown in the following table :

Year	1921	1931	1941	1951	1961
Population (in thousands)	19.96	38.65	58.81	77.21	94.61

Estimate the population in the years 1936 and 1963. Also find the rate of growth of population in 1951. (Express your results correct to two places of decimals).

7. The following table gives the values of a function at equal intervals.

x :	0.0	0.5	1.0	1.5	2.0
$f(x)$:	0.3989	0.3521	0.2420	0.1295	0.0540

Evaluate $f(1.8)$, $f'(1.5)$ and $\int_0^2 f(x)\,dx$, stating the formula used.

8. Given the following tabulated values of a function :

x :	1.0	1.2	1.4	1.6	1.8	2.0	2.2
y :	2.7183	3.3201	4.0552	4.9530	6.0496	7.3891	9.0250

Prepare a difference table and evaluate y' at $x = 1.2$.

9. Estimate the annual rate of cloth sales of 1935 from the following data :

Year	*Sale of cloth (in lakhs of metres)*
1920	250
1925	285
1930	328
1940	444

10. From the following table, find $f'(1.4)$

x :	1.2	1.3	1.4	1.5	1.6
$f(x)$:	1.5095	1.6984	1.9043	2.1293	2.3756

11. Find the numerical value of the first derivative at $x = 0.4$ of the function $f(x)$ defined as under :

x :	0.1	0.2	0.3	0.4
$f(x)$:	1.10517	1.22140	1.34986	1.49182

12. From the following table, obtain the value of $\dfrac{d^2y}{dx^2}$ at the point $x = 0.96$

x :	0.96	0.98	1.00	1.02	1.04
y :	0.7825	0.7739	0.7651	0.7563	0.7473

Answers

1. 2.0034 **2.** 0.129, – 0.005 **3.** 29.33795, 71.33
4. 2.6442250, 3.6442400 **5.** – 0.33480 **6.** 42.31, 97.95, 1.79
7. 0.0781, – 0.3911, 0.4772 by Simpson's rule **8.** 3.3205 **9.** 11.55
10. 1.9585 **11.** 1.4913 **12.** – 73.25.

1.11. NUMERICAL INTEGRATION

The process of computing the value of a definite integral $\int_a^b y\,dx$ from a set of numerical values of the integrand y is called numerical integration.

As in numerical differentiation, the function $y = f(x)$ is represented by an interpolating polynomial of certain degree [n^{th} degree polynomial if there are $(n + 1)$ entries] which is integrated within the desired limits to get an approximate value of the definite integral. Now we derive a general formula for numerical integration by using Newton's forward interpolating formula.

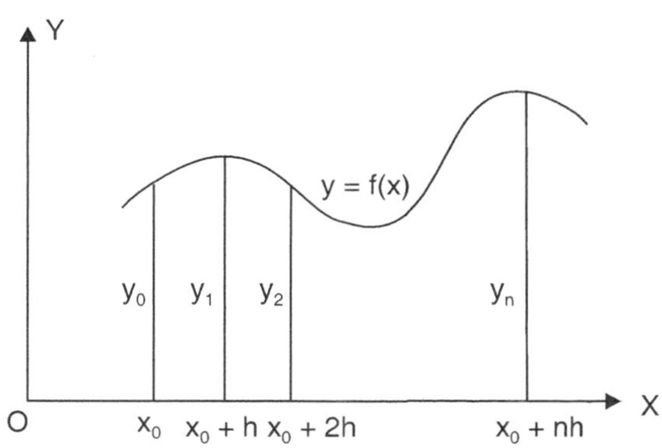

1.12. (a) Newton-cote's Quadrature Formula

Let $\quad I = \int_a^b y\,dx$ where y takes the values $y_0, y_1, y_2, \ldots\ldots, y_n$ for $x = x_0, x_1, x_2, \ldots\ldots, x_n$.

Let the interval of integration (a, b) be divided into n equal sub-interval, each of width $h = \frac{b-a}{n}$ so that $x_0 = a, x_1 = x_0 + h, x_2 = x_0 + 2h, \ldots\ldots, x_n = x_0 + nh = b$.

$$\therefore \qquad I = \int_{x_0}^{x_0 + nh} f(x)\,dx$$

Since any x is given by $x = x_0 = rh$ and $dx = hdr$

$$\therefore \qquad I = h \int_0^n f(x_0 + rh)\,dr$$

$$= h \int_0^n \left[y_0 + r\Delta y_0 + \frac{r(r-1)}{2!}\Delta^2 y_0 + \frac{r(r-1)(r-2)}{3!}\Delta^3 y_0 + \ldots\ldots \right] dr$$

[by Newton's forward interpolation formula]

$$= h \left[ry_0 + \frac{r^2}{2}\Delta y_0 + \frac{1}{2}\left(\frac{r^3}{3} - \frac{r^2}{2}\right)\Delta^2 y_0 + \frac{1}{6}\left(\frac{r^4}{4} - r^3 + r^2\right)\Delta^3 y_0 + \ldots\ldots \right]_0^n$$

$$= nh \left[y_0 + \frac{n}{2}\Delta y_0 + \frac{n(2n-3)}{12}\Delta^2 y_0 + \frac{n(n-2)^2}{24}\Delta^3 y_0 + \ldots\ldots \right] \qquad \ldots(1)$$

(M.G.U. Nov. 2008)

This is a general quadrature formula and is known as **Newton-Cote's quadrature formula.** A number of important deductions *viz.* Trapezoidal rule, Simpson's one-third and three-eighth rules, Weddle's rule can be immediately deduced by putting $n = 1, 2, 3$ and 6 respectively in formula (1).

1.12. (b) Trapezoidal Rule (n = 1)

Putting $n = 1$ in formula (1) and taking the curve through (x_0, y_0) and (x_1, y_1) as a polynomial of degree one so that differences of order higher than one vanish, we get

$$\int_{x_0}^{x_0 + h} f(x)\,dx = h\left(y_0 + \frac{1}{2}\Delta y_0\right) = \frac{h}{2}\,[2y_0 + (y_1 - y_0)] = \frac{h}{2}\,(y_0 + y_1)$$

Similarly, for the next sub-interval $(x_0 + h, x_0 + 2h)$, we get

$$\int_{x_0+h}^{x_0+2h} f(x)\,dx = \frac{h}{2}(y_1 + y_2), \ldots\ldots, \int_{x_0+(n-1)h}^{x_0+nh} f(x)\,dx = \frac{h}{2}\,(y_{n-1} + y_n)$$

Adding the above integrals, we get

$$\int_{x_0}^{x_0+nh} f(x)\,dx = \frac{h}{2}\,[(y_0 + y_n) + 2(y_1 + y_2 + \ldots\ldots + y_{n-1})]$$

which is known as Trapezoidal rule.

1.12. (c) Simpson's One-Third Rule (n = 2)

Putting $n = 2$ in formula (1) and taking the curve through (x_0, y_0), (x_1, y_1) and (x_2, y_2) as a polynomial of degree two so that differences of order higher than two vanish, we get

$$\int_{x_0}^{x_0+2h} f(x)\,dx = 2h\left[y_0 + \Delta y_0 + \frac{1}{6}\Delta^2 y_0\right]$$

$$= \frac{2h}{6}\,[6y_0 + 6(y_1 - y_0) + (y_2 - 2y_1 + y_0)] = \frac{h}{3}\,(y_0 + 4y_1 + y_2)$$

Similarly, $\displaystyle\int_{x_0+2h}^{x_0+4h} f(x)\,dx = \frac{h}{3}\,(y_2 + 4y_3 + y_4), \ldots\ldots, \int_{x_0+(n-2)h}^{x_0+nh} f(x)\,dx = \frac{h}{3}\,(y_{n-2} + 4y_{n-1} + y_n)$

Adding the above integrals, we get

$$\int_{x_0}^{x_0+nh} f(x)\,dx = \frac{h}{3}\,[(y_0 + y_n) + 4(y_1 + y_3 + \ldots\ldots + y_{n-1}) + 2(y_2 + y_4 + \ldots\ldots + y_{n-2})]$$

which is known as **Simpson's one-third rule.**

While using this formula, the given interval of integration must be divided into an even number of sub-intervals, since we find the area over two sub-intervals at a time.

1.12. (d) Simpson's Three-Eighth Rule (n = 3)

Putting $n = 3$ in formula (1) and taking the curve through (x_0, y_0), (x_1, y_1), (x_2, y_2) and (x_3, y_3) as a polynomial of degree three so that differences of order higher than three vanish, we get

$$\int_{x_0}^{x_0+3h} f(x)\,dx = 3h\left(y_0 + \frac{3}{2}\Delta y_0 + \frac{3}{4}\Delta^2 y_0 + \frac{1}{8}\Delta^3 y_0\right)$$

$$= \frac{3h}{8}\,[8y_0 + 12(y_1 - y_0) + 6(y_2 - 2y_1 + y_0) + (y_3 - 3y_2 + 3y_1 - y_0)]$$

$$= \frac{3h}{8}\,[y_0 + 3y_1 + 3y_2 + y_3]$$

Similarly, $\displaystyle\int_{x_0+3h}^{x_0+6h} f(x)\,dx = \frac{3h}{8}\,[y_3 + 3y_4 + 3y_5 + y_6], \ldots\ldots$

$$\int_{x_0+(n-3)h}^{x_0+nh} f(x)\,dx = \frac{3h}{8}\,[y_{n-3} + 3y_{n-2} + 3y_{n-1} + y_n]$$

Adding the above integrals, we get

$$\int_{x_0}^{x_0+nh} f(x)\,dx = \frac{3h}{8}\,[(y_0 + y_n) + 3(y_1 + y_2 + y_4 + y_5 + \ldots\ldots + y_{n-2} + y_{n-1}) + 2(y_3 + y_6 + \ldots\ldots\ y_{n-3})]$$

which is known as **Simpson's three-eighth rule.**

While using this formula, the given interval of integration must be divided into sub-intervals whose number n is a multiple of 3.

ILLUSTRATIVE EXAMPLES

Example 1. *Use trapezoidal rule to evaluate* $\int_0^1 x^3\,dx$ *considering five sub-intervals.*

Sol. Dividing the interval (0, 1) into five equal parts, each of width $h = \frac{1-0}{5} = 0.2$, the values of $f(x) = x^3$ are given below :

x :	0	0.2	0.4	0.6	0.8	1.0
$f(x)$:	0	0.008	0.064	0.216	0.512	1.000
	y_0	y_1	y_2	y_3	y_4	y_5

By trapezoidal rule, we have

$$\int_0^1 x^3\,dx = \frac{h}{2}\,[(y_0 + y_5) + 2(y_1 + y_2 + y_3 + y_4)]$$

$$= \frac{0.2}{2}\,[(0 + 1.000) + 2(0.008 + 0.064 + 0.216 + 0.512)] = 0.1 \times 2.6 = 0.26.$$

Example 2. *Evaluate* $\int_0^1 \frac{dx}{1+x^2}$ *using*

(*i*) *Simpson's* $\frac{1}{3}$ *rule taking* $h = \frac{1}{4}$

(*ii*) *Simpson's* $\frac{3}{8}$ *rule taking* $h = \frac{1}{6}$.

Hence compute an approximate value of π *in each case.*

Sol. (*i*) The values of $f(x) = \frac{1}{1+x^2}$ at $x = 0, \frac{1}{4}, \frac{2}{4}, \frac{3}{4}$, 1 are given below :

x :	0	$\frac{1}{4}$	$\frac{1}{2}$	$\frac{3}{4}$	1
$f(x)$:	1	0.9412	0.8000	0.6400	0.5000
	y_0	y_1	y_2	y_3	y_4

By Simpson's $\frac{1}{3}$ rule,

$$\int_0^1 \frac{dx}{1+x^2} = \frac{h}{3}\,[(y_0 + y_4) + 4(y_1 + y_3) + 2y_2]$$

$$= \frac{1}{12}\,[(1 + 0.5000) + 4(0.9412 + 0.6400) + 2(0.8000)] = 0.7854$$

Also $\int_0^1 \frac{dx}{1+x^2} = \tan^{-1} x \Big]_0^1 = \tan^{-1} 1 = \frac{\pi}{4} \quad \therefore \quad \frac{\pi}{4} \simeq 0.7854 \;\Rightarrow\; \pi \simeq 3.1416$

(*ii*) The value of $f(x) = \dfrac{1}{1+x^2}$ at $x = 0, \dfrac{1}{6}, \dfrac{2}{6}, \dfrac{3}{6}, \dfrac{4}{6}, \dfrac{5}{6}$, 1 are given below :

x :	0	$\frac{1}{6}$	$\frac{1}{3}$	$\frac{1}{2}$	$\frac{2}{3}$	$\frac{5}{6}$	1
$f(x)$:	1	0.9730	0.9000	0.8000	0.6923	0.5902	0.5000
	y_0	y_1	y_2	y_3	y_4	y_5	y_6

By Simpson's $\frac{3}{8}$ rule,

$$\int_0^1 \frac{dx}{1+x^2} = \frac{3h}{8} [(y_0 + y_6) + 3(y_1 + y_2 + y_4 + y_5) + 2y_3]$$

$$= \frac{1}{16} [(1 + 0.5000) + 3(0.9730 + 0.9000 + 0.6923 + 0.5902) + 2(0.8000)]$$

$$= 0.7854$$

Also $\displaystyle\int_0^1 \frac{dx}{1+x^2} = \frac{\pi}{4}$ $\therefore$ $\dfrac{\pi}{4} \simeq 0.7854 \Rightarrow \pi \simeq 3.1416$

Example 3. *The speed, v metres per second, of a car, t seconds after it starts, is shown in the following table :*

t	*0*	*12*	*24*	*36*	*48*	*60*	*72*	*84*	*96*	*108*	*120*
v	*0*	*3.60*	*10.08*	*18.90*	*21.60*	*18.54*	*10.26*	*5.40*	*4.50*	*5.40*	*9.00*

Using Simpson's rule, find the distance travelled by the car in 2 minutes.

Sol. If s metres is the distance covered in t seconds, then

$$\frac{ds}{dt} = v \qquad \therefore \quad s\Big]_{t=0}^{120} = \int_0^{120} v\, dt$$

$$= \frac{h}{3} [(y_0 + y_{10}) + 4(y_1 + y_3 + y_5 + y_7 + y_9) + 2(y_2 + y_4 + y_6 + y_8)] \qquad \left[\text{By Simpson's } \frac{1}{3} \text{ rule}\right]$$

$$= \frac{12}{3} [(0 + 9.00) + 4(3.60 + 18.90 + 18.54 + 5.40 + 5.40) + 2(10.08 + 21.60 + 10.26 + 4.50)]$$

$= 1236.96$ metres.

TEST YOUR KNOWLEDGE

1. Use trapezoidal rule to evaluate $\displaystyle\int_4^8 \frac{dx}{x}$, using four equal sub-intervals.
2. Apply (*i*) trapezoidal rule (*ii*) Simpson's $\frac{1}{3}$ rule, to find an approximate value of $\displaystyle\int_{-3}^3 x^4\, dx$ by taking six equal sub-intervals. Compare it with the exact value.
3. Find the value of $\displaystyle\int_1^2 \frac{dx}{x}$ by Simpson's rule. Hence find approximate value of $\log_e 2$.

4. Evaluate $\int_0^4 e^x\,dx$ by Simpson's rule, given that $e = 2.72$, $e^2 = 7.39$, $e^3 = 20.09$, $e^4 = 54.6$ and compare it with the actual value.

5. Find an approximate value of $\log_e 5$ by calculating to 4 decimal places, by Simpson's $\frac{1}{3}$ rule, $\int_0^5 \frac{dx}{4x+5}$, dividing the range into 10 equal parts.

6. Calculate the value of $\int_0^{\pi/2} \sin x\,dx$ by Simpson's $\frac{1}{3}$ rule, using 11 ordinates.

7. Evaluate $\int_0^6 \frac{dx}{1+x^2}$ by using Simpson's $\frac{3}{8}$ rule.

8. Use Simpson's rule, taking five ordinates, to find an approximate value of $\int_1^2 \sqrt{\left(x - \frac{1}{x}\right)}\,dx$ to two decimal places.

9. Evaluate $\int_0^{\pi/2} \sqrt{\sin x}\,dx$, given that

x	:	0	$\frac{\pi}{12}$	$\frac{\pi}{6}$	$\frac{\pi}{4}$	$\frac{\pi}{3}$	$\frac{5\pi}{12}$	$\frac{\pi}{2}$
$\sqrt{\sin x}$	:	0	0.5087	0.7071	0.8409	0.9306	0.9878	1

10. A river is 80 m wide. The depth d in metres at a distance x metres from one bank is given by the following table :

x	:	0	10	20	30	40	50	60	70	80
d	:	0	4	7	9	12	15	14	8	3

Find approximately the area of the cross-section.

11. Apply Simpson's rule to find the area bounded by the x-axis, the lines $x = 1$, $x = 4$ and the curve through the points

x	:	1	1.5	2	2.5	3	3.5	4
y	:	2	2.4	2.7	2.8	3	2.6	2.1

12. Estimate the length of the arc of the curve $3y = x^3$ from (0, 0) to (1, 3) using Simpson's $\frac{1}{3}$ rule taking 8 sub-intervals.

$$\left[\textbf{Hint. } s = \int_0^1 \sqrt{1+\left(\frac{dy}{dx}\right)^2}\,dx.\right]$$

13. A solid of revolution is formed by rotating about the x-axis, the area between the x-axis, the lines $x = 0$ and $x = 1$ and a curve through a points with the following coordinates :

x	:	0.00	0.25	0.50	0.75	1.00
y	:	1.0000	0.9896	0.9589	0.9089	0.8415

Estimate the volume of the solid formed using Simpson's rule.

$$\left[\textbf{Hint. } \text{volume of solid} = \int_0^1 \pi y^2\,dx = \pi\,.\,\frac{h}{3}\left\{(y_0^2 + y_4^2) + 4(y_1^2 + y_3^2) + 2y_2^2\right\}\right]$$

14. The velocity v (km/min) of a moped which starts from rest, is given at fixed intervals of time t (min) as follows :

t :	2	4	6	8	10	12	14	16	18	20
v :	10	18	25	29	32	20	11	5	2	0

Estimate approximately the distance covered in 20 minutes.

15. A rocket is launched from the ground. Its acceleration is registered during the first 80 seconds and is given in the table below. Using Simpson's $\frac{1}{3}$ rd rule, find the velocity of the rocket at $t = 80$ seconds.

$t(sec)$:	0	10	20	30	40	50	60	70	80
$f(cm/sec^2)$:	30	31.63	33.34	35.47	37.75	40.33	43.25	46.69	50.67

16. Evaluate $\int_0^1 e^{-x^2}\, dx$ by means of trapezoidal rule with $n = 10$.

(M.G.U. Nov. 2008 ; M.G.U. May 2008)

Answers

1. 0.698 **2.** (*i*) 115, error = 17.8 (*ii*) 98, error = 0.8 **3.** 0.693

4. 53.87, 53.60 **5.** 1.61 **6.** 0.9985 **7.** 1.3571

8. 0.84 **9.** 1.1615 **10.** 710 m^2 **11.** 7.78

12. 1.0893 **13.** 2.8192 **14.** 5.16 km **15.** 3086.1 cm/sec

16. 0.7468.

MODULE 2

Z-Transforms

2.1. DEFINITION

If the function u_n is defined for discrete values ($n = 0, 1, 2, \ldots$) and $u_n = 0$ for $n < 0$. Then its Z-transform is defined to be:

$$Z(u_n) = u(z) = \sum_{n=0}^{\infty} u_n z^{-n}, \text{ whenever the infinite series converges.}$$

The inverse Z-transform is written as $Z^{-1}[u(z)] = u_n$.

2.2. SOME STANDARD Z-TRANSFORMS

1. $Z(a^n) = \dfrac{z}{z-a}$.

Proof.

$$Z(a^n) = \sum_{n=0}^{\infty} a^n z^{-n} = \sum_{n=0}^{\infty} (a/z)^n$$

$$= 1 + (a/z) + (a/z)^2 + \ldots = (1 - a/z)^{-1}$$

$$= \frac{\mathbf{z}}{\mathbf{z - a}}.$$

2. $Z(n^p) = -z \dfrac{d}{dz} z(n^{p-1})$, p being a +ve integer.

Proof. $Z(n^p) = \sum_{n=0}^{\infty} n^p z^{-n} = z \sum_{n=0}^{\infty} n^{p-1}.n.z^{-(n+1)}$ ...(1)

Now consider $Z(n^{p-1}) = \sum_{n=0}^{\infty} n^{p-1}.z^{-n}$ ...(2)

Differentiate equation (2).

$$\frac{d}{dz}[Z(n^{p-1})] = \sum_{n=0}^{\infty} n^{p-1}.z^{-n-1}.(-n)$$

$$= -\sum_{n=0}^{\infty} n^{p-1}.n.z^{-(n+1)} \quad \ldots(3)$$

By (1), $Z(n^p) = -\mathbf{z}.\dfrac{\mathbf{d}}{\mathbf{dz}}[Z(n^{p-1})]$ which is the required recurrence formula.

In particular,

1. $Z(1) = \dfrac{\mathbf{z}}{\mathbf{z-1}}$

$\because \quad Z(a^n) = \dfrac{z}{z-a}$, put $a = 1$.

$Z(1) = \dfrac{z}{z-1}$

2. $$Z(n) = -z\frac{d}{dz}[Z(1)] = -z\left\{\frac{d}{dz}\left(\frac{z}{z-1}\right)\right\}$$

$$= -z\left\{\frac{(z-1)-z}{(z-1)^2}\right\} = \frac{\mathbf{z}}{(\mathbf{z-1})^2}$$

3. $$Z(n^2) = -z\frac{d}{dz}[z(n)] = -z\left\{\frac{d}{dz}\left(\frac{z}{(z-1)^2}\right)\right\}$$

$$= -z\left\{\frac{(z-1)^2 - z.2(z-1)}{(z-1)^4}\right\} = \frac{z(z+1)}{(z-1)^3} = \frac{\mathbf{z^2+z}}{(\mathbf{z-1})^3}$$

4. $$Z(n^3) = -z\frac{d}{dz}[Z(n^2)] = -z\frac{d}{dz}\left(\frac{z^2+z}{(z-1)^3}\right)$$

$$= -z\left\{\frac{(z-1)^3(2z+1) - (z^2+z).3(z-1)^2}{(z-1)^6}\right\} = \frac{\mathbf{z^3+4z^2+z}}{(\mathbf{z-1})^4}$$

5. Similarly $$Z(n^4) = \frac{\mathbf{z^4+11z^3+11z^2+z}}{(\mathbf{z-1})^5}.$$

2.3. PROPERTIES

1. **Linearity Property:** If a, b be any constants and u_n and v_n be any discrete functions, then

$$Z[a\,u_n \pm b\,v_n] = a\,Z(u_n) \pm b\,Z(v_n).$$

Proof. By definition:

$$Z[au_n \pm bv_n] = \sum_{n=0}^{\infty}[a\,u_n \pm b\,v_n]z^{-n}$$

$$= \sum_{n=0}^{\infty} a\,u_n z^{-n} \pm \sum_{n=0}^{\infty} bv_n z^{-n} = a\sum_{n=0}^{\infty} u_n z^{-n} \pm b\sum v_n z^{-n}$$

$$= \mathbf{a\,Z(u_n) \pm b\,Z(v_n)}.$$

2. **Damping Rule:** If $Z(u_n) = u(z)$, then $Z(a^{-n}\,u_n) = u(az)$

Proof. $$Z(a^{-n}\,u_n) = \sum_{n=0}^{\infty} a^{-n}.u_n z^{-n} = \sum_{n=0}^{\infty} u_n (az)^{-n}.$$

$$= \mathbf{u(az)}.$$

Note. $z(a^n u_n) = u(z/a)$.

The geometric factor a^{-n}, when $|a| < 1$, damps the function u_n, hence the some *damping rule.*

Some Standard Results:

1. $$Z(n\, a^n) = \frac{az}{(z-a)^2}.$$

Proof. $$Z(n) = \frac{z}{(z-1)^2}, \text{ applying damping rule,}$$

$$Z(n\, a^n) = u(z/a) = \frac{z/a}{(z/a-1)^2} = \frac{\mathbf{az}}{(\mathbf{z}-\mathbf{a})^2}.$$

2. $$Z(n^2 a^n) = \frac{az^2 + a^2 z}{(z-a)^3}.$$

Proof. $$Z(n^2) = \frac{z^2+z}{(z-1)^3}.$$

$\therefore$ $$Z(n^2 a^n) = u(z/a) = \frac{(z/a)^2 + (z/a)}{(z/a-1)^3}$$

$$= \frac{\mathbf{az^2 + a^2 z}}{(\mathbf{z}-\mathbf{a})^3}.$$

3. $$Z(\cos n\theta) = \frac{z(z-\cos\theta)}{z^2 - 2z\cos\theta + 1}$$

and $$Z(\sin n\theta) = \frac{z\sin\theta}{z^2 - 2z\cos\theta + 1}.$$

Proof. $$Z(1) = z/(z-1).$$

$$Z(e^{-in\theta}) = z[(e^{i\theta})^{-n} \,.\, 1] = \frac{ze^{i\theta}}{ze^{i\theta}-1} = \frac{z}{z-e^{-i\theta}}$$

$$= \frac{z\,(z-e^{i\theta})}{(z-e^{-i\theta})(z-e^{i\theta})} = \frac{z[z-\cos\theta - i\sin\theta]}{z^2 - z(e^{i\theta}+e^{-i\theta})+1}$$

$$= \frac{z[(z-\cos\theta) - i\sin\theta]}{z^2-2z\cos\theta+1} = \frac{z(z-\cos\theta)}{z^2-2z\cos\theta+1} - i\frac{z\sin\theta}{z^2-2z\cos\theta+1}$$

$\therefore$ $$\mathbf{Z[\cos n\theta]} = \frac{z(z-\cos\theta)}{z^2-2z\cos\theta+1}$$

and $$\mathbf{Z[\sin n\theta]} = \frac{\mathbf{z\sin\theta}}{\mathbf{z^2 - 2z\cos\theta + 1}}$$

4. $$Z[a^n \cos n\theta] = \frac{z(z-a\cos\theta)}{z^2-2az\cos\theta+a^2}$$

$$Z[a^n \sin n\theta] = \frac{az \sin\theta}{z^2 - 2az\cos\theta + a^2}.$$

Proof. $$Z[\cos n\theta] = \frac{z(z-\cos\theta)}{z^2 - 2z\cos\theta + 1}$$

$\therefore$ $$Z[a^n \cos n\theta] = u(z/a)$$

$$= \frac{z/a\,(z/a - \cos\theta)}{(z/a)^2 - 2(z/a)\cos\theta + 1}$$

$$= \frac{\mathbf{z(z - a\cos\theta)}}{\mathbf{z^2 - 2az\cos\theta + a^2}}$$

$$Z[a^n \sin n\theta] = \frac{z/a \sin\theta}{\frac{z^2}{a^2} - \frac{2z}{a}\cos\theta + 1} = \frac{az\sin\theta}{z^2 - 2az\cos\theta + a^2}.$$

ILLUSTRATIVE EXAMPLES

Example 1. *Find the Z-transform of the following:*

(i) $3n - 4\sin\frac{n\pi}{4} + 5a$ *(ii)* $(n+1)^2$ *(iii)* $\sin(3n+5)$.

Sol. (*i*) $$Z[3n - 4\sin\frac{n\pi}{4} + 5a] = 3z(n) - 4z\left[\sin\frac{n\pi}{4}\right] + 5z[a]$$

$$= 3.\frac{z}{(z-1)^2} - 4.\frac{z\sin\frac{\pi}{4}}{z^2 - 2z\cos\frac{\pi}{4} + 1} + 5a.\frac{z}{z-1}$$

$$= \frac{3z}{(z-1)^2} + \frac{5az}{(z-1)} - \frac{4.z\frac{1}{\sqrt{2}}}{z^2 - 2z\frac{1}{\sqrt{2}} + 1}$$

$$= \frac{\mathbf{3z + 5az\,(z-1)}}{\mathbf{(2-1)^2}} - \frac{\mathbf{2\sqrt{2}\,z}}{\mathbf{z^2 - \sqrt{2}\,z + 1}}.$$

(*ii*) $$z[(n+1)^2] = z[n^2 + 2n + 1] = z[n^2] + 2\,z[n] + z[1].$$

$$= \frac{z(z+1)}{(z-1)^3} + 2\frac{z}{(z-1)^2} + \frac{z}{(z-1)}$$

$$= \frac{z^2 + z + 2z(z-1) + z(z-1)^2}{(z-1)^3} = \frac{z[z + 1 + 2z - 2 + z^2 - 2z + 1]}{(z-1)^3}$$

$$= \frac{z[z^2 + z]}{(z-1)^3} = \frac{\mathbf{z^2[z+1]}}{\mathbf{(z-1)^3}}.$$

(*iii*)
$$\begin{aligned}Z[\sin(3n+5)] &= Z[\sin 3n \cos 5 + \cos 3n \sin 5]\\ &= \cos 5\, Z[\sin 3n] + \sin 5\, Z[\cos 3n]\\ &= \cos 5 \frac{z \sin 3}{z^2 - 2z\cos 3 + 1} + \sin 5 \frac{z(z-\cos 3)}{z^2 - 2z\cos 3+1}\\ &= \frac{z[\cos 5 \sin 3 + z \sin 5 - \sin 5 \cos 3]}{z^2 - 2z \cos 3 + 1}\\ &= \frac{z[z\sin 5 + \sin(3-5)]}{z^2 - 2z\cos 3 + 1} = \mathbf{\frac{z[z\sin 5 - \sin 2]}{z^2 - 2z\cos 3 + 1}}.\end{aligned}$$

Example 2. *Find the Z-transform of the following:*

(*i*) e^{an} (*ii*) ne^{an} (*iii*) n^2e^{an}.

Sol. (*i*) $Z[e^{an}] = z[1 \,.\, (e^{-a})^{-n}]$.

$$Z(1) = \frac{z}{z-1} \qquad \therefore \quad Z[1\,.\,(e^{-a})^{-n}] = u(e^{-a}z)$$

$$\therefore \quad Z[e^{an}] = \frac{ze^{-a}}{ze^{-a}-1} = \mathbf{\frac{z}{z-e^a}}$$

(*ii*) $Z[ne^{an}] = z[n\,.\,(e^{-a})^{-n}]$ $\qquad Z(n) = \dfrac{z}{(z-1)^2}$

$$\therefore \quad Z[ne^{an}] = u(e^{-a}z) = \frac{ze^{-a}}{(ze^{-a}-1)^2} = \frac{ze^a}{(z-e^a)^2}.$$

(*iii*) $Z[n^2e^{an}] = z[n^2(e^{-a})^{-n}] = u(ze^{-a})$

$$Z(n^2) = \frac{z^2+z}{(z-1)^3} \qquad \therefore \quad Z[n^2(e^{-a})^{-n}] = \frac{(ze^{-a})^2 + ze^{-a}}{(ze^{-a}-1)^3}.$$

$$\therefore \quad Z[n^2e^{an}] = \mathbf{\frac{ze^a(z+e^a)}{(z-e^a)^3}}.$$

Example 3. *Find the Z-transform of (i) cosh nθ (ii) a^n cosh nθ.*

Sol. (*i*)
$$Z[\cosh n\theta] = z\left[\frac{e^{n\theta}+e^{-n\theta}}{2}\right] = \frac{1}{2}[z(e^{n\theta}) + z(e^{-n\theta})]$$

$$= \frac{1}{2}\left\{\{z[1.(e^{-\theta})^{-n}]\} + z[1.(e^{\theta})^{-n}]\right\} \qquad \Bigg|\; Z(1) = \frac{z}{z-1}$$

$$= \frac{1}{2}\left\{\frac{ze^{-\theta}}{ze^{-\theta}-1} + \frac{ze^{\theta}}{ze^{\theta}-1}\right\} = \frac{1}{2}\left\{\frac{2z^2 - z(e^{\theta}+e^{-\theta})}{z^2 - z(e^{\theta}+e^{-\theta})+1}\right\}$$

$$= \frac{1}{2}\left\{\frac{2(z^2 - z\cosh\theta)}{z^2 - 2z\cosh\theta + 1}\right\} = \mathbf{\frac{z(z-\cosh\theta)}{z^2 - 2z\cosh\theta + 1}}.$$

(*ii*) $Z[a^n \cosh n\theta] = z[(a^{-1})^{-n} \cosh n\theta]$

$= za^{-1}\,[za^{-1} - \cosh\theta]/(za^{-1})^2 - 2(za^{-1})\cosh\theta + 1$

$$= \mathbf{\frac{z(z - a\cosh\theta)}{z^2 - 2az\cosh\theta + a^2}}.$$

Example 4. *Find the Z-transforms of:*

(*i*) $e^t \sin 2t$ (*ii*) $e^k \cos k\alpha\ (k \geq 0)$.

Sol. (*i*) $Z(e^t \sin 2t) = Z\,((e^{-1})^{-t} \sin 2t)$

$$Z(e^t \sin 2t) = \frac{e^{-1}z\sin 2}{(e^{-1}z)^2 - 2(e^{-1}z)\cos 2 + 1} \qquad \left|\ Z(\sin 2t) = \frac{z\sin 2}{z^2 - 2z\cos 2 + 1}\right.$$

$$= \mathbf{\frac{ez\sin 2}{z^2 - 2ze\cos 2 + e^2}}$$

(*ii*) $Z(\cos k\alpha) = z(z - \cos\alpha)/z^2 - 2z\cos\alpha + 1$

$Z(e^k \cos k\alpha) = z((e^{-1})^{-k} \cos k\alpha)$

$$= \frac{(e^{-1}z)(e^{-1}z - \cos\alpha)}{(e^{-1}z)^2 - 2(e^{-1}z)\cos\alpha + 1}$$

$$= \mathbf{\frac{z(z - e\cos\alpha)}{z^2 - 2ez\cos\alpha + e^2}}.$$

Example 5. *Find the Z-transforms of:*

(*i*) $\cos\left(\frac{n\pi}{2} + \frac{\pi}{4}\right)$ (*ii*) $\cosh\left(\frac{n\pi}{2} + \theta\right)$.

Sol. (*i*) $$Z\left[\cos\left(\frac{n\pi}{2} + \frac{\pi}{4}\right)\right] = z\left[\cos\frac{n\pi}{2}\cos\frac{\pi}{4} - \sin\frac{n\pi}{2}\sin\frac{\pi}{4}\right]$$

$$= \cos\frac{\pi}{4}\, z\left[\cos\frac{n\pi}{2}\right] - \sin\frac{\pi}{4}\, z\left[\sin\frac{n\pi}{2}\right]$$

$$= \frac{1}{\sqrt{2}}\left\{\frac{z(z - \cos\pi/2)}{z^2 - 2z\cos\pi/2 + 1}\right\} - \frac{1}{\sqrt{2}}\left\{\frac{z\sin\pi/2}{z^2 - 2z\cos\pi/2 + 1}\right\}$$

$$= \frac{1}{\sqrt{2}}\left\{\frac{z^2 - z}{z^2 + 1}\right\} = \mathbf{\frac{z(z-1)}{\sqrt{2}\,(z^2 + 1)}}$$

(*ii*) $$Z\left[\cosh\left(\frac{n\pi}{2} + \theta\right)\right] = z\left[\frac{e^{\left(\frac{n\pi}{2} + \theta\right)} + e^{-\left(\frac{n\pi}{2} + \theta\right)}}{2}\right]$$

$$= \frac{1}{2}\left\{z\left[e^{\theta}\cdot e^{\frac{n\pi}{2}}\right] + z\left[e^{-\theta}\cdot e^{-n\pi/2}\right]\right\}$$

$$= \frac{1}{2}\left\{e^{\theta}\cdot\frac{z}{z-e^{\pi/2}} + e^{-\theta}\cdot\frac{z}{z-e^{-\pi/2}}\right\}$$

$$Z(a^n) = \frac{z}{z-a}$$

$$Z(e^{n\pi/2}) = \frac{z}{z-e^{\pi/2}}$$

$$Z(e^{-n\pi/2}) = \frac{z}{z-e^{-\pi/2}}$$

$$= \frac{z}{2}\left\{\frac{e^{\theta}(z-e^{-\pi/2}) + e^{-\theta}(z-e^{\pi/2})}{(z-e^{-\pi/2})(z-e^{\pi/2})}\right\}$$

$$= \frac{z}{2}\left\{\frac{z(e^{\theta}+e^{-\theta}) - \left[e^{(\pi/2-\theta)} + e^{-(\pi/2-\theta)}\right]}{z^2 - z(e^{\pi/2}+e^{-\pi/2})+1}\right\}$$

$$= \frac{\mathbf{z^2 \cosh \theta - z \cosh (\pi/2 - \theta)}}{\mathbf{z^2 - 2z \cosh (\pi/2) + 1}}.$$

Example 6. *Find the Z-transform of:*

(i) ^nC_p $\quad (0 \le p \le n)$ $\quad$ *(ii)* $^{n+p}C_p$.

Sol. *(i)* $Z(^nC_p) = \sum_{p=0}^{n} {}^nC_p\, z^{-p} = 1 + {}^nC_1\, z^{-1} + {}^nC_2\, z^{-2} + \ldots + {}^nC_n\, z^{-n}$.

$$= (1 + z^{-1})^n = \left(1 + \frac{1}{z}\right)^n = \left(\frac{\mathbf{z+1}}{\mathbf{z}}\right)^{\mathbf{n}}.$$

(ii) $$Z[^{n+p}C_p] = \sum_{p=0}^{\infty} {}^{n+p}C_p\, z^{-p}$$

$$= 1 + {}^{n+1}C_1\, z^{-1} + {}^{n+2}C_2\, z^{-2} + {}^{n+3}C_3\, z^{-3} + \ldots$$

$$= 1 + (n+1)z^{-1} + \frac{(n+2)(n+1)}{1.2}z^{-2} + \frac{(n+3)(n+2)(n+1)}{3!}z^{-3} + \cdots \infty$$

$$= 1 + (-n-1)(-z^{-1}) + \frac{(-n-1)(-n-2)}{2!}(-z^{-1})^2 + \cdots \infty$$

$$= (1 - z^{-1})^{-n-1} = \mathbf{(1 - z^{-1})^{-(n+1)}}.$$

Example 7. *Find the Z-transform of:*

(i) Unit impulse function $\delta(n) = \begin{cases} 1, & n = 0 \\ 0, & n \neq 0 \end{cases}$

(ii) Unit step sequence $u(n) = \begin{cases} 0, & n < 0 \\ 1, & n \geq 0 \end{cases}$.

Sol. *(i)* $$Z(\delta(n)) = \sum_{n=0}^{\infty} \delta(n)\, z^{-n} = 1 + 0 + \ldots + 0 = 1.$$

(ii) $$Z(u(n)) = \sum_{n=0}^{\infty} u(n)\, z^{-n} = \sum_{n=0}^{\infty} z^{-n} = (1 + z^{-1} + z^{-2} + \ldots) = (1 - z^{-1})^{-1}.$$

$$= \frac{\mathbf{z}}{\mathbf{z-1}}$$

3. Shifting Theorems:

(*a*) *Shifting* u_n *to right:* If $Z(u_n) = u(z)$. Then

$$Z(u_{n-k}) = z^{-k}\, u(z), \quad k > 0.$$

Proof.
$$Z(u_{n-k}) = \sum_{n=0}^{\infty} u_{n-k} \cdot z^{-n} \qquad \left| \begin{aligned} n-k &= m \\ n &= m+k \end{aligned} \right.$$

$$= \sum_{m=0}^{\infty} u_m z^{-(m+k)} = z^{-k} \sum_{n=0}^{\infty} u_m z^{-m} = z^{-k} \cdot u(z)$$

$\therefore$
$$\mathbf{Z(u_{n-k}) = z^{-k} \cdot u(z).}$$

Note: This rule will be very useful in applications to difference equation.

(*b*) *Shifting* u_n *to left:* If $Z(u_n) = u(z)$, then

$$Z(u_{n+k}) = z^k[u(z) - u_0 - u_1 z^{-1} - u_2 z^{-2} - \ldots - u_{k-1} z^{-(k-1)}].$$

Proof.
$$Z(u_{n+k}) = \sum_{n=0}^{\infty} u_{n+k} z^{-n} = z^k \cdot \sum_{n=0}^{\infty} u_{n+k}\, z^{-(n+k)}$$

$$= z^k \left[\sum_{n=0}^{\infty} u_n z^{-n} - \sum_{n=0}^{k-1} u_n z^{-n} \right].$$

$$= z^k\, [u(z) - u_0 - u_1 z^{-1} - u_2 z^{-2} - \ldots - u_{k-1} z^{-(k-1)}].$$

Note: In particular, we have the following results:

(*i*) $Z(u_{n+1}) = z[u(z) - u_0]$.

(*ii*) $Z(u_{n+2}) = z^2[u(z) - u_0 - u_1 z^{-1}]$.

(*iii*) $Z(u_{n+3}) = z^3[u(z) - u_0 - u_1 z^{-1} - u_2 z^{-2}]$.

Example 8. *Show that* $Z\left(\frac{1}{n!}\right) = e^{1/z}$. *Hence evaluate* $= Z\left(\frac{1}{(n+1)!}\right)$ *and* $Z\left(\frac{1}{(n+2)!}\right)$.

Sol.
$$Z(1/n!) = \sum_{n=0}^{\infty} \left(\frac{1}{n!}\right) z^{-n} = 1 + \frac{z^{-1}}{1!} + \frac{z^{-2}}{2!} + \cdots = e^{+z^{-1}} = \mathbf{e^{1/z}}$$

Shifting $(1/n!)$ one unit left:
$$Z\left(\frac{1}{(n+1)!}\right) = z\left(z\left(\frac{1}{n!}\right) - 1\right) = z(e^{1/z} - 1)$$

Similarly,
$$Z\left(\frac{1}{(n+2)!}\right) = \mathbf{z^2(e^{1/z} - 1 - z^{-1}).}$$

4. Multiplication by '*n*': If $Z(u_n) = u(z)$, then $Z(nu_n) = -z\dfrac{d}{dz}u(z)$.

Proof.
$$Z(nu_n) = \sum_{n=0}^{\infty} nu_n \cdot z^{-n} = -z \sum_{n=0}^{\infty} u_n \cdot (-n)\, z^{-n-1}$$

$$Z(u_n) = \sum_{n=0}^{\infty} u_n z^{-n} = u(z).$$

$$\frac{d}{dz} u(z) = \sum_{n=0}^{\infty} u_n (-n) z^{-n-1}.$$

$$\therefore \qquad Z(nu_n) = -\mathbf{z} \cdot \frac{\mathbf{d}}{\mathbf{dz}} \mathbf{u(z)}.$$

Note: By Mathematical Inductions

$$Z(n^m u_n) = (-z)^m \frac{d^m}{dz^m} u(z)$$

Example 9. *Find the Z-transform of (i) n sin nθ (ii) $n^2 e^{n\theta}$.*

Sol. (*i*) $\quad Z(\sin n\theta) = z \sin\theta / z^2 - 2z\cos\theta + 1.$ $\qquad \left| \; Z(nu_n) = -z \dfrac{d}{dz} u(z) \right.$

$$Z(n \sin n\theta) = -z \frac{d}{dz}\left[\frac{z \sin\theta}{z^2 - 2z\cos\theta + 1}\right]$$

$$= \frac{\mathbf{z(z^2 - 1)\sin\theta}}{\mathbf{(z^2 - 2z\cos\theta + 1)^2}}$$

(*ii*)
$$Z(e^{n\theta}) = \frac{z}{z - e^{\theta}}$$

$$Z(n^2 u_n) = (-z)^2 \frac{d^2}{dz^2} u(z)$$

$$\therefore \qquad Z(n^2 e^{n\theta}) = z^2 \frac{d}{dz}\left(\frac{d}{dz}\left(\frac{z}{z - e^{\theta}}\right)\right) = z^2 \frac{d}{dz}\left(\frac{-e^{\theta}}{(z - e^{\theta})^2}\right).$$

$$= -z^2 \left\{\frac{(z - e^{\theta})^2 \times \theta - e^{\theta} \cdot 2(z - e^{\theta})}{(z - e^{\theta})^4}\right\}$$

$$Z(n^2 e^{n\theta}) = \frac{\mathbf{2e^{\theta} z^2}}{\mathbf{(z - e^{\theta})^3}}.$$

5. Two Basic Theorems:

(*i*) **Initial value theorem:** If $Z(u_n) = u(z)$, then

$$u_0 = \underset{z \to \infty}{\text{Lt}}\, u(z).$$

Proof.
$$u(z) = z(u_n) = \sum_{n=0}^{\infty} u_n z^{-n}.$$

$$= u_0 + u_1 z^{-1} + u_2 z^{-2} + u_3 z^{-3} + \ldots$$

Taking limit as $z \to \infty$. then, $\frac{1}{z} \to 0$.

$$\therefore \qquad \underset{z \to \infty}{\text{Lt}}\ u(z) = u_0 + 0 + \ldots = u_0.$$

$$\therefore \qquad u_0 = \underset{\mathbf{z} \to \infty}{\textbf{Lt}}\ \mathbf{u(z)}.$$

Note: Similarly, additional initial values can be found successively.

$$u_1 = \underset{z \to \infty}{\text{Lt}}\ \{z\,[u(z) - u_0]\}$$

$$u_2 = \underset{z \to \infty}{\text{Lt}}\ \{z^2\,[u(z) - u_0 - u_1 z^{-1}]\}\ldots$$

(*ii*) **Final value theorem:** If $Z(u_n) = u(z)$, then

$$\underset{n \to \infty}{\text{Lt}}\ u_n = \underset{n \to 1}{\text{Lt}}\ (z-1)\,u(z).$$

Proof.

$$Z(u_{n+1} - u_n) = \sum_{n=0}^{\infty} (u_{n+1} - u_n)\, z^{-n}.$$

$$Z(u_{n+1}) - z(u_n) = \sum_{n=0}^{\infty} (u_{n+1} - u_n)\, z^{-n}$$

$$Z[u(z) - u_0] - u(z) = \sum_{n=0}^{\infty} (u_{n+1} - u_n)\, z^{-n}$$

$$u(z)\,(z-1) - u_0 z = \sum_{n=0}^{\infty} (u_{n+1} - u_n)\, z^{-n}.$$

Taking limits of both sides as $z \to 1$.

$$\underset{z \to 1}{\text{Lt}}\ [(z-1)\,u(z)] - u_0 = \sum_{n=0}^{\infty} (u_{n+1} - u_n) \qquad \ldots(1)$$

$$= \underset{n \to \infty}{\text{Lt}}\ [(u_1 - u_0) + (u_2 - u_1) + (u_3 - u_2) + \ldots + (u_{n+1} - u_n)]$$

$$= \underset{n \to \infty}{\text{Lt}}\ u_{n+1} - u_0 = u_\infty - u_0.$$

$$\therefore \qquad \underset{z \to 1}{\text{Lt}}\ [(z-1)\,u(z)] = u_\infty.$$

$$\therefore \qquad \underset{n \to \infty}{\text{Lt}}\ u_n = \underset{z \to 1}{\text{Lt}}\ [(z-1)\,u(z)]$$

Example 10. *If* $u(z) = \dfrac{2z^2 + 5z + 14}{(z-1)^4}$, *evaluate* u_2 *and* u_3.

Sol.

$$u(z) = \frac{1}{z^2}\,\frac{2 + 5z^{-1} + 14z^{-2}}{(1 - z^{-1})^4}$$

By initial value theorem,

$$u_0 = \underset{z \to \infty}{\text{Lt}}\ u(z) = 0.$$

$$u_1 = \underset{z \to \infty}{\text{Lt}} \{z[u(z) - u_0]\} = 0.$$

$$u_2 = \underset{z \to \infty}{\text{Lt}} \{z^2 [u(z) - u_0 - u_1 z^{-1}]\} = 2 - 0 - 0 = 2$$

$$u_3 = \underset{z \to \infty}{\text{Lt}} \{z^3 [u(z) - u_0 - u_1 z^{-1} - u_2 z^{-2}]\}$$

$$= \underset{z \to \infty}{\text{Lt}} \{z^3 u(z) - z^3 u_0 - z^2 u_1 - z u_2\}.$$

$$= \underset{z \to \infty}{\text{Lt}} \left\{z^3 . \left(\frac{2z^2 + 5z + 14}{(z-1)^4}\right) - 0 - 0 - 2z\right\} = 13$$

2.4. CONVOLUTIONS THEOREM

If $Z^{-1}[U(z)] = u_n$

$Z^{-1}(V(z)) = v_n$, *then* $Z^{-1}[U(z) . V(z)] = \sum_{m=0}^{n} u_m . v_{n-m} = u_n * v_n$,

where the symbol '' denotes the convolutions operations.*

Proof. $U(z) = Z(u_n) = \sum_{n=0}^{\infty} u_n z^{-n}$ $\quad V(z) = z(V_n) = \sum_{n=0}^{\infty} u_n . z^{-n}$.

$$U(z) . V(z) = (u_0 + u_1 z^{-1} + u_2 z^{-2} + \ldots)(v_0 + v_1 z^{-1} + v_2 z^{-2} + \ldots)$$

$$= \sum_{n=0}^{\infty} (u_0 v_n + u_1 v_{n-1} + u_2 v_{n-2} + \ldots + u_n v_0) z^{-n}$$

$$= Z[u_0 v_n + u_1 v_{n-1} + u_2 v_{n-2} + \ldots + u_n v_0] = Z\left[\sum_{m=0}^{n} u_m v_{n-m}\right]$$

$\therefore$ $Z^{-1}[U(z) . V(z)] = u_0 v_n + u_1 v_{n-1} + u_2 v_{n-2} + \ldots + u_n v_0 = \mathbf{u_n * v_n}$.

Example 11. *Use convolutions theorem to evaluate:* $Z^{-1}\left\{\frac{z^2}{(z-a)(z-b)}\right\}$.

Sol. $Z^{-1}\left(\frac{z}{z-a}\right) = a^n \qquad Z^{-1}\left(\frac{z}{z-b}\right) = b^n.$

$$\therefore \quad Z^{-1}\left(\frac{z^2}{(z-a)(z-b)}\right) = a^n * b^n.$$

$$= \sum_{m=0}^{n} a^m . b^{n-m} = b^n . \sum_{n=0}^{n} (a/b)^m.$$

$$= b^n \left\{\frac{(a/b)^{n+1} - 1}{a/b - 1}\right\} = \frac{\mathbf{a^{n+1} - b^{n+1}}}{\mathbf{a - b}}.$$

2.5. EVALUATION OF INVERSE Z-TRANSFORMS

I. Convolutions Method: We know that

If $Z^{-1}[u(z)] = u_n$ and $Z^{-1}[v(z)] = v_n$. then

$$Z^{-1}[u(z) \,.\, v(z)] = u_n * v_n.$$

Example 12. *Find* $Z^{-1}\left\{\dfrac{z^2}{(z-4)(z-3)}\right\}$.

Sol. $Z^{-1}\left\{\dfrac{z}{z-4}\right\} = 4^n \qquad Z^{-1}\left\{\dfrac{z}{z-3}\right\} = 3^n.$

$$Z^{-1}\left\{\frac{z^2}{(z-4)(z-3)}\right\} = 4^n * 3^n.$$

$$= \sum_{m=0}^{n} 4^m \,.\, 3^{n-m} = 3^n \sum_{m=0}^{n}\left(\frac{4}{3}\right)^m = 3^n\left\{\frac{(4/3)^{n+1}-1}{4/3-1}\right\}$$

$$= \mathbf{4^{n+1} - 3^{n+1}}$$

II. Power Series Method: If $u(z)$ is expressed as the ratio of two polynomials which cannot be factorized, divide the numerator by the denominator and take inverse Z-transforms of each term in the quotient.

Example 13. *Find* $Z^{-1}\left\{\log\left(\dfrac{z}{z+1}\right)\right\}$ *by power series method.*

Sol. Let $u(z) = \log\left(\dfrac{z}{z+1}\right)$. Let $z = \dfrac{1}{y}$.

Then $u(z) \,.\, \log\left(\dfrac{1/y}{1/y+1}\right) = -\log(1+y) = -y + \dfrac{y^2}{2} - \dfrac{y^3}{3} + \dfrac{y^4}{4} - \ldots\ldots$

$$= \frac{-1}{z} + \frac{1}{2}\cdot\frac{1}{z^2} - \frac{1}{3}\cdot\frac{1}{z^3} + \ldots\ldots = -1\,(z^{-1}) + \frac{1}{2}z^{-2} - \frac{1}{3}z^{-3} + \ldots\ldots$$

$$\therefore \qquad u_n = \begin{cases} \mathbf{0,} & \textbf{for n = 0} \\ \mathbf{(-1)^n/n,} & \textbf{elsewhere} \end{cases}.$$

III. Long Division Method: Since Z-transforms is defines by the series $u(z) = \sum_{0}^{\infty} u_n z^{-n}$, to find $Z^{-1}(u(z))$, expand $u(z)$ is the proper power series and collect the coefficient of z^{-n} to get $u(n)$.

Example 14. *Find* $Z^{-1}\left[\dfrac{10z}{z^2-3z+2}\right]$.

Sol. $u(z) = \dfrac{10z}{z^2-3z+2} = \dfrac{10z^{-1}}{1-3z^{-1}+2z^{-2}}$

By actual divisions:

$$\begin{array}{r|l} & 10z^{-1}+30z^{-2}+70z^{-3} \\ \hline 1-3z^{-1}+2z^{-2} & 10z^{-1} \\ & 10z^{-1}-30z^{-2}+20z^{-3} \\ \hline & \quad 30z^{-2}-20z^{-3} \\ & \quad 30z^{-2}-90z^{-3}+60z^{-4} \\ \hline & \qquad 70z^{-3}-60z^{-4} \\ & \qquad 70z^{-3}-210z^{-4}+140z^{-5} \\ \hline & \qquad\quad 150z^{-4}-140z^{-5} \end{array}$$

$\therefore$ $$u(z) = 10z^{-1} + 30z^{-2} + 70z^{-3} + \ldots\ldots$$

Comparing the quotients with

$$\sum_{n=0}^{\infty} u_n z^{-n} = u_0 + u_1 z^{-1} + u_2 z^{-2} + u_3 z^{-3} + \ldots\ldots$$

$$u(0) = 0 \quad u(1) = 10 \quad u(2) = 30 \quad u(3) = 70 \ldots\ldots$$

i.e., $$\mathbf{u(n) = 10(2^n - 1)}.\ n = 0, 1, 2, \ldots\ldots$$

Example 15. *Find* $z^{-1}\left(\dfrac{2(z^3 - z)}{(z^2 + 1)^2}\right)$.

Sol. $$u(z) = \frac{2z(z^2 - 1)}{(z^2 + 1)^2} = \frac{2z^{-1} - 2z^{-3}}{1 + 2z^{-2} + z^{-4}}$$

By actual divisions.

$$u(z) = 2z^{-1} - 6z^{-3} + 10z^{-5} - 14z^{-7} + \ldots\ldots$$

Comparing with $\sum u_n z^{-n} = u_0 + u_1 z^{-1} + u_2 z^{-2} + u_3 z^{-3} + \ldots$

$$u(0) = 0,\quad u(1) = 2 \quad u(2) = 0,\quad u(3) = -6,\quad u(4) = 0,\quad u(5) = 10, \ldots\ldots, u(n) = 2n \sin\frac{n\pi}{2}$$

In general, $$\mathbf{u(n) = 2n \sin \frac{n\pi}{2}},\ n = 0, 1, 2, 3, \ldots\ldots$$

IV. Partial Fractions Method: This method consists of decomposing $\dfrac{u(z)}{z}$ into partial fraction, multiplying the resulting expression by z and then inverting the same.

Example 16. *Find* $Z^{-1}\left\{\dfrac{2z^2 + 3z}{(z + 2)(z - 4)}\right\}$.

Sol. $$Z^{-1}\left\{\frac{2z^2 + 3z}{(z + 2)(z - 4)}\right\} \Rightarrow \frac{u(z)}{z} = \frac{2z + 3}{(z + 2)(z - 4)}$$

i.e., $$\frac{u(z)}{z} = \frac{A}{(z + 2)} + \frac{B}{(z - 4)} = \frac{1/6}{(z + 2)} + \frac{11/6}{(z - 4)}$$

$\therefore \quad u(z) = \frac{1}{6} \cdot \frac{z}{(z+2)} + \frac{11}{6} \cdot \frac{z}{z-4}$

$\therefore \quad Z^{-1}[u(z)] = \mathbf{\frac{1}{6} \cdot (-2)^n + \frac{n}{6} (4)^n} = u_n .$

Example 17. *Find* $Z^{-1}\left(\dfrac{z^3 - 20z}{(z-2)^3 (z-4)}\right)$

Sol. $u(z) = \dfrac{z^3 - 20z}{(z-2)^3 (z-4)} \quad \therefore \quad \dfrac{u(z)}{z} = \dfrac{z^2 - 20}{(z-2)^3 (z-4)} = \dfrac{A + Bz + Cz^2}{(z-2)^3} + \dfrac{D}{(z-4)}$

$$\frac{u(z)}{z} = \frac{12 + z^2}{2(z-2)^3} - \frac{1}{2}\frac{1}{(z-4)} \qquad \left| \begin{array}{l} A = 6 \quad B = 0 \\ C = 1/2 \\ D = -1/2 \end{array} \right.$$

$$= \frac{8 + 4 + 4z - 4z + z^2}{2(z-2)^3} - \frac{1}{2}\frac{1}{(z-4)}$$

$$= \frac{1}{2}\left\{\frac{1}{(z-2)} + \frac{4(z+2)}{(z-2)^3}\right\} - \frac{1}{2}\left(\frac{1}{z-4}\right).$$

$$u(z) = \frac{1}{2}\left\{\frac{z}{z-2} + 2 \cdot \frac{2z^2 + 4z}{(z-2)^3} - \frac{z}{z-4}\right\}.$$

$$\therefore \quad u_n = \frac{1}{2}\{2^n + 2 \cdot n^2 \cdot 2^n - 4^n\} \qquad \left| \because \quad z(n^2 a^n) = \frac{az^2 + a^2 z}{(z-a)^3}. \right.$$

or $\quad u_n = \mathbf{2^{n-1} + n^2 2^n - 2^{2n-1}}$

Example 18. *Find* $Z^{-1}\left\{\dfrac{8z^2}{(2z-1)(4z-1)}\right\}.$

Sol. $u(z) = \dfrac{8z^2}{8(z-1/2)(z-1/4)} \quad \therefore \quad \dfrac{u(z)}{z} = \dfrac{z}{(z-1/2)(z-1/4)}.$

$$\frac{u(z)}{z} = \frac{A}{(z-1/2)} + \frac{B}{(z-1/4)} = \frac{2}{(z-1/2)} - \frac{1}{(z-1/4)}$$

$\therefore \quad u(z) = 2 \cdot \dfrac{z}{(z-1/2)} - \dfrac{z}{(z-1/4)}$

$\therefore \quad u(n) = z^{-1}(u(z) = \mathbf{2(1/2)^n - (1/4)^n}, \quad n = 0, 1, 2, \ldots$

V. Inverse Integral Method (or Residue Method): The inverse Z-transforms of $u(z)$ is given by the formula: $u_n = \dfrac{1}{2\pi i} \int_C u(z) z^{n-1} dz$

= sum of residues of $U(z)\, z^{n-1}$ at the poles of $U(z)$ which are inside the contour C, drawn according to the regions of convergence gives.

Example 19. *Using inverse integral method, find* $Z^{-1}\left\{\dfrac{10z}{(z-1)(z-2)}\right\}$.

Sol. $U(z) = \dfrac{10z}{(z-1)(z-2)}$. Its poles are at $z = 1$, $z = 2$.

Now, $u_n = \dfrac{1}{2\pi i}\int_C u(z)\, z^{n-1} dz$ = Sum of residues

$\therefore$ Residue at $z = 1 \Rightarrow \quad \underset{z\to 1}{\text{Lt}}\ (z-1)\,[U(z)\, z^{n-1}] = \underset{z\to 1}{\text{Lt}}\left\{\dfrac{(z-1)\,10\,z\,.\,z^{n-1}}{(z-1)(z-2)}\right\}$.

$$= -\mathbf{10}$$

Residue at $z = 2 \Rightarrow \quad \underset{z\to 2}{\text{Lt}}\dfrac{(z-2)\,.\,10z^n}{(z-1)(z-2)} = 10(z)^n$.

$\therefore \quad u_n = 10(2^n) - 10 = \mathbf{10\ [2^n - 1]}, \quad n = 0, 1, 2, \ldots$

Example 20. *Find* $Z^{-1}\left\{\dfrac{2z}{(z-1)(z^2+1)}\right\}$.

Sol. Let $\quad U(z) = \dfrac{2z}{(z-1)(z+i)(z-i)}$

It has three poles $\quad z = \mathbf{1, +\,i, -\,i}$

$$u_n = \frac{1}{2\pi i}\int_C z^{n-1}\,.\,\frac{2z}{(z-1)(z+i)(z-i)}\,dz = \text{Sum of residues.}$$

Residue at $z = 1 \quad \Rightarrow \underset{z\to 1}{\text{Lt}}\left\{\dfrac{(z-1)\,.\,2z^n}{(z-1)(z+i)(z-i)}\right\} = \dfrac{2}{1^2+1} = \mathbf{1}$

Residue at $z = i \quad \Rightarrow \underset{z\to i}{\text{Lt}}\left\{\dfrac{(z-i)\,2z^n}{(z-1)(z+i)(z-i)}\right\} = \dfrac{+(i)^n}{i(i-1)} = \dfrac{\mathbf{-(i)^n}}{\mathbf{(1+i)}}$

Residue at $z = -\,i \quad \Rightarrow \underset{z\to -i}{\text{Lt}}\left\{\dfrac{(z+i)\,2z^n}{(z-1)(z+i)(z-i)}\right\} = \dfrac{2(-i)^n}{(-i-1)(-2i)} = \dfrac{\mathbf{(-i)^n}}{\mathbf{(i-1)}}$

$\therefore \quad u_n = 1 - \dfrac{(i)^n}{(1+i)} + \dfrac{(-i)^n}{(i-1)} = \mathbf{1 - \dfrac{(i)^n}{(1+i)} - \dfrac{(-i)^n}{(1-i)}}$

Example 21. *Find* $Z^{-1}\left\{\dfrac{z(z+1)}{(z-1)^3}\right\}$.

Sol. $\quad U(z) = \dfrac{z(z+1)}{(z-1)^3}$. $\quad \therefore \quad z = 1$ is a pole of order 3.

$$u_n = \frac{1}{2\pi i}\int_C z^{n-1}\,.\,\frac{z(z+1)}{(z-1)^3}\,dz = \text{Sum of residues.}$$

Residue at $z = 1$ $\Rightarrow \frac{1}{2!} \underset{z \to 1}{\text{Lt}} \frac{d^2}{dz^2} \cdot \left\{ \frac{(z-1)^3 \cdot z^n \cdot (z+1)}{(z-1)^3} \right\}.$

$$\Rightarrow \quad \frac{1}{2} \cdot \underset{z \to 1}{\text{Lt}} \cdot \left[\frac{d}{dz} [(n+1) z^n + nz^{n-1}] \right]$$

$$= \frac{1}{2} \cdot \underset{z \to 1}{\text{Lt}} \ \{(n+1)\, n\, z^{n-1} + n(n-1)\, z^{n-2}\}$$

$$= \frac{1}{2} \ [n(n+1) + (n-1)n]$$

$$= \frac{1}{2} \ (2n^2) = \mathbf{n}^2$$

$$\therefore \quad u_n = \mathbf{n}^2, \quad n = 0, 1, 2, \ldots .$$

2.6. APPLICATIONS TO DIFFERENCE EQUATIONS

Z-transforms are quite useful for solving linear difference equations.

Working procedure to solve a linear difference equations with constant coefficients by Z-transforms:

(*i*) Take the Z-transforms of both sides of the difference equations using the formulas:

$$u_{n+1} = z(u(z) - u_0)$$
$$u_{n+2} = z^2(u(z) - u_0 - u_1 z^{-1})$$
$$u_{n+3} = z^3[u(z) - u_0 - u_1 z^{-1} - u_1 z^{-2}] \ \ldots\ldots$$

and the given initial conditions.

(*ii*) Transpose all terms without $u(z)$ to the right

(*iii*) Divide the coefficient of $u(z)$, getting $u(z)$ as function of z.

(*iv*) Express this function in terms of the Z-transforms of known functions and take the inverse Z-transform of both sides. This gives u_n as a function of 'n' which is the desired solutions.

Example 22. *Using Z-transforms solve:* $u_{n+2} + 4u_{n+1} + 3u_n = 3^n$, *with* $u_0 = 0$, $u_1 = 1$.

Sol. Take Z-transforms on both sides: $\text{Z}[u_{n+2}] + 4z(u_{n+1}) + 3z(u_n) = z(3^n)$.

i.e., $$z^2[\text{U}(z) - u_0 - u_1 z^{-1}] + 4z[\text{U}(z) - u_0] + 3\text{U}(z) = \frac{z}{(z-3)}$$

Using initial conditions:

$$u_0 = 0,\ u_1 = 1,\ u(z)\ [z^2 + 4z + 3] = z + \frac{z}{z-3}.$$

$$\frac{u(z)}{z} = \frac{1}{(z+1)(z+3)} + \frac{1}{(z-3)(z+1)(z+3)}.$$

$$\frac{u(z)}{z} = \frac{z-2}{(z-3)(z+1)(z+3)} = \frac{\text{A}}{(z-3)} + \frac{\text{B}}{(z+1)} + \frac{\text{C}}{(z+3)}.$$

$$= \frac{3/8}{z+1} + \frac{1/24}{(z-3)} + \frac{-5/12}{z+3}$$

$$u(z) = \frac{3}{8}\frac{z}{z+1} + \frac{1}{24}\cdot\frac{z}{(z-3)} - \frac{5}{12}\frac{z}{(z+3)}$$

$$\therefore \quad z^{-1}(u(z)) = u_n = \mathbf{\frac{3}{8}(-1)^n + \frac{1}{24}(3)^n - \frac{5}{12}(-3)^n}.$$

Example 23. *Solve* $y_{n+2} + 6y_{n+1} + 9y_n = 2^n$, *with* $y_0 = y_1 = 0$, *using Z-transforms.*

Sol. Take Z-transforms on both sides

$Z(y_{n+2}) + 6z(y_{n+1}) + 9z(y_0) = z(2^n).$

$$z^2(Y(z) - y_0 - y_1 z^{-1}) + 6z[Y(z) - y_0] + 9Y(z) = \frac{z}{z-2}$$

Given $y_0 = y_1 = 0 \quad \therefore \quad (z^2 + 6z + 9)\,Y(z) = \dfrac{z}{(z-2)}.$

$$\therefore \quad \frac{Y(z)}{z} = \frac{1}{(z-2)(z+3)^2} = \frac{A}{(z-2)} + \frac{B}{(z+3)} + \frac{C}{(z+3)^2}$$

i.e.,

$$\frac{Y(z)}{z} = \frac{1}{25}\left[\frac{1}{z-2} - \frac{1}{z+3} - \frac{5}{(z+3)^2}\right]$$

or

$$Y(z) = \frac{1}{25}\left\{\frac{z}{z-2} - \frac{z}{(z+3)} - \frac{5z}{(z+3)^2}\right\}$$

$$\therefore \quad y_n = Z^{-1}[Y(z)] = \frac{1}{25}\left\{(2)^n - (-3)^n + \frac{5}{3}z^{-1}\left[\frac{-3z}{(z+3)^2}\right]\right\}$$

$$\therefore \quad y_n = \mathbf{\frac{1}{25}\left\{2^n - (-3)^n + \frac{5}{3}n(-3)^n\right\}} \qquad \left|\; Z^{-1}\left(\frac{az}{(z-a)^2}\right) = na^n\right.$$

Example 24. *Find the response of the system* $y_{n+2} - 5y_{n+1} + 6y_n = u_n$, *with* $y_0 = 0$, $y_1 = 1$ *and* $u_n = 1$ *for* $n = 0, 1, 2, 3, \ldots$ *6y Z-transform method.*

Sol. $Z[y_{n+2} - 5y_{n+1} + 6y_n] = Z(u_n)$

$$z^2[Y(z) - y_0 - y_1 z^{-1}] - 5z[Y(z) - y_0] + 6Y(z) = \frac{z}{z-1}$$

$$(z^2 - 5z + 6)\,Y(z) = z + \frac{z}{z-1}$$

$$\frac{Y(z)}{z} = \frac{1}{(z-2)(z-3)} + \frac{1}{(z-1)(z-2)(z-3)} = \frac{z}{(z-1)(z-2)(z-3)}$$

$$= \frac{A}{z-1} + \frac{B}{z-2} + \frac{C}{z-3} = \frac{1/2}{z-1} + \frac{(-2)}{(z-2)} + \frac{3/2}{(z-3)}.$$

$$\therefore \quad Y(z) = \frac{1}{2}\cdot\frac{z}{(z-1)} - 2\cdot\frac{z}{(z-2)} + \frac{3}{2}\cdot\frac{z}{(z-3)}$$

$\therefore \qquad y_n = Z^{-1}(Y(z)) = \frac{1}{2} \times 1 - 2(2)^n + \frac{3}{2} \cdot (3)^n.$

$$y_n = \frac{1}{2} - 2(2)^n + \frac{3}{2}(3)^n.$$

Example 25. *Solve the difference equations:* $y_n + \frac{1}{4} y_{n-1} = \delta_n + \frac{1}{3}\delta_{n-1}$, *where* δ_n *is a unit impulse sequence.*

Sol. Taking Z-transforms, $Y(z) + \frac{1}{4} z^{-1} \cdot Y(z) = 1 + \frac{1}{3} z^{-1}$.

$$Y(z) = \frac{\left(1 + \frac{1}{3} z^{-1}\right)}{\left(1 + \frac{1}{4} z^{-1}\right)} = \frac{z + 1/3}{z + 1/4}.$$ There is only one

Pole: $z = \frac{-1}{4}$, $\therefore$ Residue at $z = \frac{-1}{4}$,

$$= \operatorname*{Lt}_{z \to -1/4} \left\{ \frac{(z + 1/4).(z + 1/3)\, z^{n-1}}{(z + 1/4)} \right\}.$$

$$= \operatorname*{Lt}_{z \to -1/4} (z + 1/3)\, z^{n-1} = \left(\frac{-1}{4} + \frac{1}{3}\right)\left(\frac{-1}{4}\right)^{n-1} = \frac{1}{12}\left(\frac{-1}{4}\right)^{n-1}$$

$\therefore \qquad y_n = \frac{1}{12}\left(\frac{-1}{4}\right)^{n-1}.$

Example 26. *Using the Z-transform, solve* $u_{n+2} - 2u_{n+1} + u_n = 3n + 5$.

Sol. Taking Z-transforms on both sides:

$$z^2[u(z) - u_0 - u_1 z^{-1}] - 2z\,[u(z) - u_0] + u(z) = 3z(n) + 5z \qquad \ldots(1)$$

$$u(z)\,(z^2 - 2z + 1) - u_0(z^2 - 2z) - u_1(z) = \frac{3z}{(z-1)^2} + \frac{5z}{(z-1)}$$

$$u(z)\,(z-1)^2 = \frac{5z^2 - 3z}{(z-1)^2} + u_0\,(z^2 - 2z) + u_1 z$$

$$\frac{u(z)}{z} = \frac{(5z-3)}{(z-1)^4} + u_0 \frac{(z-2)}{(z-1)^2} + u_1 \frac{1}{(z-1)^2}.$$

$$u(z) = \frac{(5z^2 - 3z)}{(z-1)^4} + u_0 \frac{(z^2 - 2z)}{(z-1)^2} + u_1 \frac{z}{(z-1)^2}.$$

$\therefore \qquad u_n = z^{-1}(u(z))$

$$= z^{-1}\left\{\frac{5z^2 - 3z}{(z-1)^4}\right\} + u_0 \cdot z^{-1}\left\{\frac{z^2 - 2z}{(z-1)^2}\right\} + u_1 z^{-1}\left\{\frac{z}{(z-1)^2}\right\}$$

We have $z(1) = \dfrac{z}{(z-1)}$ $z(n) = \dfrac{z}{(z-1)^2}$

$$z(n^2) = \frac{z^2+2}{(z-1)^3} \qquad z(n^3) = \frac{z^3+4z^2+z}{(z-1)^4}.$$

$$z^{-1}\left(\frac{z}{(z-1)^2}\right) = n \qquad \left\{\frac{z(z-2)}{(z-1)^2} = \frac{z(z-1-1)}{(z-1)^2} = \frac{z(z-1)}{(z-1)^2} - \frac{z}{(z-1)^2}\right.$$

$$z^{-1}\left(\frac{z^2-2z}{(z-1)^2}\right) = z^{-1}\left(\frac{z}{(z-1)}\right) - z^{-1}\left(\frac{z}{(z-1)^2}\right)$$

$$= \mathbf{1 - n}.$$

$$z^{-1}\left(\frac{5z^2-2z}{(z-1)^4}\right) = \frac{1}{2}n^3 + n^2 - \frac{3}{2}n.$$

$$= \frac{1}{2}n(n-1)(n+3)$$

$$\frac{5z^2-2z}{(z-1)^4} = A\frac{(z^3+4z^2+z)}{(z-1)^4} + B\frac{z^2+2}{(z-1)^3} + C\frac{z}{(z-1)^2} + D\frac{z}{(z-1)^2}$$

$$\therefore\ A = \frac{1}{2},\quad B = 1,\quad C = -\frac{3}{2},\quad D = 0$$

$$\therefore \qquad u_n = \frac{1}{2}\, n(n-1)(n+3) + u_0(1-n) + u_1 n$$

$$u_n = \frac{1}{2}\, n(n-1)(n+3) + C_1 n + C_0.$$

$$u_0 = C_0$$

$$\mathbf{u_1 - u_0 = C_1}.$$

Example 27. *Solve:* $y_{n+2} - 4y_n = 0,\ y_0 = 0,\ y_1 = 2$

Sol. $Z(y_{n+2}) - 4Z(y_n) = 0$

$$z^2[Y(z) - y_0 - y_1 z^{-1}] - 4Y(z) = 0$$

$$(z^2-4)\,Y(z) - 2z = 0 \qquad Y(z) = \frac{2z}{(z^2-4)}$$

$$\frac{Y(z)}{z} = \frac{2}{z^2-4} = \frac{1/2}{z-2} - \frac{1/2}{z+2}$$

$$Y(z) = \frac{1}{2}\left\{\frac{z}{z-2} - \frac{z}{z+2}\right\}.$$

$$\therefore \qquad y_n = Z^{-1}(Y(z)) = \frac{1}{2}((2)^n - (-2)^n) = \mathbf{2^{n-1} - (-2)^{n-1}}.$$

TEST YOUR KNOWLEDGE

1. Find

(*a*) $Z\{\delta(n)\}$ (*b*) $Z\{n^2\}$ (*c*) $Z\{1/n\}$

2. Find

(*a*) $Z\{u(n-1)\}$ (*b*) $Z\{e^{-zt}\, t^3\}$ (*c*) $Z\{a^n \cos n\pi\}$

3. Using $Z(n^2) = \dfrac{z(z+1)}{(z-1)^3}$, show that $Z(n+1)^2 = \dfrac{z^2(z+1)}{(z-1)^3}$.

4. Find the inverse Z-transform of $f(n)$:

(*i*) $\dfrac{z^2+z}{(z-1)^2}$ (*ii*) $\dfrac{z}{(z-1)(z-2)(z-3)}$ (*iii*) $\dfrac{z^2}{(z+2)(z^2+4)}$

(*iv*) $\dfrac{4z^{-1}}{(1-z^{-1})^2}$ (*v*) $\dfrac{4z^2-2z}{z^3-5z^2+8z-4}$

5. Using convolutions theorem, find Z^{-1} of:

(*i*) $\dfrac{z^2}{(z-4)(z-3)}$ (*ii*) $\dfrac{8z^2}{(2z-1)(4z-1)}$ (*iii*) $\dfrac{z^2}{(z-a)^2}$

6. Solve the following difference equations:

(*i*) $y(n) + y(n-1) - 4y(n-2) = 0$, $n = 2$, $y(0) = 3$, $y(1) = -2$.

(*ii*) $u_{x+2} + u_x = 5.2^x$, $u_0 = 1$, $u_1 = 0$.

(*iii*) $y_{n+2} - 4y_n = 0$.

(*iv*) $u_{n+2} - 2u_{n+1} + u_n = z^n$, $u_0 = 2$, $u_1 = 1$.

(*v*) $y_{n+3} + y_{n+2} - 8y_{n+1} - 12y_n = 0$, $y_0 = 1$, $y_1 = y_2 = 0$.

MODULE **3**

Discrete Numeric Functions and Generating Functions

3.1. INTRODUCTION

A function is a binary relation that assigns to each element in the domain, a unique value which is an element in the range. A class of functions whose domain is the set of natural numbers and whose range is the set of real numbers is referred to as ***discrete numeric functions*** or ***numeric functions***. They are very often used in digital computations.

The lower case letters are used to denote numeric functions. For a numeric function 'a', $a_0, a_1, a_2, \ldots, a_r, \ldots$ to denote the values of the function at 0, 1, 2, ..., r, ...

For example: $a_r = 7r^3 + 1,\ r \geq 0$

$$b_r = \begin{cases} 2r, & 0 \leq r \leq 11 \\ 3^r - 1, & r \geq 11. \end{cases}$$

$$c_r = \begin{cases} -4, & r = 3, 5, 7 \\ 0, & \text{otherwise.} \end{cases} \qquad d_r = \begin{cases} 2 + r, & 0 \leq r \leq 5. \\ 2 - r, & r > 5 \text{ and } r, \text{ odd} \\ \frac{2}{r}, & r > 5 \text{ and } r, \text{ even} \end{cases}$$

When there is one simple expression for the value of the numeric function for every 'r' use the notation: $\mathbf{a} = 7r^3 + 1$.

For example: Let a_r denote the altitude of an aircraft, in thousands of feet, at the rth minute. Suppose the aircraft takes off after spending 10 minutes on the ground, climbs up at a uniform speed to a cruising altitude of 30,000 feet in 10 minutes, starts to descend uniformly after 110 minutes of flying time and lands 10 minutes later. Then:

$$a_r = \begin{cases} 0, & 0 \leq r \leq 10 \\ 3(r - 10), & 11 \leq r \leq 20 \\ 30, & 21 \leq r \leq 120 \\ 3(130 - r), & 121 \leq r \leq 130 \\ 0, & r \geq 131. \end{cases}$$

3.2. MANIPULATION OF NUMERIC FUNCTIONS

(*i*) *Sum:* The sum of two numeric functions is a numeric function whose values at r is equal to the sum of the values of the two numeric functions at 'r'.

For example: Consider two functions **a** and **b** where:

$$a_r = \begin{cases} 0, & 0 \le r \le 2 \\ 2^{-r} + 5, & r \ge 3 \end{cases} \text{ and } \quad b_r = \begin{cases} 3 - 2^r, & 0 \le r \le 1 \\ r + 2, & r \ge 2 \end{cases}.$$

Let **c** = **a** + **b**, the sum of two functions.

Then $$c_r = a_r + b_r = \begin{cases} 3 - 2^r, & 0 \le r \le 1 \\ 4, & r = 2 \\ 2^{-r} + r + 7, & r \ge 3 \end{cases}.$$

(*ii*) *Product:* The product of two numeric functions is a numeric function whose value at r is equal to the product of the values of the two numeric functions at 'r'.
For example: Consider two functions **a** and **b** where:

$$a_r = \begin{cases} 0, & 0 \le r \le 2 \\ 2^{-r} + 5, & r \ge 3 \end{cases} \text{ and } b_r = \begin{cases} 3 - 2^r, & 0 \le r \le 1 \\ r + 2, & r \ge 2. \end{cases}.$$

Let **d** be the product of two functions a and b, *i.e.*, **d** = **a** . **b**.

Then $$d_r = a_r \times b_r = \begin{cases} 0, & 0 \le r \le 2 \\ r \cdot 2^{-r} + 2^{-r+1} + 5r + 10, & r \ge 3 \end{cases}.$$

(*iii*) *Scaled Product:* Let **a** be a numeric function and α be a real number. Then α**a**, is a numeric function whose value at r is equal to 'α' times a_r. The numeric function α**a** is called a scaled version of **a** with scaling factor α.

For example: Let **a** be a numeric function such that $a_r = (1.07)^r$. Then 100**a** is a numeric function whose value at r is 100 $(1.07)^r$.

(*iv*) *Absolute value (modulus value) function:* Let **a** be a numeric function. Then $|a|$ is a numeric function whose value at r is equal to a_r, if a_r is non-negative, and is equal to $-a_r$ if a_r is negative.

i.e., $$|a_r| = \begin{cases} a_r, & a_r \ge 0 \\ -a_r, & a_r < 0 \end{cases}.$$

For example: Let a be a numeric function defined by $a_r = (-1)^r \left(\frac{2}{r^2}\right)$, $r \ge 0$.

Let $b = |a|$ then

$$b_r = \left(\frac{2}{r^2}\right), \; r \ge 0.$$

(*v*) S^i *function:* Let **a** be a numeric function and 'i' a positive integer. $\mathbf{s^i a}$ is a numeric function defined such that its value at r is 0 for $r = 0, 1, 2, \ldots (i-1)$ and is a_{r-i} for $r \ge i$.

For example: Let $a_r = \begin{cases} 1, & 0 \le r \le 10 \\ 2, & r \ge 11 \end{cases}$. Let $\mathbf{b} = \mathbf{S^5}$ **a**, then $b_r = \begin{cases} 0, & 0 \le r \le 4 \\ 1, & 5 \le r \le 15 \\ 2, & r \ge 16 \end{cases}$

(*vi*) S^{-i} *function:* Let **a** be a numeric function and 'i' is a positive integer. Then $\mathbf{S^{-i}}$ **a** is a numeric function such that its value at r is a_{r+i} for $r \ge 0$.

For example: Let $a_r = \begin{cases} 1, & 0 \le r \le 10 \\ 2, & r \ge 11 \end{cases}$. Let $\mathbf{b} = \mathbf{S^{-7}}$ **a**, then $b_r = \begin{cases} 1, & 0 \le r \le 3 \\ 2, & r \ge 4 \end{cases}$.

(*vii*) *Accumulated Sum:* The accumulated sum of a numeric function **a** is a numeric function whose value at r is equal to $a_r = \sum_{i=0}^{r} a_i$.

For example: Let $a_r = 100\,(1.07)^r$, $r \geq 0$, and let b is the accumulated sum of a.

$$\text{Then } b_r = \sum_{i=0}^{r} a_r = \sum_{i=0}^{r} 100(1.07)^r = 100\,[1 + 1.07 + 1.07^2 + \ldots + 1.07^r]$$

$$= 100\left[\frac{1.07^{r+1} - 1}{1.07 - 1}\right] = \frac{10{,}000}{7}(1.07^{r+1} - 1).$$

(*viii*) *Forward Difference* (Δ)*:* The forward difference of a numeric function **a** is a numeric function denoted by $\mathbf{\Delta a}$, whose value at r is defined as $a_r = a_{r+1} - a_r$.

(*ix*) *Backward Difference* (∇)*:* The backward difference of a numeric function **a** is a numeric function, denoted by $\mathbf{\nabla a}$, whose value is equal to a_0 at 0 and equal to $a_r = a_r - a_{r-1}$, at $r \geq 1$.

For example: Let **a** be a numeric function such that

$$a_r = \begin{cases} 0, & 0 \leq r \leq 2 \\ 2^{-r} + 5, & r \geq 3. \end{cases}$$

Let **b** denote the forward difference of a. *i.e.*, $\mathbf{b} = \mathbf{\Delta a}$, then

$$b_r = \begin{cases} 0, & 0 \leq r \leq 1 \\ \dfrac{41}{8}, & r = 2 \\ -2^{-(r+1)}, & r \geq 3. \end{cases}$$

Let **c** denote the backward difference of **a**. *i.e.*, $\mathbf{c} = \mathbf{\nabla a}$, then

$$c_r = \begin{cases} 0, & 0 \leq r \leq 2 \\ \dfrac{41}{8}, & r = 3 \\ -2^{-r}, & r \geq 4. \end{cases}$$

Note: $S^{-1}(\nabla a) = \Delta a$.

(*x*) *Convolution:* Let **a** and **b** be two numeric functions. The convolution of **a** and **b**, denoted by **a*b**, is a numeric function **c** such that:

$$c_r = a_0 b_r + a_1 b_{r-1} + a_2 b_{r-2} + \ldots\ldots + a_i b_{r-i} + \ldots\ldots + a_{r-1} b_1 + a_r b_0 = \sum_{i=0}^{r} a_i b_{r-i}$$

For example: Let **a** and **b** be the two numeric functions such that $a_r = 3^r$, $r \geq 0$, and $b_r = 2^r$, $r \geq 0$. Then $\mathbf{c} = \mathbf{a*b}$, such that $c_r = \sum_{i=0}^{r} 3^i 2^{r-i}, r \geq 0$.

ILLUSTRATIVE EXAMPLES

Example 1. *Let* **a** *be a numeric function such that a_r is the remainder when the integer i is divided by 17. Let* **b** *be a numeric function such that $b_r = 0$, if the integer r is divisible by 3, and is equal to 1 otherwise.*

(*i*) *Let $c_r = a_r + b_r$. For what values of r, $c_r = 0$? For what values of r, $c_r = 1$?*

(*ii*) *Let $d_r = a_r \cdot b_r$. For what values of r, $d_r = 1$?*

Sol. From the definition of **a** $a_r = \{0, 1, 2, 3, ..., 16\}$ and from the definition of b

$$b_r = \begin{cases} 0, & r = 0, 3, 6, 9, 12, 15 \\ 1, & \text{otherwise.} \end{cases}$$

(*i*) Given $c_r = a_r + b_r$. Therefore $c_r = 0$ only when $a_r = 0 = b_r$. *i.e.*, when $r = 0$.
$c_r = 1$, when $a_r + b_r = 1$. *i.e.*, when $a_r = 0$ and $b_r = 1$ or $a_r = 1$ and $b_r = 0$, which will never happens. Therefore $c_r \neq 1$.

(*ii*) Given $d_r = a_r \times b_r$. Now $d_r = 0$ either of a_r or b_r or both are equal to zero. Therefore $d_r = 0$, when, $r = 0, 3, 9, 12, ...$ *i.e.*, $d_r = 0$, when r is a multiple of 3. $d_r = 1$, if $a_r = 1 = b_r$, and that will happens only when $r = 1$. $\therefore \quad d_r = 1, r = 1$.

Example 2. *Let a be a numeric function such that* $a_r = \begin{cases} 2, & 0 \le r \le 3 \\ 2^{-r} + 5, & r \ge 4 \end{cases}$. *Determine:*

(*i*) *S^2a and $S^{-2}a$* (*ii*) *Δa and ∇a?*

Sol. Given

$$a_r = \begin{cases} 2, & 0 \le r \le 3 \\ 2^{-r} + 5, & r \ge 4 \end{cases}.$$

(*i*) Let $b = S^2a$. Then $b_r = \begin{cases} 0, & 0 \le r \le 1 \\ 2, & 2 \le r \le 5 \\ 2^{-r} + 5, & r \ge 6 \end{cases}$.

Let $c = S^{-2}a$, then $c_r = \begin{cases} 2, & 0 \le r \le 1 \\ 2^{-r} + 5, & r \ge 2 \end{cases}$.

(*ii*) Let $d = \Delta a$. Then $d_r = \begin{cases} 0, & 0 \le r \le 2 \\ 2^{-4} + 3, & r = 3 \\ 2^{-(r+1)} - 2^{-r}, & r \ge 4 \end{cases}$.

Let $e = \nabla a$. Then $e_r = \begin{cases} 0, & 0 \le r \le 3 \\ 2^{-4} - 3, & r = 4 \\ 2^{-(r+1)} - 2^{-r}, & r \ge 5 \end{cases}$.

3.3. GENERATING FUNCTIONS

Generating function is an alternative way to represent numeric functions. For a numeric function **a** $(a_0, a_1, a_2, ..., a_r)$ define an infinite series $a_0 + a_1z + a_2z^2 + ... + a_rz^r + ...$, which is called the generating function of the numeric function **a**. *i.e.,* instead of writing down the values of a numeric function one by one and using commas as separators as in $(a_0, a_1, a_2, ..., a_r)$, we choose a formal variable z and use the powers of z as indicators in an infinite series such that the coefficient of z^r is the value of the numeric function at r.

For a numeric function **a**, A(z) is used to denote the generating function of **a**.

Clearly, given a numeric function, we can easily obtain its generating function and conversely.

For example: The generating function of the numeric function $(3^0, 3^1, 3^2, ..., 3^r, ...)$ is:

$$3^0 + 3^1z + 3^2z^2 + ... + 3^rz^r + ... = (1-3z)^{-1} = \frac{1}{(1-3z)}.$$

Note: The generating function representation of numeric functions is for expressing infinite series in closed form so that they can be manipulated conveniently.

3.4. PROPERTIES OF GENERATING FUNCTIONS

(*i*) $B(z) = \alpha A(z)$, corresponding to $\mathbf{b} = \alpha\mathbf{a}$.

(*ii*) $C(z) = A(z) + B(z)$, corresponding to $\mathbf{c} = \mathbf{a} + \mathbf{b}$.

(*iii*) Let A(z) be the generating function of the numeric function **a** and let **b** be a numeric function such that $b_r = \alpha^r a_r$, then the generating function of **b**

$B(z) = A(\alpha z)$.

Note: *Unfortunately, if* $\mathbf{c} = \mathbf{a}.\mathbf{b}$, *there is no simple form in which C(z) in terms of A(z) and B(z).*

(*iv*) (*i*) Let A(z) be the generating function of **a**. It follows that z^i A(z) is the generating function of S^i **a** for positive integer i.

(*ii*) Also z^{-i} $[A(z) - a_0 - a_1z + a_2z^2 - ...... - a_{i-1}z^{i-1}]$ is the generating function of S^{-i} **a**.

(*v*) (*i*) For $\mathbf{b} = \Delta\mathbf{a}$, $B(z) = \frac{1}{z}[A(z) - a_0] - A(z)$.

(*ii*) For $\mathbf{c} = \nabla\mathbf{a}$, $C(z) = A(z) - zA(z)$.

(*vi*) Let $\mathbf{c} = \mathbf{a}*\mathbf{b}$,

$$c_r = a_0b_r + a_1b_{r-1} + a_2b_{r-2} + ... + a_ib_{r-i} + ... + a_{r-1}b_1 + a_rb_0 = \sum_{i=0}^{r} a_ib_{r-i}$$

is the coefficient of z^r in the product:

$(a_0 + a_1z + a_2z^2 + ... + a_rz^r + ...)(b_0 + b_1z + b_2z^2 + ... + b_rz^r + ...)$. Therefore the generating function is $C(z) = A(z) . B(z)$.

Example 3. *Let* **a** *be a numeric function with* $a_r = 1$, $r \geq 0$. *Find the generating function of* **a**?

Sol. Given $a_r = 1$, $r \geq 0$, *i.e.,* (1, 1, 1, ..., 1, ...).

$$A(z) = a_0 + a_1z + a_2z^2 + ... + a_rz^r + ... = 1 + z + z^2 + ... + z^r + ...$$

$$= (1-z)^{-1} = \frac{1}{(1-z)}.$$

Example 4. *Let* $\boldsymbol{a}$ *be a numeric function with* $a_r = \alpha^r$, $r \geq 0$. *Find the generating function of* $\boldsymbol{a}$?

Sol. Given $a_r = \alpha^r$, $r \geq 0$ *i.e.*, $(1, \alpha, \alpha^2, \alpha^3, \ldots\ldots, \alpha^r, \ldots\ldots)$. Then

$$A(z) = a_0 + a_1 z + a_2 z^2 + \ldots\ldots + a_r z^r + \ldots\ldots = 1 + \alpha z + \alpha^2 z^2 + \ldots\ldots + \alpha^r z^r + \ldots$$

$$= (1 - \alpha z)^{-1} = \frac{1}{(a - \alpha z)}$$

Example 5. *Given* $A(z) = \dfrac{2}{(1 - 4z^2)}$. *Find the numeric function* $\boldsymbol{a}$?

Sol. Given $A(z) = \dfrac{2}{(1 - 4z^2)}$ *i.e.*, $A(z) = \dfrac{1}{(1 - 2z)} + \dfrac{1}{(1 + 2z)}$.

$\therefore$ $a_r = 2^r + (-2)^r$, $r \geq 0$.

or $$a_r = \begin{cases} 0, & r, \text{odd} \\ 2^{r+1}, & r, \text{even} \end{cases}.$$

Example 6. *Given* $A(z) = \dfrac{z^4}{(1 - 2z)}$. *Find the numeric function* $\boldsymbol{a}$?

Sol. Given $A(z) = \dfrac{z^4}{(1 - 2z)}$ *i.e.*, $A(z) = z^4(1 + 2z + (2z)^2 + \ldots + (2z)^r + \ldots)$.

i.e., $A(z) = (z^4 + 2z^5 + 2^2 z^6 + \ldots + 2^r z^{r+4} + \ldots)$

i.e., $A(z) = 0 + 0.z + 0.z^2 + 0.z^3 + 1.z^4 + 2z^5 + 2^2 z^6 + \ldots + 2^r z^{r+4} + \ldots$

$\therefore$ $$a_r = \begin{cases} 0, & 0 \leq r \leq 3 \\ 2^{r-4}, & r \geq 4 \end{cases}.$$

i.e., $z^i A(z)$ ***is the generating function of*** $S^i a$, ***for any positive integer 'i'.***

Example 7. *Find the generating function of* $a_r = 3^{r+2}$, $r \geq 0$?

Sol. Given $a_r = 3^{r+2}$, $r \geq 0$. Generating function of 3^{r+2} can be calculated as:

$$A(z) = z^{-2}\left[\frac{1}{1 - 3z} - 1 - 3z\right]$$

(since $\dfrac{1}{1 - 3z}$ is the generating function of $a_r = 3^r$)

Also we know that $S^{-i} a = z^{-i}\,[A(z) - a_0 - a_1 z - \ldots - z_{i-1} z^{i-1}]$.

$$A(z) = z^{-2}\left[\frac{1}{1 - 3z} - \frac{(1 + 3z)(1 - 3z)}{1 - 3z}\right] = z^{-2}\left[\frac{9z^2}{1 - 3z}\right] = \frac{9}{1 - 3z}.$$

Example 8. *Given* $a_r = 3^r$, $r \geq 0$, $b_r = 2^r$, $r \geq 0$. Compute $c = a * b$?

Sol. Given $a_r = 3^r$, $r \geq 0$, $\therefore$ $A(z) = \dfrac{1}{1 - 3z}$.

$b_r = 2^r$, $r \geq 0$ $\therefore$ $B(z) = \dfrac{1}{1 - 2z}$.

Now let $$C(z) = A(z)B(z) = \frac{1}{1-3z} \cdot \frac{1}{1-2z} = \frac{1}{(1-3z)(1-2z)} = \frac{3}{(1-3z)} - \frac{2}{(1-2z)}$$

i.e., $$C(z) = \frac{3-2}{(1-3z)(1-2z)} = \frac{3}{(1-3z)} - \frac{2}{(1-2z)}$$

or $$c_r = 3(3)^r - 2(2)^r = (3)^{r+1} - (2)^{r+1}.$$

Example 9. *Let* **a** *be an arbitrary numeric function and* **b** *be the numeric function (1, 1, 1, ...).*

*Let c = a*b. Then find the generating function of* **c**?

Sol. Let $c = a*b$. Then $c_r = \sum_{i=0}^{r} a_i b_{r-i} = \sum_{i=0}^{r} a_i$ $\Rightarrow$ **c is the accumulated sum of a.**

Therefore the generating function of **c** is $C(z) = \frac{1}{(1-z)} A(z)$.

Note: Let $A(z) = \frac{1}{(1-z)}$, in the above result, then $C(z) = \frac{1}{(1-z)^2}$ and which is the generating function of the numeric function (1, 2, 3, ..., r, ...).

Example 10. *Evaluate* $1^2 + 2^2 + 3^2 + ... + r^2$?

Sol. Here first we have to determine the generating function of the numeric function $(0^2, 1^2, 2^2, ..., r^2, ...)$. For that let us consider:

$$\frac{1}{1-z} = 1 + z + z^2 + ... + z^r + ... \quad ...(1)$$

Differentiating both sides of (1) we get:

$$\frac{1}{(1-z)^2} = 1 + 2z + 3z^2 + ... + rz^{r-1} + ...$$

$$\therefore \quad \frac{z}{(1-z)^2} = z + 2z^2 + 3z^3 + ... + rz^r + ...$$

Now $$\frac{d}{dz}\left(\frac{z}{(1-z)^2}\right) = 1 + 2^2 z + 3^2 z^2 + ... + r^2 z^{r-1} + ...$$

$$\Rightarrow \quad z\left(\frac{d}{dz}\left(\frac{z}{(1-z)^2}\right)\right) = 1^2 z + 2^2 z^2 + 3^2 z^3 + ... + r^2 z^r + ... \quad ...(2)$$

Now, $$z\left(\frac{d}{dz}\left(\frac{z}{(1-z)^2}\right)\right) = z\left\{\frac{(1-z)^2 + z^2(1-z)}{(1-z)^4}\right\} = \frac{z(1+z)}{(1-z)^3}.$$

i.e., $\frac{z(1+z)}{(1-z)^3}$ is the generating function of $(0^2, 1^2, 2^2, ..., r^2, ...)$.

Now $$C(z) = \frac{1}{(1-z)} A(z),$$

is the generating function of the accumulated sum function,

$$C(z) = \frac{1}{(1-z)}\left\{\frac{z(1+z)}{(1-z)^3}\right\} = \frac{z(1+z)}{(1-z)^4},$$

is the generating function of the accumulated sum function $(0^2, 0^2 + 1^2, 0^2 + 1^2, + 2^2 ..., 0^2 + 1^2 + 2^2 + r^2, ...)$.

According to binomial theorem, the coefficient of z^r in $\frac{1}{(1-z)^4}$ is:

$$\frac{4.5.6...(r+3)}{r!} = \frac{(r+1)(r+2)(r+3)}{1.2.3}.$$

Therefore coefficient of z^r in $\frac{1}{(1-z)^4}$ is:

$$\frac{(r+1)(r+2)(r+3)}{1.2.3} + \frac{(r-1)r(r+1)}{1.2.3} = \frac{r(r+1)(2r+1)}{6}.$$

i.e., $1^2 + 2^2 + 3^2 + ... + r^2 = \frac{r(r+1)(2r+1)}{6}.$

Example 11. *Find the generating function for the following sequences.*

(i) $a_r = b\alpha^r$ *(ii)* $a_r = r$

(iii) $a_r = \frac{1}{r!}$ *(iv)* $a_r = \begin{cases} rC_k, & \text{for, } 0 \le k \le r \\ 0, & \text{for, } k > r \end{cases}$

Sol. (*i*) $A(z) = \sum_{r=0}^{\infty} b\alpha^r z^r = b\sum_{r=0}^{\infty} (\alpha z)^r = \frac{1}{1-\alpha z}.$

(*ii*) $A(z) = \sum_{r=0}^{\infty} rz^r = z + 2z^2 + 3z^3 + ... = z(1 + 2z + 3z^2 + ...) = \frac{z}{(1-z)^2}.$

(*iii*) $A(z) = \sum_{r=0}^{\infty} \frac{1}{r!}z^r = 1 + \frac{z}{1!} + \frac{z^2}{2!} + \frac{z^3}{3!} + \frac{z^4}{4!} + ... = e^z.$

(*iv*) $A(z) = \sum_{r=0}^{r} rC_k z^r = (1+z)^r.$

Note: Table of some generating functions:

Sequence	*Generating Function*
1	$\frac{1}{1-z}$
$(-1)^r$	$\frac{1}{1+z}$
a^r	$\frac{1}{1-az}$
$(-a)^r$	$\frac{1}{1+az}$

$r+1$	$\dfrac{1}{1-(z)^2}$
r	$\dfrac{z}{(1-z)^2}$
r^2	$\dfrac{z(1+z)}{(1-z)^3}$
ra^r	$\dfrac{az}{(1+az)^2}$
$\dfrac{1}{n!}$	e^z
${}^nC_r$	$(1+z)^r$

3.5. RECURRENCE RELATIONS

Consider the numeric function $a = (3^0, 3^1, 3^2, ..., 3^r, ...)$, *i.e.*, $a_r = 3^r$, $r \geq 0$. This function can be specified by its generating function $A(z) = \dfrac{1}{1-3z}$. There is still another way to specify the numeric function. As by definition, the value of a_r is three times the value of a_{r-1}, for all r. So once we know the value of a_{r-1}, we can compute the value of a_r. The value of a_{r-1}, be computed as three times the value of a_{r-2}, which again, is equal to 3 times the value of a_{r-3}. Eventually, we need the value of a_0, which is known to be 1. Then the relation becomes: $a_r = 3a_{r-1}$, $a_0 = 1$, completely specifies the numeric function **a**.

For example: *Find the recurrence relation for the Fibonacci series: 1, 1, 2, 3, 5, 8, 13, ...?*

Sol. The recurrence relation is:

$$a_r = a_{r-1} + a_{r-2},$$
$$a_0 = 1, a_1 = 1.$$

Note: The general expression is quite difficult as it is:

$$a_r = \frac{1}{\sqrt{5}}\left(\frac{1+\sqrt{5}}{2}\right)^{r+1} - \frac{1}{\sqrt{5}}\left(\frac{1-\sqrt{5}}{2}\right)^{r+1}.$$

and its generating function is: $A(z) = \dfrac{1}{1-z-z^2}$. Hence it is too difficult to find the expressions, but it is easy if we denote this by the recurrence relation.

Definition: For a numeric function $a = (a_0, a_1, a_2, ..., a_r, ...)$, an equation relating a_r, for any r, in terms of one or more of the a_i's, $i < r$, is called a ***recurrence relation***. A recurrence relation is also called a ***difference equation.***

According to the definition, a step-by-step computation is to be carried out to determine a_r, from $a_{r-1}, a_{r-2}, ...$, to determine a_{r+1} from $a_r, a_{r-1}, ...$ and so on., provided that the value of the function at one or more points is given so that the computation can be initiated. These given values of the function are called ***boundary conditions.*** *i.e.*, a numeric function can be described by a recurrence relation together with an appropriate set of boundary conditions. The numeric function is also referred to as the solution of recurrence relation.

3.6. LINEAR RECURRENCE RELATION WITH CONSTANT COEFFICIENTS

A recurrence relation of the form $f(r) = c_0a_r + c_1a_{r-1} + c_2a_{r-2} + \ldots + c_ka_{r-k}$, where c_i's are constants, is called a linear recurrence relation with constant coefficients. The above relation is known as k^{th} order recurrence relation, provided c_0 and c_k are non-zero.

For example (*i*) $2a_r + 3a_{r-1} = 2^r$ .... is 1st order linear recurrence relation with constant coefficients.

(*ii*) $3a_r + 5a_{r-1} + 2a_{r-2} = r^2 + 5 \rightarrow$ is 2nd order linear recurrence relation with constant coefficients.

(*iii*) $a_r + 7a_{r-2} = 0 \rightarrow$ is 2nd order linear recurrence relation with constant coefficients.

Note. For a kth order linear recurrence relation with constant coefficients, fewer than k values of the numeric function will not be sufficient to determine the numeric function uniquely.

3.7. HOMOGENEOUS SOLUTION

The ***total solution*** (complete solution) of a linear difference equation with constant coefficient is the sum of two parts, the ***homogeneous solution***, which satisfies the difference equation when the right hand side of the equation is set to zero, and ***particular solution*** which satisfies the difference equation with '$f(r)$' on the right–hand side.

In other words, the discrete numeric function that is the solution of the difference equation is the sum of two discrete numeric functions – one is the homogeneous solution and the other is the particular solution.

Let $a^{(h)} = \left(a_0^{(h)}, a_1^{(h)}, a_2^{(h)}, \ldots\ldots, a_r^{(h)}, \ldots\ldots\right)$ denotes the homogeneous solution and $a^{(p)} = \left(a_0^{(p)}, a_1^{(p)}, a_2^{(p)}, \ldots\ldots, a_r^{(p)}, \ldots\ldots\right)$, denotes the particular solution to the difference equation. Then the total solution is $a = a^{(h)} + a^{(p)}$ satisfies the difference equation.

A homogeneous solution of a linear difference equation with constant coefficients is of the form $A\alpha_1^r$, where α_1 is called a characteristic root and A is a constant determined by the boundary conditions. Substituting $A\alpha^r$ for a_r, in the difference equation with right hand side of the equation set to zero, we get:

$c_0A\alpha^r + c_1A\alpha^{r-1} + c_2A\alpha^{r-2} + \ldots + c_kA\alpha^{r-k} = 0$. This equation can be simplified to:

$c_0\alpha^k + c_1\alpha^{k-1} + c_2\alpha^{k-2} + \ldots + c_k = 0$, which is called the ***characteristic equation*** of the difference equation.

Therefore if α_1 is one of the roots of the characteristic equation (known as characteristic root), $A\alpha_1{}^r$ is a homogeneous solution to the difference equation.

A characteristic equation of kth degree has k characteristic roots.

Case (*i*): *The roots of the characteristic equation are distinct:* If the roots are distinct, then $a_r^{(h)} = A_1\alpha_1^r + A_2\alpha_2^r + A_3\alpha_3^r + \ldots\ldots + A_k\alpha_k^r$, is also a homogeneous solution to the difference equation, where α_i's are distinct characteristic roots and $A_1, A_2, \ldots, A_k$ are constants which are to be determined by the boundary conditions.

Example 12. *Determine the homogeneous solution for the Fibonacci Sequence.*

Sol. The recurrence relation for the Fibonacci sequence of numbers is: $a_r = a_{r-1} + a_{r-2}$. Therefore the corresponding characteristic equation is: $\alpha^2 - \alpha - 1 = 0$, which has two distinct roots: $\alpha_1 = \frac{1+\sqrt{5}}{2}$ and $\alpha_2 = \frac{1-\sqrt{5}}{2}$. $\therefore \quad a_r^{(h)} = A_1\left(\frac{1+\sqrt{5}}{2}\right)^r + A_2\left(\frac{1-\sqrt{5}}{2}\right)^r$, is a homogeneous solution where A_1 and A_2 are constants to be determined from the boundary conditions.

Case (*ii*). *Some of the roots of the characteristic equations are multiple roots:* Let α_1 be a root of multiplicity m. Then the corresponding homogeneous solution is:

$a_r^{(h)} = (A_1 r^{m-1} + A_2 r^{m-2} + A_3 r^{m-3} + \ldots + A_{m-1} r + A_m)\alpha_1^r$, where A_i's are constants to be determined by the boundary conditions.

Example 13. *Solve* $a_r + 6a_{r-1} + 12a_{r-2} + 8a_{r-3} = 0$

Sol. The characteristic equation is:

$$\alpha^3 + 6\alpha^2 + 12\alpha + 8 = 0 \quad i.e., \quad (\alpha + 2)^3 = 0, \ \alpha = -2, -2, -2.$$

i.e., -2 is a triple characteristic root. $\therefore$ $a_r^{(h)} = (A_1 r^2 + A_2 r + A_3)(-2)^r$, is a homogeneous solution.

Example 14. *Find the homogeneous solution to:* $4a_r - 20a_{r-1} + 17a_{r-2} - 4a_{r-3} = 0$?

Sol. The characteristic equation is:

$$4\alpha^3 - 20\alpha^2 + 17\alpha - 4 = 0 \quad i.e., \quad (\alpha - 4)\left(\alpha - \frac{1}{2}\right)^2 = 0, \ \alpha = 4, \frac{1}{2}, \frac{1}{2}$$

are characteristic roots.

Therefore the homogeneous solution is:

$$a_r^{(h)} = (A_1 r + A_2)\left(\frac{1}{2}\right)^r + A_3 4^r .$$

Example 15. *Solve the following recurrence relations:*

(*i*) $a_r - 7a_{r-1} + 10a_{r-2} = 0$, *given* $a_0 = 0$, $a_1 = 3$.

(*ii*) $a_r - 4a_{r-1} + 4a_{r-2} = 0$, *given* $a_0 = 1$, $a_1 = 6$.

Sol. (*i*) $a_r - 7a_{r-1} + 10a_{r-2} = 0$, then the characteristic equation is:

$$\alpha^2 - 7\alpha + 10 = 0 \quad i.e., \quad (\alpha - 2)(\alpha - 5) = 0$$

i.e., $\alpha = 2, 5$, are characteristic roots.

Therefore the solution is: $a_r = a_r^{(h)} = A_1 2^r + A_2 5^r$.

Applying initial conditions $a_0 = 0$, $a_1 = 3$ we get $A_1 = -1$, $A_2 = 1$.

Hence the solution is: $a_r = a_r^{(h)} = (-1)\, 2^r + 5^r$.

(*ii*) $a_r - 4a_{r-1} + 4a_{r-2} = 0$, then the characteristic equation is:

$(\alpha - 2)^2 = 0$, $\alpha = 2, 2$, *i.e.*, characteristic roots are repeated roots.

Therefore the solution is: $a_r = a_r^{(h)} = (A_1 + A_2 r)2^r$.

Applying initial conditions $a_0 = 1$, $a_1 = 6$, we get $A_1 = 1$, $A_2 = 2$.

Hence the required solution is: $a_r = a_r^{(h)} = (1 + 2r)\, 2^r$.

3.8. PARTICULAR SOLUTION

There is no general procedure for determining the particular solution of difference equation. However, in simple cases, this solution can be obtained by the method of inspection.

Let $c_0 a_r^{(p)} + c_1 a_{r-1}^{(p)} + c_2 a_{r-2}^{(p)} + \ldots\ldots + c_k a_{r-k}^{(p)} = f(r)$, be the given equation.

Case (*i*). *Let f(r) is a constant.*

If $f(r)$ is constant, the particular solution also will be a constant 'P'.

Example 16. *Find the total solution to:* $a_r - 5a_{r-1} + 6a_{r-2} = 1$.

Sol. The characteristic equation is: $\alpha^2 - 5\alpha + 6 = 0$ *i.e.*, $(\alpha - 2)(\alpha - 3) = 0$, $\alpha = 2, 3$.

Therefore the homogeneous solution is: $a_r^{(h)} = A_1 2^r + A_2 3^r$.

To find particular solution $f(r) = 1$, a constant. Therefore substituting P in the given equation, we get: $P - 5P + 6P = 1 \Rightarrow 2P = 1 \Rightarrow P = \frac{1}{2}$. $\therefore\ a_r^{(P)} = \frac{1}{2}$.

Total solution is: $a_r = a_r^{(h)} + a_r^{(P)} = A_1 2^r + A_2 3^r + \frac{1}{2}$.

Case (*ii*): *Let f(r) is of the form of a polynomial of degree 't' in r.*

Such as: $F_1 r^t + F_2 r^{t-1} + F_3 r^{r-2} + \ldots\ldots + F_1 r + F_{t+1}$. The corresponding particular solution will be of the form: $P_1 r^t + P_2 r^{t-1} + P_3 r^{t-2} + \ldots\ldots + P_t r + P_{t+1}$.

Example 17. *Find the total solution to:* $a_r + 5a_{r-1} + 6a_{r-2} = 3r^2$.

Sol. The characteristic equation is: $\alpha^2 + 5\alpha + 6 = 0$ *i.e.*, $(\alpha + 2)(\alpha + 3) = 0$, $\alpha = -2, -3$.

Therefore the homogeneous solution is: $a_r^{(h)} = A_1(-2)^r + A_2(-3)^r$.

To find particular solution, since $f(r) = 3r^2$ the general form of particular solution is: $P_1 r^2 + P_2 r + P_3$, where P_1, P_2, P_3 are constants to be determined. Substituting in the given form we get,

$$a_r + 5a_{r-1} + 6a_{r-2} = 3r^2$$

$$\Rightarrow (P_1 r^2 + P_2 r + P_3) + 5(P_1(r-1)^2 + P_2(r-1) + P_3) + 6(P_1(r-2)^2 + P_2(r-2) + P_3) = 3r^2.$$

i.e.,
$$12P_1 r^2 - (34P_1 - 12P_2) r + (29P_1 - 17P_2 + 12P_3) = 3r^2.$$

Solving we get: $P_1 = \frac{1}{4}, P_2 = \frac{17}{24}, P_3 = \frac{115}{288}$, $\therefore\ a_r^{(P)} = \frac{1}{4}r^2 + \frac{17}{24}r + \frac{115}{288}$

Total solution is: $a_r = a_r^{(h)} + a_r^{(P)} = A_1(-2)^r + A_2(-3)^r + \frac{1}{4}r^2 + \frac{17}{24}r + \frac{115}{288}$.

Example 18. *Find the total solution to:* $a_r + 5a_{r-1} + 6a_{r-2} = 3r^2 - 2r + 1$.

Sol. The homogeneous solution is: $a_r^{(h)} = A_1(-2)^r + A_2(-3)^r$.

The particular solution is:

$$a_r^{(P)} = \frac{1}{4}r^2 + \frac{13}{24}r + \frac{71}{288}.$$

Total solution is: $a_r = a_r^{(h)} + a_r^{(P)} = A_1(-2)^r + A_2(-3)^r + \frac{1}{4}r^2 + \frac{13}{24}r + \frac{71}{228}$.

Case (*iii*) (*a*): *Let f(r) is of the form* β^r.

Then the corresponding particular solution is of the form $P\beta^r$, of β is not a characteristic root of the difference equation.

Further more, when $f(r)$ is of the form $(F_1 r^t + F_2 r^{t-1} + F_3 r^{t-2} + \ldots\ldots + F_t r + F_{t+1})\beta^r$, the corresponding particular solution is of the form:

$(P_1 r^t + P_2 r^{t-1} + P_3 r^{t-2} + \ldots\ldots + P_t r + P_{t+1})\beta^r$, if β is not a characteristic root of the difference equation.

Example 19. *Solve* $a_r + a_{r-1} = 3r2^r$.

Sol. The characteristic equation is: $\alpha + 1 = 0$ *i.e.*, $\alpha = -1$.

Therefore the homogeneous solution is: $a_r^{(h)} = A_1(-1)^r$.

To find the particular solution, let the general form of particular solution is: $(P_1 r + P_2)2^r$.

Then the given equation becomes: $(P_1 r + P_2)2^r + (P_1(r-1) + P_2)2^{r-1} = 3r2^r$. Solving we get,

$$P_1 = 2, P_2 = \frac{2}{3}. \quad \therefore\ a_r^{(P)} = \left(2r + \frac{2}{3}\right)2^r.$$

Total solution is: $a_r = a_r^{(h)} + a_r^{(P)} = A_1(-1)^r + \left(2r + \frac{2}{3}\right)2^r$.

Case (*iii*). *When f(r) is of the form* $(F_1r^t + F_2r^{t-1} + F_3r^{t-2} + ... + F_tr + F_{t+1})\,\beta^r$, *and* β *is a characteristic root:*

If β is a characteristic root of multiplicity $(m - 1)$. Then the corresponding particular solution is of the form:

$$r^{m-1}\,(P_1r^t + P_2r^{t-1} + P_3r^{t-2} + ... + P_tr + P_{t+1})\,B^r.$$

Example 20. *Solve the difference equation:* $a_r - 2a_{r-1} = 3.(2)^r$.

Sol. The characteristic equation is: $\alpha - 2 = 0$. *i.e.,* $\alpha = 2$

Therefore the homogeneous solution is: $a_r^{(h)} = A_1(2)^r$.

To find the particular solution, since here 2 is a characteristic root of multiplicity '1', the general form of particular solution is $P_r(2)^r$. Substituting in the given equation, we get:

$$P_r\, 2^r - 2.P.(r - 1)\, 2^{r-1} = 3.(2)^r. \text{ Solving, we get } P = 3. \quad \therefore \quad a_r^{(P)} = 3r2^r.$$

Total solution is: $a_r = a_r^{(h)} + a_r^{(P)} = A_1(2)^r + 3r2^r$.

Example 21. *Solve the difference equation:* $a_r - 4a_{r-1} + 4a_{r-2} = (r + 1)\,(2)^r$.

Sol. The characteristic equation is: $\alpha^2 - 4\alpha + 4 = 0$ *i.e.,* $(\alpha - 2)^2 = 0$ or $\alpha = 2, 2$.

Therefore the homogeneous solution is: $a_r^{(h)} = (A_1r + A_2)\,(2)^r$.

Since 2 is a characteristic root of multiplicity 2, the general form of particular solution is: $r^2\,(P_1r + P_2)\,2^r$.

Substituting in the given equation, we get:

$$r^2(P_1r + P_2)\,2^r - 4\,((r - 1)^2\,(P_1(r - 1) + P_2)\,2^{r-1}) + 4\,((r - 2)^2\,(P_1(r - 2) + P_2)\,2^{r-2}) = (r + 1)\,(2)^r.$$

On simplification, we get: $P_1 = \frac{1}{6}$, $P_2 = 1$. $\therefore$ $a_r^{(P)} = r^2\left(\frac{1}{6}r + 1\right)2^r$.

Total solution is: $a_r = a_r^{(h)} + a_r^{(P)} = (A_1r + A_2)\,(2)^r + r^2\left(\frac{1}{6}r + 1\right)2^r$.

Example 22. *Solve the difference equation:* $a_r = a_{r-1} + 7$

Sol. The characteristic equation is: $\alpha - 1 = 0$ *i.e.,* $\alpha = 1$.

Therefore the homogeneous solution is: $a_r^{(h)} = A_1(1)^r$.

Since 7 is a constant, if we put the general form of the particular solution as P, it is impossible to find P. Therefore take the general form of the particular solution as P_r as 7 can be written as $7(1)^r$. Substituting in the given equation we get.,

$$P_r = P(r - 1) + 7 \;\Rightarrow\; P = 7. \quad \therefore \quad a_r^{(P)} = 7r.$$

Total solution is: $a_r = a_r^{(h)} + a_r^{(P)} = A_1(1)^r + 7r$.

Example 23. *Solve the difference equation:* $a_r - 5a_{r-1} + 6a_{r-2} = 2^r + r$.

Sol. The characteristic equation is: $\alpha^2 - 5\alpha + 6 = 0$ *i.e.,* $(\alpha - 2)\,(\alpha - 3) = 0$, $\alpha = 2, 3$.

Therefore the homogeneous solution is: $a_r^{(h)} = A_1(2)^r + A_2(3)^r$.

Particular solution (*i*) is for 2^r, and since 2 is a root its general form is $P_1r(2)^r$. Particular solution (*ii*) is for 'r' and its general form is $P_2r + P_3$.

Therefore the particular solution is of the form $P_1r\,(2)^r + P_2r + P_3$. Substituting this in the given equation and solving, we get:

$$P_1 = -2,\; P_2 = \frac{1}{2},\; P_3 = \frac{7}{4}.$$

$$\therefore \qquad a_r^{(P)} = -2r2^r + \frac{1}{2}r + \frac{7}{4} = -r2^{r+1} + \frac{1}{2}r + \frac{7}{4}.$$

Therefore the total solution is:

$$a_r = a_r^{(h)} + a_r^{(P)} = A_1(2)^r + A_2(3)^r - r2^{r+1} + \frac{1}{2}r + \frac{7}{4}.$$

Note. *In total solution a_r, if boundary conditions are given, we can find out the constants A_1, A_2.*

Example 24. *Solve the following recurrence relation:*

$$a_r - 7a_{r-1} + 10a_{r-2} = 3^r,\ a_0 = 0,\ a_1 = 1.$$

Sol. $a_r - 7a_{r-1} + 10a_{r-2} = 3^r$. The characteristic equation is:

$$\alpha^2 - 7\alpha + 10 = 0 \text{ i.e., } (\alpha - 2)(\alpha - 5) = 0,\ \alpha = 2, 5.$$

$$a_r^{(h)} = A_1(2)^r + A_2(5)^r.$$

The general form of particular solution is $P(3)^r$. Substituting in the given equation we get $P = \frac{-9}{2}$. Therefore $a_r^{(P)} = \frac{-9}{2}(3)^r$.

$$a_r = a_r^{(h)} + a_r^{(P)} = A_1(2)^r + A_2(5)^r + \frac{-9}{2}(3)^r.$$

Applying initial conditions:

$$a_0 = 0,\ a_1 = 1, \text{ we get } A_1 = \frac{8}{3},\ A_2 = \frac{11}{6}.$$

$$\therefore \qquad a_r = a_r^{(h)} + a_r^{(P)} = \frac{8}{3}(2)^r + \frac{11}{6}(5)^r + \frac{-9}{2}(3)^r.$$

3.9. SOLUTION BY THE METHOD OF GENERATING FUNCTIONS

Instead of solving a difference equation for an expression for the value of a numeric function, we can determine the generating function of the numeric function from the difference equation. In many cases, once the generating function is determined, an expression for the value of the numeric function can easily be obtained.

A general procedure for determining the generating function of the numeric function **a** form the difference equation:

$c_0a_r + c_1a_{r-1} + c_2a_{r-2} + \ldots\ldots + c_ka_{r-k} = f(r)$, which is valid for $r \geq s$ where $s \geq k$. Multiplying both sides of this equation by z^r, and summing form $r = s$ to $r = \infty$,

$$\sum_{u=s}^{\infty} (c_0a_r + c_1a_{r-1} + c_2a_{r-2} + \ldots\ldots + c_ka_{r-k})z^r = \sum_{r=s}^{\infty} f(r)z^r.$$

$$\therefore \quad A(z) = \frac{1}{c_0 + c_1z + c_2z^2 + \ldots\ldots + c_kz^k}\left\{\sum_{r=s}^{\infty} f(r)z^r + c_0\left[a_0 + a_1z + \ldots + a_{s-1}z^{s-1}\right]\right.$$

$$\left. + c_1z\left[a_0 + a_1z + \ldots + a_{s-2}z^{s-2}\right] + \ldots + c_kz_k\left[a_0 + a_1z + \ldots + a_{s-k-1}z^{s-k-1}\right]\right\}$$

Since we have

$$\sum_{r=s}^{\infty} c_0a_rz^r = c_0\,[A(z) - a_0 - a_1z - \ldots - a_{s-1}z^{s-1}]$$

$$\sum_{r=s}^{\infty} c_1 a_{r-1} z^r = c_1 z\,[\mathrm{A}(z) - a_0 - a_1 z - \ldots - a_{s-2} z^{s-2}]$$

$$\sum_{r=s}^{\infty} c_2 a_{r-2} z^r = c_2 z^2\,[\mathrm{A}(z) - a_0 - a_1 z - \ldots - a_{s-3} z^{s-3}]$$

$$\ldots\ldots \qquad \ldots\ldots \qquad \ldots\ldots$$

$$\sum_{r=s}^{\infty} c_k a_{r-k} z^r = c_k z^k\,[\mathrm{A}(z) - a_0 - a_1 z - \ldots - a_{s-k-1} z^{s-k-1}].$$

The Procedure used for solving recurrence relation by generating function is:

1. *Multiply both sides of the relation by z^r and sum from $r = s$ to, $r = \infty$.*
2. *From the above se of equations find A(z) and simplify.*
3. *Decompose A(z) into partial fractions.*
4. *Express A(z) as a sum of familiar series.*
5. *Express a_r as the coefficient of z^r in A(z).*

Example 25. *Solve the difference equation: $a_r - 5a_{r-1} + 6a_{r-2} = 2^r + r$, by finding its generating function? (Given that the boundary conditions are $a_0 = 1$, $a_1 = 1$).*

Sol. Given $a_r - 5a_{r-1} + 6a_{r-2} = 2^r + r$. Multiplying both sides by z^r and summing up we get:

$$\sum_{r=2}^{\infty} a_r z^r - 5\sum_{r=2}^{\infty} a_{r-1} z^r + 6\sum_{r=2}^{\infty} a_{r-2} z^r = \sum_{r=2}^{\infty} 2^r z^r + \sum_{r=2}^{\infty} r z^r$$

$$(\mathrm{A}(z) - a_0 - a_1 z) - 5z(\mathrm{A}(z) - a_0) + 6z^2\mathrm{A}(z) = 2^2 z^2 \cdot \frac{1}{1-2z} + z\left(\frac{1}{(1-z)^2} - 1\right).$$

i.e.,
$$\mathrm{A}(z) = \frac{1 - 8z + 27z^2 - 35z^3 + 14z^4}{(1-z)^2\,(1-2z)^2\,(1-3z)}$$

i.e.,
$$\mathrm{A}(z) = \frac{5/4}{(1-z)} + \frac{1/2}{(1-z)^2} - \frac{3}{(1-2z)} - \frac{2}{(1-2z)^2} + \frac{17/4}{(1-3z)}.$$

From this expression we have:

$$a_r = \frac{7}{4} + \frac{r}{2} - r2^{r+1} - 52^r + \frac{17}{4}3^r.$$

Example 26. *Solve the recurrence relation $a_r = a_{r-1} + 2\,(r - 1)$, with $a_0 = 3$, $a_1 = 1$ by finding its generating function?*

Sol. Let A(z) be the generating function. Then $\mathrm{A}(z) = \sum_{r=0}^{\infty} a_r z^r$.

Now the given relation is $a_r - a_{r-1} - 2r + 2 = 0$, $r \geq 1$. Therefore,

$$\sum_{r=1}^{\infty} [a_r - a_{r-1} - 2r + 2] z^r = 0.$$

Hence,
$$\sum_{r=1}^{\infty} a_r z^r - \sum_{r=1}^{\infty} a_{r-1} z^r - 2\sum_{r=1}^{\infty} r z^r + 2\sum_{r=1}^{\infty} z^r = 0$$

$$[A(z) - a_0] - z\left[\sum_{r=1}^{\infty} a_{r-1}z^{r-1}\right] - 2[z + 2z^2 + 3z^3 + \ldots] + 2\left[\sum_{r=0}^{\infty} z^r - 1\right] = 0$$

$$A(z) - 3 - zA(z) - 2z\left[\frac{1}{(1-z)^2}\right] + 2\left[\frac{1}{(1-z)} - 1\right] = 0$$

$$(1 - z)\,A(z) = \frac{2z}{(1-z)^2} - \frac{2}{(1-z)} + 5.$$

$$\therefore \qquad A(z) = \frac{2z}{(1-z)^3} - \frac{2}{(1-z)^2} + \frac{5}{(1-z)}.$$

Example 27. *Solve the recurrence relation* $a_r - 7a_{r-1} + 10a_{r-2} = 0$ *for* $r \geq 2$, *given that* $a_0 = 10$, $a_1 = 41$ *using generating function?*

Sol. Given $\qquad a_r - 7a_{r-1} + 10a_{r-2} = 0$

Multiplying both sides of the given equation by z^r and summing from 2 to ∞, we get

$$\sum_{r=2}^{\infty} a_r z^r - 7\sum_{r=2}^{\infty} a_{r-1}z^r + 10\sum_{r=2}^{\infty} a_{r-2}z^r = 0$$

$$[A(z) - a_0 - a_1 z] - 7z\,[A(z) - a_0] + 10z^2\,[A(z)] = 0$$

Solving for A(z) we get,

$$A(z) = \frac{a_0 + (a_1 - 7a_0)z}{1 - 7z + 10z^2} = \frac{a_0 + (a_1 - 7a_0)z}{(1-2z)(1-5z)^2} = \frac{C_1}{(1-2z)} + \frac{C_2}{(1-5z)}$$

i.e.,

$$A(z) = C_1\sum_{r=0}^{\infty} 2^r z^r + C_2\sum_{r=0}^{\infty} 5^r z^r.$$

Thus $a_r = C_1 2^r + C_2 5^r$, $r \geq 2$. Now given $a_0 = 10$, $a_1 = 41$. Substituting we get $C_1 = 3$ and $C_2 = 7$. Thus we have, $a_r = 3.2^r + 7.5^r$.

3.10. SIMULTANEOUS DIFFERENCE EQUATIONS

We can solve a set of simultaneous difference equation by the technique of generating functions. Form a set of simultaneous difference equations, relating several numeric functions, we can obtain a set of simultaneous algebraic equations relating their generating functions. These equations can be solved for closed form expressions for the generating functions.

Example 28. *Let a and b be two numeric functions with:*

$$a_r = 3a_{r-1} + 2b_{r-1},$$
$$b_r = a_{r-1} + b_{r-1}$$

solve these simultaneous difference equations. (Given $a_0 = 1$, $b_0 = 0$*).*

Sol. By the method of generating functions:

$$a_r = 3a_{r-1} + 2b_{r-1}$$
$$b_r = a_{r-1} + b_{r-1}$$

we have:

$$\sum_{r=1}^{\infty} a_r z^r = 3\sum_{r=1}^{\infty} a_{r-1}z^r + 2\sum_{r=1}^{\infty} b_{r-1}z^r$$

$$\sum_{r=1}^{\infty} b_r z^r = \sum_{r=1}^{\infty} a_{r-1}z^r + \sum_{r=1}^{\infty} b_{r-1}z^r$$

i.e., $A(z) - a_0 = 3zA(z) + 2zB(z)$

i.e., $B(z) - b_0 = zA(z) + zB(z).$

i.e., $A(z) - 1 = 3zA(z) + 2zB(z)$

i.e., $B(z) = zA(z) + zB(z)$

Solving:

$$A(z) = \frac{(3+\sqrt{3})/6}{1-(2+\sqrt{3})z} + \frac{(3-\sqrt{3})/6}{1-(2-\sqrt{3})z}$$

$$B(z) = \frac{\sqrt{3}/6}{1-(2+\sqrt{3})z} - \frac{\sqrt{3}/6}{1-(2-\sqrt{3})z}$$

Therefore the solution is:

$$a_r = \frac{(3+\sqrt{3})}{6}(2+\sqrt{3})^r + \frac{(3-\sqrt{3})}{6}(2-\sqrt{3})^r$$

$$b_r = \frac{\sqrt{3}}{6}(2+\sqrt{3})^r - \frac{\sqrt{3}}{6}(2-\sqrt{3})^r.$$

TEST YOUR KNOWLEDGE

1. Find the general solution of $a_r + a_{r-1} + a_{r-2} = 0$.
2. Solve: $u_x + 6u_{x-1} + 12u_{x-2} + 8u_{x-3} = 0$.
3. Using generating function solve: $a_r = 3a_{r-1} + 2, r \geq 1$ and $a_0 = 1$.
4. Solve the recurrence relation $u_r - u_{r-1} + 9u_{r-2} = 3^r$.
5. Solve using generating function: $a_{r+2} - 3a_{r+1} + 2a_r = 0$, given $a_0 = 2, a_1 = 3$.
6. Solve the recurrence relation $2a_{n+3} = a_{n+2} + 2a_{n+1} - a_n$ for $n \geq 2, a_1 = 1, a_2 = 2$.
7. Find the generating function (*i*) $a^r = r^2$ (*ii*) (0, 1, 0, – 1, 0, 1, 0, – 1, ...).
8. Find the generating function of (1, 1, 0, 1, 1, 0, ...)?
9. Find the discrete numeric function corresponding to the genertaing function $\frac{32-22z}{2-3z+z^2}$
10. Obtain the d.n.f. corresponding to the generating function: $A(z) = \frac{2}{1-4z^2}$.
11. Obain the numeric function corresponding to the generating function:
$$A(z) = \frac{2-3z}{z^2-7z+12}.$$
12. Obtain the sequence corresponding to the generating function $f(x) = \frac{1}{1-x^2}$.
13. Using generating function solve: $a_n - a_{n-1} - a_{n-2} = 0$, given $a_0 = a_1 = 1$.
14. Find the particular solution for the recurrence relation $a_{r+2} - 5a_{r+1} + 6a_r = 5^r$.
15. Obtain the sequence given by the generating function: $A(z) = \frac{2-3z}{z^2-7z+12}$.

MODULE 4
Complex Integration

4.1. INTRODUCTION

A complex number z is an ordered pair (x, y) of real numbers and is written as

$$z = x + iy, \quad \text{where } i = \sqrt{-1}.$$

The real numbers x and y are called the real and imaginary parts of z. In the Argand's diagram, the complex number z is represented by the point $P(x, y)$. If (r, θ) are the polar coordinates of P, then $r = \sqrt{x^2 + y^2}$ is called the modulus of z and is denoted by $|z|$. Also $\theta = \tan^{-1} \frac{y}{x}$ is called the argument of z and is denoted by arg. z. Every non-zero complex number z can be expressed as

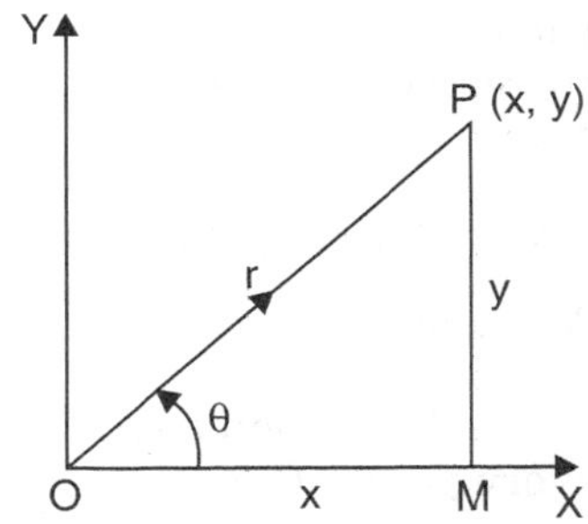

$$z = r(\cos\theta + i\sin\theta) = re^{i\theta}$$

If $z = x + iy$, then the complex number $x - iy$ is called the conjugate of the complex number z and is denoted by $\bar{z}$.

Clearly, $|\bar{z}| = |z|, |z|^2 = z\bar{z}$,

$$R(z) = \frac{z + \bar{z}}{2}, \quad I(z) = \frac{z - \bar{z}}{2i}.$$

4.2. FUNCTION OF A COMPLEX VARIABLE

If x and y are real variables, then $z = x + iy$ is called a **complex variable.** If corresponding to each value of a complex variable $z(= x + iy)$ in a given region R, there correspond one or more values of another complex variable w $(= u + iv)$, then w is called a function of the complex variable z and is denoted by

$$w = f(z) = u + iv$$

For example, if $\quad w = z^2$, where $z = x + iy$ and $w = f(z) = u + iv$

then $\quad u + iv = (x + iy)^2 = (x^2 - y^2) + i(2xy)$

$\Rightarrow \quad u = x^2 - y^2$ and $v = 2xy$

Thus u and v, the real and imaginary parts of w, are functions of the real variables x and y.

$\therefore \quad w = f(z) = u(x, y) + iv(x, y)$

If to each value of z, there corresponds one and only one value of w, then w is called a *single-valued function* of z. If to each value of z, there correspond more than one values of w, then w is called a *multi-valued function of z*.

To represent $w = f(z)$ graphically, we take two Argand diagrams: one to represent the point z and the other to represent w. The former diagram is called the xoy-plane or the z-plane and the latter uov-plane or the w-plane.

4.3. LIMIT OF f(z)

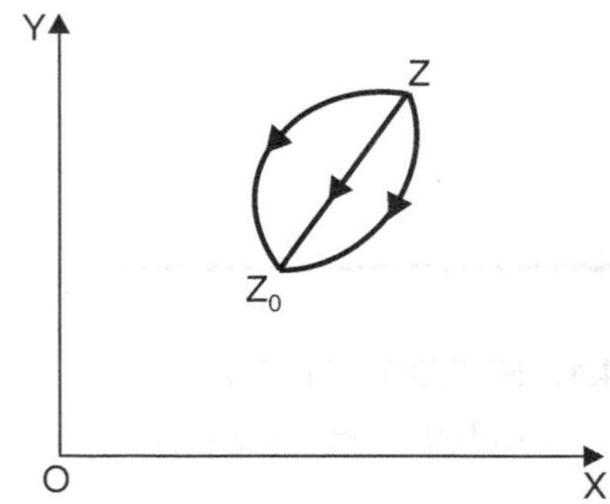

A function $f(z)$ tends to the limit l as z tends to z_0 *along any path,* if to each positive arbitrary number ε, however small, there corresponds a positive number δ, such that

$$| f(z) - l | < \varepsilon \quad \text{whenever} \quad 0 < | z - z_0 | < \delta$$

i.e., $$l - \varepsilon < f(z) < l + \varepsilon$$

whenever $$z_0 - \delta < z < z_0 + \delta, \; z \neq z_0$$

and we write $\underset{z \to z_0}{\text{Lt}} f(z) = l.$

Note. In real variables, $x \to x_0$ implies that x approaches x_0 along the number line, either from left or from right. In complex variables, $z \to z_0$ implies that z approaches z_0 along any path, straight or curved, since the two points representing z and z_0 in a complex plane can be joined by an infinite number of curves.

4.4. CONTINUITY OF f(z)

A single-valued function $f(z)$ is said to be continuous at a point $z = z_0$ if $\underset{z \to z_0}{\text{Lt}} f(z) = f(z_0)$.

A function $f(z)$ is said to be continuous in a region R of the z-plane if it is continuous at every point of the region.

4.5. DERIVATIVE OF f(z)

Let $w = f(z)$ be a single-valued function of the variable $z (= x + iy)$, then the derivative or differential co-efficient of $w = f(z)$ is defined as

$$\frac{dw}{dz} = f'(z) = \underset{\delta z \to 0}{\text{Lt}} \frac{f(z + \delta z) - f(z)}{\delta z}$$

provided the limit exists, independent of the manner in which $\delta z \to 0$.

4.6. ANALYTIC FUNCTION

If a single valued function $f(z)$ possesses a unique derivative at every point of a neighbourhood of the point z_0 in the region R, then $f(z)$ is analytic at z_0. If $f(z)$ is analytic at all points of a region R, then $f(z)$ is called an analytic function or a regular function or a holomorphic function of z in R.

A point where the function ceases to be analytic is called a **singular point.**

4.7. NECESSARY AND SUFFICIENT CONDITIONS FOR f(z) TO BE ANALYTIC

The necessary and sufficient conditions for the function

$$w = f(z) = u(x, y) + iv(x, y)$$

to be analytic in a region R, are

(*i*) $\frac{\partial u}{\partial x}, \frac{\partial u}{\partial y}, \frac{\partial v}{\partial x}, \frac{\partial v}{\partial y}$ *are continuous functions of x and y in the region R.*

(*ii*) $\dfrac{\partial u}{\partial x} = \dfrac{\partial v}{\partial y}, \dfrac{\partial u}{\partial y} = -\dfrac{\partial v}{\partial x}$.

The conditions in (*ii*) are known as **Cauchy-Riemann equations** or briefly **C-R equations.**

Proof. (*a*) Necessary Condition. Let $w = f(z) = u(x, y) + iv(x, y)$ be analytic in a region R, then $\dfrac{dw}{dz} = f'(z)$ exists uniquely at every point of that region.

Let δx and δy be the increments in x and y respectively. Let δu, δv and δz be the corresponding increments in u, v and z respectively. Then,

$$f'(z) = \underset{\delta z \to 0}{\text{Lt}} \frac{f(z+\delta z) - f(z)}{\delta z} = \underset{\delta z \to 0}{\text{Lt}} \frac{(u+\delta u) + i(v+\delta v) - (u+iv)}{\delta z}$$

$$= \underset{\delta z \to 0}{\text{Lt}} \left(\frac{\delta u}{\delta z} + i\frac{\delta v}{\delta z}\right) \qquad \text{...(1)}$$

Since the function $w = f(z)$ is analytic in the region R, the limit (1) must exist independent of the manner in which $\delta z \to 0$, *i.e.*, along whichever path δx and $\delta y \to 0$.

First, let $\delta z \to 0$ along a line parallel to x-axis so that $\delta y = 0$ and $\delta z = \delta x$.

[Since $z = x + iy$, $z + \delta z = (x + \delta x) + i(y + \delta y)$ and $\delta z = \delta x + i\delta y$]

$$\therefore \quad \text{From (1)}, \quad f'(z) = \underset{\delta x \to 0}{\text{Lt}} \left(\frac{\delta u}{\delta x} + i\frac{\delta v}{\delta x}\right) = \frac{\partial u}{\partial x} + i\frac{\partial v}{\partial x} \qquad \text{...(2)}$$

Now, let $\delta z \to 0$ along a line parallel to y-axis so that $\delta x = 0$ and $\delta z = i\,\delta y$.

$$\therefore \quad \text{From (1)}, \quad f'(z) = \underset{\delta y \to 0}{\text{Lt}} \left(\frac{\delta u}{i\,\delta y} + i\frac{\delta v}{i\,\delta y}\right) = \frac{1}{i}\frac{\partial u}{\partial y} + \frac{\partial v}{\partial y}$$

$$= \frac{\partial v}{\partial y} - i\frac{\partial u}{\partial y} \qquad \text{...(3)} \qquad \left|\ \because \frac{1}{i} = -i\right.$$

From (2) and (3), we have $\dfrac{\partial u}{\partial x} + i\dfrac{\partial v}{\partial x} = \dfrac{\partial v}{\partial y} - i\dfrac{\partial u}{\partial y}$

Equating the real and imaginary parts, $\dfrac{\partial u}{\partial x} = \dfrac{\partial v}{\partial y}$ and $\dfrac{\partial u}{\partial y} = -\dfrac{\partial v}{\partial x}$.

Hence the necessary condition for f(z) to be analytic is that the C-R equations must be satisfied.

(*b*) Sufficient Condition. Let $f(z) = u + iv$ be a single-valued function possessing partial derivatives $\dfrac{\partial u}{\partial x}, \dfrac{\partial u}{\partial y}, \dfrac{\partial v}{\partial x}, \dfrac{\partial v}{\partial y}$ at each point of a region R and satisfying C-R equations.

i.e., $$\frac{\partial u}{\partial x} = \frac{\partial v}{\partial y} \quad \text{and} \quad \frac{\partial u}{\partial y} = -\frac{\partial v}{\partial x}.$$

We shall show that $f(z)$ is analytic, *i.e.*, $f'(z)$ exists at every point of the region R.

By Taylor's theorem for functions of two variables, we have, on omitting second and higher degree terms of δx and δy.

$$f(z + \delta z) = u(x + \delta x, y + \delta y) + iv(x + \delta x, y + \delta y)$$

$$= \left[u(x, y) + \left(\frac{\partial u}{\partial x}\delta x + \frac{\partial u}{\partial y}\delta y\right)\right] + i\left[v(x, y) + \left(\frac{\partial v}{\partial x}\delta x + \frac{\partial v}{\partial y}\delta y\right)\right]$$

$$= [u(x, y) + iv(x, y)] + \left(\frac{\partial u}{\partial x} + i\frac{\partial v}{\partial x}\right)\delta x + \left(\frac{\partial u}{\partial y} + i\frac{\partial v}{\partial y}\right)\delta y$$

$$= f(z) + \left(\frac{\partial u}{\partial x} + i\frac{\partial v}{\partial x}\right)\delta x + \left(\frac{\partial u}{\partial y} + i\frac{\partial v}{\partial y}\right)\delta y$$

or
$$f(z + \delta z) - f(z) = \left(\frac{\partial u}{\partial x} + i\frac{\partial v}{\partial x}\right)\delta x + \left(\frac{\partial u}{\partial y} + i\frac{\partial v}{\partial y}\right)\delta y$$

$$= \left(\frac{\partial u}{\partial x} + i\frac{\partial v}{\partial x}\right)\delta x + \left(-\frac{\partial v}{\partial x} + i\frac{\partial u}{\partial x}\right)\delta y \qquad | \text{ Using C-R equations}$$

$$= \left(\frac{\partial u}{\partial x} + i\frac{\partial v}{\partial x}\right)\delta x + \left(\frac{\partial u}{\partial x} + i\frac{\partial v}{\partial x}\right)i\delta y \qquad | \because \; -1 = i^2$$

$$= \left(\frac{\partial u}{\partial x} + i\frac{\partial v}{\partial x}\right)(\delta x + i\delta y) = \left(\frac{\partial u}{\partial x} + i\frac{\partial v}{\partial x}\right)\delta z \qquad | \because \; \delta x + i\delta y = \delta z$$

$$\Rightarrow \qquad \frac{f(z + \delta z) - f(z)}{\delta z} = \frac{\partial u}{\partial x} + i\frac{\partial v}{\partial x}$$

$$\therefore \qquad f'(z) = \underset{\delta z \to 0}{\text{Lt}} \frac{f(z + \delta z) - f(z)}{\delta z} = \frac{\partial u}{\partial x} + i\frac{\partial v}{\partial x}$$

Thus $f'(z)$ exists, because $\frac{\partial u}{\partial x}, \frac{\partial v}{\partial x}$ exist.

Hence $f(z)$ is analytic.

Note 1. The real and imaginary parts of an analytic function are called **conjugate functions.** Thus, if $f(z) = u(x, y) + iv(x, y)$ is an analytic function, then $u(x, y)$ and $v(x, y)$ are conjugate functions. The relation between two conjugate functions is given by C-R equations.

Note 2. When a function $f(z)$ is known to be analytic, it can be differentiated in the ordinary way as if z is a real variable.

Thus, $\quad f(z) = z^2 \quad \Rightarrow \quad f'(z) = 2z$

$\quad f(z) = \sin z \quad \Rightarrow \quad f'(z) = \cos z$ etc.

4.8. CAUCHY-RIEMANN EQUATIONS IN POLAR COORDINATES

Let (r, θ) be the polar coordinates of the point whose cartesian coordinates are (x, y), then

$$x = r\cos\theta, \; y = r\sin\theta,$$

$$z = x + iy = r(\cos\theta + i\sin\theta) = re^{i\theta}$$

$$\therefore \qquad u + iv = f(z) = f(re^{i\theta}) \qquad \text{...(1)}$$

Differentiating (1) partially w.r.t. r, we have

$$\frac{\partial u}{\partial r} + i\frac{\partial v}{\partial r} = f'(re^{i\theta}) \, . \, e^{i\theta} \qquad \text{...(2)}$$

Differentiating (1) partially w.r.t. θ, we have

$$\frac{\partial u}{\partial \theta}+i\frac{\partial v}{\partial \theta}=f'(re^{i\theta})\,.\,ire^{i\theta}=ir\left(\frac{\partial u}{\partial r}+i\frac{\partial v}{\partial r}\right) \qquad \text{| Using (2)}$$

$$=-r\frac{\partial v}{\partial r}+ir\frac{\partial u}{\partial r}$$

Equating real and imaginary parts, we get

$$\frac{\partial u}{\partial \theta}=-r\frac{\partial v}{\partial r} \quad \text{and} \quad \frac{\partial v}{\partial \theta}=r\frac{\partial u}{\partial r}$$

or $$\frac{\partial u}{\partial r}=\frac{1}{r}\frac{\partial v}{\partial \theta} \quad \text{and} \quad \frac{\partial v}{\partial r}=-\frac{1}{r}\frac{\partial u}{\partial \theta}$$ which is the polar form of C-R equations.

4.9. HARMONIC FUNCTIONS

Any solution of the Laplace's equation, $\frac{\partial^2 \phi}{\partial x^2}+\frac{\partial^2 \phi}{\partial y^2}=0$ is called a harmonic function.

Let $f(z) = u + iv$ be analytic in some region of the z-plane, then u and v satisfy C-R equations.

∴ $$\frac{\partial u}{\partial x}=\frac{\partial v}{\partial y} \qquad ...(1)$$

and $$\frac{\partial u}{\partial y}=-\frac{\partial v}{\partial x} \qquad ...(2)$$

Differentiating (1) partially w.r.t. x and (2) w.r.t. y, we get

$$\frac{\partial^2 u}{\partial x^2}=\frac{\partial^2 v}{\partial x \partial y} \qquad ...(3)$$

and $$\frac{\partial^2 u}{\partial y^2}=-\frac{\partial^2 v}{\partial y \partial x} \qquad ...(4)$$

Assuming $\frac{\partial^2 v}{\partial x \partial y}=\frac{\partial^2 v}{\partial y \partial x}$ and adding (3) and (4), we get

$$\frac{\partial^2 u}{\partial x^2}+\frac{\partial^2 u}{\partial y^2}=0 \qquad ...(5)$$

Now, differentiating (1) partially w.r.t. y and (2) w.r.t. x, we get

$$\frac{\partial^2 u}{\partial y \partial x}=\frac{\partial^2 v}{\partial y^2} \qquad ...(6)$$

and $$\frac{\partial^2 u}{\partial x \partial y}=-\frac{\partial^2 v}{\partial x^2} \qquad ...(7)$$

Assuming $\frac{\partial^2 u}{\partial y \partial x}=\frac{\partial^2 u}{\partial x \partial y}$ and subtracting (7) from (6), we get

$$\frac{\partial^2 v}{\partial x^2}+\frac{\partial^2 v}{\partial y^2}=0 \qquad ...(8)$$

Equations (5) and (8) show that the real and imaginary parts u and v of an analytic function satisfy the Laplace's equation.

Hence u and v are known as harmonic functions.

4.10. ORTHOGONAL SYSTEM

Every analytic function $f(z)=u+iv$ defines two families of curves $u(x, y)=c_1$ and $v(x, y)=c_2$, which form an orthogonal system.

Consider the two families of curves

$$u(x, y) = c_1 \qquad ...(1)$$

and

$$v(x, y) = c_2 \qquad ...(2)$$

Differentiating (1) w.r.t. x, we get

$$\frac{\partial u}{\partial x}+\frac{\partial u}{\partial y}\cdot\frac{dy}{dx}=0 \quad \text{or} \quad \frac{dy}{dx}=-\frac{\frac{\partial u}{\partial x}}{\frac{\partial u}{\partial y}}=m_1 \text{ (say)}$$

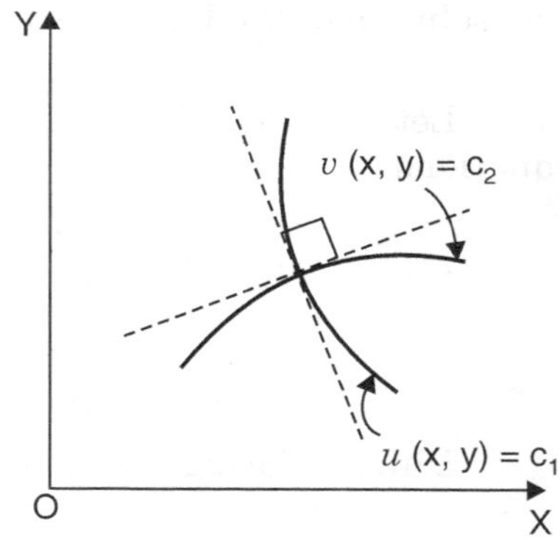

Similarly, from (2), we get $\frac{dy}{dx}=-\frac{\frac{\partial v}{\partial x}}{\frac{\partial v}{\partial y}}=m_2$ (say)

$$\therefore \quad m_1 m_2=\frac{\frac{\partial u}{\partial x}\cdot\frac{\partial v}{\partial x}}{\frac{\partial u}{\partial y}\cdot\frac{\partial v}{\partial y}} \qquad ...(3)$$

Since $f(z)$ is analytic, u and v satisfy C-R equations

i.e., $\frac{\partial u}{\partial x}=\frac{\partial v}{\partial y}$ and $\frac{\partial u}{\partial y}=-\frac{\partial v}{\partial x}$

$$\therefore \text{ From (3),} \quad m_1 m_2=\frac{\frac{\partial v}{\partial y}\cdot\frac{\partial v}{\partial x}}{-\frac{\partial v}{\partial x}\cdot\frac{\partial v}{\partial y}}=-1$$

Thus the product of the slopes of the curves (1) and (2) is – 1. Hence the curves intersect at right angles, *i.e.,* they form an orthogonal system.

4.11. APPLICATION OF ANALYTIC FUNCTIONS TO FLOW PROBLEMS

Since the real and imaginary parts of an analytic function satisfy the Laplace's equation in two variables, these conjugate functions provide solutions to a number of field and flow problems.

For example, consider the two dimensional irrotational motion of an incompressible fluid, in planes parallel to xy-plane.

Let V be the velocity of a fluid particle, then it can be expressed as

$$V=v_x\hat{i}+v_y\hat{j} \qquad ...(1)$$

Since the motion is irrotational, there exists a scalar function $\phi(x, y)$, such that

$$V = \nabla\phi(x, y) = \frac{\partial\phi}{\partial x}\hat{i} + \frac{\partial\phi}{\partial y}\hat{j} \qquad ...(2)$$

From (1) and (2), we have $v_x = \dfrac{\partial\phi}{\partial x}$ and $v_y = \dfrac{\partial\phi}{\partial y}$ ...(3)

The scalar function $\phi(x, y)$, which gives the velocity components, is called the **velocity potential function** or simply the **velocity potential.**

Also the fluid being incompressible, div V = 0

$$\Rightarrow \qquad \left(\hat{i}\frac{\partial}{\partial x} + \hat{j}\frac{\partial}{\partial y}\right)(v_x\hat{i} + v_y\hat{j}) = 0$$

$$\Rightarrow \qquad \frac{\partial v_x}{\partial x} + \frac{\partial v_y}{\partial y} = 0 \qquad ...(4)$$

Substituting the values of v_x and v_y from (3) in (4), we get

$$\frac{\partial}{\partial x}\left(\frac{\partial\phi}{\partial x}\right) + \frac{\partial}{\partial y}\left(\frac{\partial\phi}{\partial y}\right) = 0 \quad \text{or} \quad \frac{\partial^2\phi}{\partial x^2} + \frac{\partial^2\phi}{\partial y^2} = 0$$

Thus the function ϕ is harmonic and can be treated as real part of an analytic function

$$w = f(z) = \phi(x, y) + i\,\psi(x, y)$$

For interpretation of conjugate function $\psi(x, y)$, the slope at any point of the curve $\psi(x, y) = c'$ is given by

$$\frac{dy}{dx} = -\frac{\dfrac{\partial\psi}{\partial x}}{\dfrac{\partial\psi}{\partial y}} = \frac{\dfrac{\partial\phi}{\partial y}}{\dfrac{\partial\phi}{\partial x}} \qquad \text{[By C-R equations]}$$

$$= \frac{v_y}{v_x} \qquad \text{[By (3)]}$$

This shows that the resultant velocity $\sqrt{v_x^2 + v_y^2}$ of the fluid particle is along the tangent to the curve $\psi(x, y) = c'$ *i.e.*, the fluid particles move along this curve. Such curves are known as *stream lines* and $\psi(x, y)$ is called the *stream function.* The curves represented by $\phi(x, y) = c$ are called *equipotential lines.*

Since $\phi(x, y)$ and $\psi(x, y)$ are conjugate functions of analytic function $w = f(z)$, the equipotential lines $\phi(x, y) = c$ and the stream lines $\phi(x, y) = c'$, intersect each other orthogonally.

Now,
$$\frac{dw}{dz} = \frac{\partial\phi}{\partial x} + i\frac{\partial\psi}{\partial x}$$

$$= \frac{\partial\phi}{\partial x} - i\frac{\partial\phi}{\partial y} \qquad \text{[By C-R equations]}$$

$$= v_x - iv_y \qquad \text{[By (3)]}$$

$\therefore$ The magnitude of resultant velocity $= \left|\dfrac{dw}{dz}\right| = \sqrt{v_x^2 + v_y^2}$

The function $w = f(z)$ which fully represents the flow pattern is called the *complex potential.*

In the study of electrostatics and gravitational fields, the curves $\phi(x, y) = c$ and $\psi(x, y) = c'$ are called *equipotential lines* and *lines of force* respectively. In heat flow problems, the curves $\phi(x, y) = c$ and $\psi(x, y) = c'$ are known as *isothermals* and *heat flow lines* respectively.

ILLUSTRATIVE EXAMPLES

Example 1. *Find p such that the function f(z) expressed in polar coordinates as $f(z) = r^2 \cos 2\theta + ir^2 \sin p\theta$ is analytic.*

Sol. Let $f(z) = u + iv$, then $u = r^2 \cos 2\theta$, $v = r^2 \sin p\theta$

$$\frac{\partial u}{\partial r} = 2r\cos 2\theta, \quad \frac{\partial v}{\partial r} = 2r \sin p\theta$$

$$\frac{\partial u}{\partial \theta} = -2r^2 \sin 2\theta, \quad \frac{\partial v}{\partial \theta} = pr^2 \cos p\theta$$

For $f(z)$ to be analytic, $\dfrac{\partial u}{\partial r} = \dfrac{1}{r}\dfrac{\partial v}{\partial \theta}$ and $\dfrac{\partial v}{\partial r} = -\dfrac{1}{r}\dfrac{\partial u}{\partial \theta}$

$\therefore$ $2r\cos 2\theta = pr\cos p\theta$ and $2r \sin p\theta = 2r \sin 2\theta$

Both these equations are satisfied if $p = 2$.

Note. For a function $f(z)$ to be analytic, the first order partial derivatives of u and v must be continuous in addition to C-R equations.

Example 2. *Show that the function $f(z) = \sqrt{|xy|}$ is not regular at the origin, although Cauchy-Riemann equations are satisfied.*

Sol. Let $f(z) = u(x, y) + iv(x, y) = \sqrt{|xy|}$, then $u(x, y) = \sqrt{|xy|}$, $v(x, y) = 0$

At the origin (0, 0), we have

$$\frac{\partial u}{\partial x} = \underset{x \to 0}{\text{Lt}} \frac{u(x, 0) - u(0, 0)}{x} = \underset{x \to 0}{\text{Lt}} \frac{0 - 0}{x} = 0$$

$$\frac{\partial u}{\partial y} = \underset{y \to 0}{\text{Lt}} \frac{u(0, y) - u(0, 0)}{y} = \underset{y \to 0}{\text{Lt}} \frac{0 - 0}{y} = 0$$

$$\frac{\partial v}{\partial x} = \underset{x \to 0}{\text{Lt}} \frac{v(x, 0) - v(0, 0)}{x} = \underset{x \to 0}{\text{Lt}} \frac{0 - 0}{x} = 0$$

$$\frac{\partial v}{\partial y} = \underset{y \to 0}{\text{Lt}} \frac{v(0, y) - v(0, 0)}{y} = \underset{y \to 0}{\text{Lt}} \frac{0 - 0}{y} = 0$$

Clearly, $\dfrac{\partial u}{\partial x} = \dfrac{\partial v}{\partial y}, \dfrac{\partial u}{\partial y} = -\dfrac{\partial v}{\partial x}$

Hence C-R equations are satisfied at the origin.

Now $f'(0) = \underset{z \to 0}{\text{Lt}} \dfrac{f(z) - f(0)}{z} = \underset{z \to 0}{\text{Lt}} \dfrac{\sqrt{|xy|} - 0}{x + iy}$

If $z \to 0$ along the line $y = mx$, we get

$$f'(0) = \underset{x \to 0}{\text{Lt}} \frac{\sqrt{|mx^2|}}{x(1+im)} = \underset{x \to 0}{\text{Lt}} \frac{\sqrt{|m|}}{1+im}$$

Now this limit is not unique since it depends on m. Therefore, $f'(0)$ does not exist. Hence the function $f(z)$ is not regular at the origin.

Example 3. *Prove that the function $f(z)$ defined by*

$$f(z) = \frac{x^3(1+i) - y^3(1-i)}{x^2+y^2}, \; z \neq 0 \text{ and } f(0) = 0$$

is continuous and the Cauchy-Riemann equations are satisfied at the origin, yet $f'(0)$ does not exist.

Sol. Here,
$$f(z) = \frac{(x^3 - y^3) + i(x^3 + y^3)}{x^2+y^2}, \; z \neq 0$$

Let
$$f(z) = u + iv = \frac{x^3 - y^3}{x^2+y^2} + i\frac{x^3+y^3}{x^2+y^2},$$

then
$$u = \frac{x^3 - y^3}{x^2+y^2}, \; v = \frac{x^3+y^3}{x^2+y^2}$$

Since
$$z \neq 0 \;\Rightarrow\; x \neq 0, y \neq 0$$

$\therefore$ u and v are rational functions of x and y with non-zero denominators. Thus, u, v and hence $f(z)$ *are continuous functions when* $z \neq 0$. To test them for continuity at $z = 0$, on changing u, v to polar coordinates by putting $x = r\cos\theta$, $y = r\sin\theta$, we get

$$u = r(\cos^3\theta - \sin^3\theta) \text{ and } v = r(\cos^3\theta + \sin^3\theta)$$

When $z \to 0$, $r \to 0$

$$\therefore \quad \underset{z \to 0}{\text{Lt}}\; u = \underset{r \to 0}{\text{Lt}}\; r(\cos^3\theta - \sin^3\theta) = 0$$

Similarly,
$$\underset{z \to 0}{\text{Lt}}\; v = 0$$

$$\therefore \quad \underset{r \to 0}{\text{Lt}}\; f(z) = 0 = f(0)$$

$\Rightarrow$ $f(z)$ is continuous at $z = 0$.

Hence $f(z)$ is continuous for all values of z.

At the origin (0, 0), we have

$$\frac{\partial u}{\partial x} = \underset{x \to 0}{\text{Lt}} \frac{u(x,0) - u(0,0)}{x} = \underset{x \to 0}{\text{Lt}} \frac{x-0}{x} = 1$$

$$\frac{\partial u}{\partial y} = \underset{y \to 0}{\text{Lt}} \frac{u(0,y) - u(0,0)}{y} = \underset{y \to 0}{\text{Lt}} \frac{-y-0}{y} = -1$$

$$\frac{\partial v}{\partial x} = \underset{x \to 0}{\text{Lt}} \frac{v(x,0) - v(0,0)}{x} = \underset{x \to 0}{\text{Lt}} \frac{x-0}{x} = 1$$

$$\frac{\partial v}{\partial y} = \underset{y \to 0}{\text{Lt}} \frac{v(0,y) - v(0,0)}{y} = \underset{y \to 0}{\text{Lt}} \frac{y-0}{y} = 1$$

$$\therefore \qquad \frac{\partial u}{\partial x} = \frac{\partial v}{\partial y} \quad \text{and} \quad \frac{\partial u}{\partial y} = -\frac{\partial v}{\partial x}$$

Hence C-R equations are satisfied at the origin.

Now, $$f'(0) = \underset{z \to 0}{\text{Lt}} \frac{f(z) - f(0)}{z} = \underset{z \to 0}{\text{Lt}} \frac{(x^3 - y^3) + i(x^3 + y^3) - 0}{(x^2 + y^2)(x + iy)}$$

Let $z \to 0$ along the line $y = x$, then

$$f'(0) = \underset{x \to 0}{\text{Lt}} \frac{0 + 2ix^3}{2x^3(1+i)} = \frac{i}{1+i} = \frac{i(1-i)}{2} = \frac{1+i}{2} \qquad \ldots(1)$$

Also, let $z \to 0$ along the x-axis (*i.e.*, $y = 0$), then

$$f'(0) = \underset{x \to 0}{\text{Lt}} \frac{x^3 + ix^3}{x^3} = 1 + i \qquad \ldots(2)$$

Since the limits (1) and (2) are different, $f'(0)$ does not exist.

Example 4. *Prove that the function sinh z is analytic and find its derivative.*

Sol. Here $\quad f(z) = u + iv = \sinh z = \sinh(x + iy) = \sinh x \cos y + i \cosh x \sin y$

$\therefore \quad u = \sinh x \cos y \quad \text{and} \quad v = \cosh x \sin y$

$$\frac{\partial u}{\partial x} = \cosh x \cos y, \quad \frac{\partial u}{\partial y} = -\sinh x \sin y$$

$$\frac{\partial v}{\partial x} = \sinh x \sin y, \quad \frac{\partial v}{\partial y} = \cosh x \cos y$$

$$\therefore \qquad \frac{\partial u}{\partial x} = \frac{\partial v}{\partial y} \quad \text{and} \quad \frac{\partial u}{\partial y} = -\frac{\partial v}{\partial x}$$

Thus C-R equations are satisfied.

Since sinh x, cosh x, sin y and cos y are continuous functions, $\frac{\partial u}{\partial x}, \frac{\partial u}{\partial y}, \frac{\partial v}{\partial x}$ and $\frac{\partial v}{\partial y}$ are also continuous functions satisfying C-R equations.

Hence $f(z)$ is analytic everywhere.

Now $$f'(z) = \frac{\partial u}{\partial x} + i\frac{\partial v}{\partial x}$$
$$= \cosh x \cos y + i \sinh x \sin y = \cosh(x + iy) = \cosh z.$$

Example 5. *Determine the analytic function whose real part is* $e^{2x}(x \cos 2y - y \sin 2y)$.

Sol. Let $f(z) = u + iv$ be the analytic function,

where $\quad u = e^{2x}(x \cos 2y - y \sin 2y)$

$$\therefore \qquad \frac{\partial u}{\partial x} = 2e^{2x}(x \cos 2y - y \sin 2y) + e^{2x} \cos 2y$$
$$= e^{2x}(2x \cos 2y - 2y \sin 2y + \cos 2y) \qquad \ldots(1)$$

$$\frac{\partial u}{\partial y} = e^{2x}(-2x \sin 2y - \sin 2y - 2y \cos 2y)$$
$$= -e^{2x}(2x \sin 2y + \sin 2y + 2y \cos 2y) \qquad \ldots(2)$$

Since $f(z)$ is analytic, u and v must satisfy C-R equations

$$\frac{\partial u}{\partial x} = \frac{\partial v}{\partial y} \quad \text{and} \quad \frac{\partial u}{\partial y} = -\frac{\partial v}{\partial x}$$

Now $$\frac{\partial v}{\partial y} = \frac{\partial u}{\partial x} = e^{2x}\,(2x \cos 2y - 2y \sin 2y + \cos 2y)$$

Integrating w.r.t. y, treating x as constant, we get

$$v = e^{2x}\left[2x \cdot \frac{\sin 2y}{2} - \left\{2y\left(-\frac{\cos 2y}{2}\right) - (2)\left(-\frac{\sin 2y}{4}\right)\right\} + \frac{\sin 2y}{2}\right] + \phi(x)$$

$$= e^{2x}\,(x \sin 2y + y \cos 2y) + \phi(x) \qquad \ldots(3)$$

where $\phi(x)$ is an arbitrary function of x.

$\therefore$ $$\frac{\partial v}{\partial x} = 2e^{2x}\,(x \sin 2y + y \cos 2y) + e^{2x}\,(\sin 2y) + \phi'(x)$$

$$= e^{2x}\,(2x \sin 2y + \sin 2y + 2y \cos 2y) + \phi'(x)$$

But $$\frac{\partial v}{\partial x} = -\frac{\partial u}{\partial y} = e^{2x}\,(2x \sin 2y + \sin 2y + 2y \cos 2y) \qquad \text{[From (2)]}$$

$\therefore$ $\phi'(x) = 0$

$\Rightarrow$ $\phi(x) = c$, an arbitrary constant.

$\therefore$ From (3), $v = e^{2x}\,(x \sin 2y + y \cos 2y) + c$

$$f(z) = u + iv = e^{2x}\,(x \cos 2y - y \sin 2y) + ie^{2x}\,(x \sin 2y + y \cos 2y) + ic$$

$$= e^{2x}\,[(x + iy) \cos 2y + i(x + iy) \sin 2y] + c'$$

$$= (x + iy)\, e^{2x}\,(\cos 2y + i \sin 2y) + c'$$

$$= ze^{2z} \cdot e^{2iy} + c' = ze^{2(x + iy)} + c' = ze^{2z} + c'.$$

(Milne Thomson's Method)

This method determines the analytic function $f(z)$ when u or v is given.

Since $z = x + iy$, $\bar{z} = x - iy$ so that $x = \dfrac{z + \bar{z}}{2}$, $y = \dfrac{z - \bar{z}}{2i}$

Let $$f(z) = u(x, y) + iv\,(x, y) \qquad \ldots(1)$$

$$= u\left(\frac{z + \bar{z}}{2}, \frac{z - \bar{z}}{2i}\right) + iv\left(\frac{z + \bar{z}}{2}, \frac{z - \bar{z}}{2i}\right)$$

Considering this as an identity in the two independent variables z, $\bar{z}$ and putting $\bar{z} = z$, we get

$$f(z) = u(z, 0) + iv\,(z, 0)$$

which is the same as (1) if we replace x by z and y by 0.

Now $f(z) = u + iv$

$\Rightarrow$ $$f'(z) = \frac{\partial u}{\partial x} + i\frac{\partial v}{\partial x} = \frac{\partial u}{\partial x} - i\frac{\partial u}{\partial y} \qquad \text{[C-R equations]}$$

$$= e^{2x}\,(2x \cos 2y - 2y \sin 2y + \cos 2y) + ie^{2x}\,(2x \sin 2y + \sin 2y + 2y \cos 2y)$$

On replacing x by z and y by 0 on R.H.S., we get $f'(z) = e^{2z}(2z + 1)$

Integrating w.r.t. z, we have $f(z) = (2z + 1)\frac{e^{2z}}{2} - 2 \cdot \frac{e^{2z}}{4} + c = ze^{2z} + c.$

Example 6. *Determine the analytic function $w = u + iv$, if $v = \log(x^2 + y^2) + x - 2y$.*

Sol. Here $v = \log(x^2 + y^2) + x - 2y$

$$\therefore \quad \frac{\partial v}{\partial x} = \frac{2x}{x^2 + y^2} + 1$$

$$\frac{\partial v}{\partial y} = \frac{2y}{x^2 + y^2} - 2$$

Since $w = u + iv$

$$\frac{dw}{dz} = \frac{\partial u}{\partial x} + i\frac{\partial v}{\partial x} = \frac{\partial v}{\partial y} + i\frac{\partial v}{\partial x} \qquad \text{[C-R equations]}$$

$$= \left(\frac{2y}{x^2 + y^2} - 2\right) + i\left(\frac{2x}{x^2 + y^2} + 1\right)$$

Replacing x by z and y by 0, we get $\frac{dw}{dz} = -2 + i\left(\frac{2}{z} + 1\right) = (i - 2) + \frac{2i}{z}$

Integrating w.r.t. z, we have $w = (i - 2)z + 2i \log z + c.$

Example 7. *Show that the function $u = e^{-2xy} \sin(x^2 - y^2)$ is harmonic. Find the conjugate function v and express $u + iv$ as an analytic function of z.*

Sol. Here $u = e^{-2xy} \sin(x^2 - y^2)$

$$\therefore \quad \frac{\partial u}{\partial x} = -2y\, e^{-2xy} \sin(x^2 - y^2) + 2x\, e^{-2xy} \cos(x^2 - y^2)$$

$$\frac{\partial^2 u}{\partial x^2} = 4y^2 e^{-2xy} \sin(x^2 - y^2) - 4xy\, e^{-2xy} \cos(x^2 - y^2) + 2e^{-2xy} \cos(x^2 - y^2)$$
$$- 4xy\, e^{-2xy} \cos(x^2 - y^2) - 4x^2 e^{-2xy} \sin(x^2 - y^2) \qquad \ldots(1)$$

$$\frac{\partial u}{\partial y} = -2x\, e^{-2xy} \sin(x^2 - y^2) - 2y\, e^{-2xy} \cos(x^2 - y^2)$$

$$\frac{\partial^2 u}{\partial y^2} = 4x^2 e^{-2xy} \sin(x^2 - y^2) + 4xy\, e^{-2xy} \cos(x^2 - y^2) - 2e^{-2xy} \cos(x^2 - y^2)$$
$$+ 4xy\, e^{-2xy} \cos(x^2 - y^2) - 4y^2 e^{-2xy} \sin(x^2 - y^2) \qquad \ldots(2)$$

Adding (1) and (2), we get

$$\frac{\partial^2 u}{\partial x^2} + \frac{\partial^2 u}{\partial y^2} = 0 \qquad \text{which proves that } u \text{ is harmonic.}$$

Now, let $f(z) = u + iv$

then

$$f'(z) = \frac{\partial u}{\partial x} + i\frac{\partial v}{\partial x} = \frac{\partial u}{\partial x} - i\frac{\partial u}{\partial y} \qquad \text{[C-R equations]}$$

$$= [-2y\, e^{-2xy} \sin (x^2 - y^2) + 2x\, e^{-2xy} \cos (x^2 - y^2)] + i\, [2x\, e^{-2xy} \sin (x^2 - y^2) + 2y\, e^{-2xy} \cos (x^2 - y^2)]$$

Replacing x by z and y by 0, we get

$$f'(z) = 2z \cos z^2 + 2iz \sin z^2 = 2z (\cos z^2 + i \sin z^2) = 2ze^{iz^2}$$

Integrating w.r.t. z, we have

$$f(z) = -i\, e^{iz^2} + C \text{ (C = A + } i\text{B is a complex constant)}$$

which expresses $u + iv$ as an analytic function of z.

Since $\quad u + iv = -ie^{iz^2} + C = -ie^{i(x+iy)^2} + C$

$$= -ie^{i(x^2-y^2+2ixy)} + C = -ie^{-2xy} \cdot e^{i(x^2-y^2)} + C$$

$$= -ie^{-2xy} [\cos (x^2 - y^2) + i \sin (x^2 - y^2)] + C$$

$$= e^{-2xy} \sin (x^2 - y^2) + i[-e^{-2xy} \cos (x^2 - y^2)] + C$$

$\therefore \quad v = -e^{-2xy} \cos (x^2 - y^2) + B.$

Example 8. *An electrostatic field in the xy-plane is given by the potential function* $\phi = 3x^2y - y^3$, *find the stream function.*

Sol. Let $\psi(x, y)$ be a stream function.

By C-R equations $\quad \dfrac{\partial \psi}{\partial x} = -\dfrac{\partial \phi}{\partial y} = -3x^2 + 3y^2 \quad$ ...(1)

$$\frac{\partial \psi}{\partial y} = \frac{\partial \phi}{\partial x} = 6xy \quad \text{...(2)}$$

Integrating (1) w.r.t.x, treating y as constant, we get

$$\psi = -x^3 + 3xy^2 + F(y)$$

so that $\quad \dfrac{\partial \psi}{\partial y} = 6xy + F'(y) \quad$ ...(3)

From (2) and (3), $\quad 6xy + F'(y) = 6xy \quad$ or $\quad F'(y) = 0 \quad \therefore \quad F(y) = c$

Hence $\quad \psi = -x^3 + 3xy^2 + c.$

Example 9. *If* $u - v = (x - y)(x^2 + 4xy + y^2)$ *and* $f(z) = u + iv$ *is an analytic function of* $z = x + iy$, *find* $f(z)$ *in terms of* z.

Sol. Here $\quad f(z) = u + iv$

$\therefore \quad i\, f(z) = iu + v$

Adding $\quad (1 + i) f(z) = (u - v) + i(u + v)$

Let $\quad (1 + i) f(z) = F(z),\ u - v = U,\ u + v = V$, then

$$F(z) = U + iV$$

Now $\quad U = u - v = (x - y)(x^2 + 4xy + y^2)$

$$\Rightarrow \quad \frac{\partial U}{\partial x} = x^2 + 4xy + y^2 + (x - y)(2x + 4y) = 3x^2 + 6xy - 3y^2$$

and $\quad \dfrac{\partial U}{\partial y} = -(x^2 + 4xy + y^2) + (x - y)(4x + 2y) = 3x^2 - 6xy - 3y^2$

$$\therefore \quad F'(z) = \frac{\partial U}{\partial x} + i\frac{\partial V}{\partial x} = \frac{\partial U}{\partial x} - i\frac{\partial U}{\partial y} \quad \text{[C-R equations]}$$

$$= (3x^2 + 6xy - 3y^2) - i(3x^2 - 6xy - 3y^2)$$

Replacing x by z and y by 0, we get

$$F'(z) = 3z^2 - 3iz^2 = 3(1 - i)z^2$$

Integrating both sides,

$$F(z) = (1 - i)\, z^3 + c$$

$$\Rightarrow \quad (1 + i)\, f(z) = (1 - i)\, z^3 + c$$

$$f(z) = \frac{1-i}{1+i} z^3 + \frac{c}{1+i} = \frac{(1-i)^2}{1-i^2} z^3 + \frac{c}{1+i}$$

Hence $\quad f(z) = -\,iz^3 + A.$

Example 10. *If f(z) is a regular function of z, prove that*

$$\left(\frac{\partial^2}{\partial x^2} + \frac{\partial^2}{\partial y^2}\right) |f(z)|^2 = 4\, |f'(z)|^2.$$

Sol. Let $f(z) = u + iv$ so that $|f(z)| = \sqrt{u^2 + v^2}$

or $\quad |f(z)|^2 = u^2 + v^2 = \phi(x, y) \quad$ (say)

$$\therefore \quad \frac{\partial \phi}{\partial x} = 2u\frac{\partial u}{\partial x} + 2v\frac{\partial v}{\partial x}$$

$$\frac{\partial^2 \phi}{\partial x^2} = 2\left[u\frac{\partial^2 u}{\partial x^2} + \left(\frac{\partial u}{\partial x}\right)^2 + v\frac{\partial^2 v}{\partial x^2} + \left(\frac{\partial v}{\partial x}\right)^2\right]$$

Similarly,

$$\frac{\partial^2 \phi}{\partial y^2} = 2\left[u\frac{\partial^2 u}{\partial y^2} + \left(\frac{\partial u}{\partial y}\right)^2 + v\frac{\partial^2 v}{\partial y^2} + \left(\frac{\partial v}{\partial y}\right)^2\right]$$

Adding, we get

$$\frac{\partial^2 \phi}{\partial x^2} + \frac{\partial^2 \phi}{\partial y^2} = 2\left[u\left(\frac{\partial^2 u}{\partial x^2} + \frac{\partial^2 u}{\partial y^2}\right) + \left(\frac{\partial u}{\partial x}\right)^2 + \left(\frac{\partial u}{\partial y}\right)^2 + v\left(\frac{\partial^2 v}{\partial x^2} + \frac{\partial^2 v}{\partial y^2}\right) + \left(\frac{\partial v}{\partial x}\right)^2 + \left(\frac{\partial v}{\partial y}\right)^2\right] \quad ...(1)$$

Since $f(z) = u + iv$ is a regular function of z, u and v satisfy C-R equations and Laplace's equation.

$$\therefore \quad \frac{\partial u}{\partial x} = \frac{\partial v}{\partial y}, \frac{\partial u}{\partial y} = -\frac{\partial v}{\partial x} \quad \text{and} \quad \frac{\partial^2 u}{\partial x^2} + \frac{\partial^2 u}{\partial y^2} = 0 = \frac{\partial^2 v}{\partial x^2} + \frac{\partial^2 v}{\partial y^2}$$

$\therefore$ From (1), we get

$$\frac{\partial^2 \phi}{\partial x^2} + \frac{\partial^2 \phi}{\partial y^2} = 2\left[0 + \left(\frac{\partial u}{\partial x}\right)^2 + \left(\frac{\partial v}{\partial x}\right)^2 + 0 + \left(\frac{\partial v}{\partial x}\right)^2 + \left(\frac{\partial u}{\partial x}\right)^2\right]$$

$$= 4\left[\left(\frac{\partial u}{\partial x}\right)^2 + \left(\frac{\partial v}{\partial x}\right)^2\right] \quad ...(2)$$

Now, $f(z) = u + iv$

$\therefore$ $f'(z) = \dfrac{\partial u}{\partial x} + i\dfrac{\partial v}{\partial x}$ and $|f'(z)|^2 = \left(\dfrac{\partial u}{\partial x}\right)^2 + \left(\dfrac{\partial v}{\partial x}\right)^2$

From (2), we get

$$\left(\frac{\partial^2}{\partial x^2} + \frac{\partial^2}{\partial y^2}\right)\phi = 4\,|f'(z)|^2 \quad \text{or} \quad \left(\frac{\partial^2}{\partial x^2} + \frac{\partial^2}{\partial y^2}\right)|f(z)|^2 = 4\,|f'(z)|^2.$$

TEST YOUR KNOWLEDGE

1. Determine a, b, c, d so that the function $f(z) = (x^2 + axy + by^2) + i(cx^2 + dxy + y^2)$ is analytic.
2. Determine p such that the function $f(z) = \dfrac{1}{2}\log(x^2 + y^2) + i\tan^{-1}\dfrac{px}{y}$ be an analytic function.
3. Show that the polar form of Cauchy-Riemann equations are $\dfrac{\partial u}{\partial r} = \dfrac{1}{r}\dfrac{\partial v}{\partial \theta}, \dfrac{\partial v}{\partial r} = -\dfrac{1}{r}\dfrac{\partial u}{\partial \theta}$.

   Deduce that $\dfrac{\partial^2 u}{\partial r^2} + \dfrac{1}{r}\dfrac{\partial u}{\partial r} + \dfrac{1}{r^2}\dfrac{\partial^2 u}{\partial \theta^2} = 0.$
4. If $f(z) = \dfrac{x^3 y(y - ix)}{x^6 + y^2}, z \neq 0, f(0) = 0$, prove that $\dfrac{f(z) - f(0)}{z} \to 0$ as $z \to 0$ along any radius vector but not as $z \to 0$ in any manner.
5. Show that the function $f(z)$ defined by $f(z) = \dfrac{x^3 y^5 (x + iy)}{x^6 + y^{10}}$, $z \neq 0$, $f(0) = 0$, is not analytic at the origin even though it satisfies Cauchy-Riemann equations at the origin.
6. Determine which of the following functions are analytic:

   (i) e^z (ii) $\sin z$ (iii) $\cosh z$

   (iv) $\dfrac{1}{z}$ (v) $\dfrac{x + iy}{x^2 + y^2}$ (vi) $\dfrac{1}{2}\log(x^2 + y^2) + i\tan^{-1}\dfrac{y}{x}$.
7. Show that $|z|^2$ is not analytic at any point.
8. Show that $u + iv = \dfrac{x - iy}{x - iy + a}$ where $a \neq 0$, is not an analytic function of $z = x + iy$ whereas $u - iv$ is such a function.
9. Determine the analytic function whose real part is

   (i) $x^3 - 3xy^2 + 3x^2 - 3y^2 + 1$ (ii) $\log\sqrt{x^2 + y^2}$

   (M.G.U., June 2006)

   (iii) $e^x (x\cos y - y\sin y)$ (iv) $\cos x \cosh y$

   (M.G.U., Jan. 2007)

   (v) $e^{-x}(x\sin y - y\cos y)$ (vi) $\dfrac{\sin 2x}{\cosh 2y - \cos 2x}$.

10. Find the regular function whose imaginary part is

(*i*) $\dfrac{x-y}{x^2+y^2}$ (*ii*) $\cos x \cosh y$ (*iii*) $\sinh x \cos y$.

11. Prove that $u = x^2 - y^2 - 2xy - 2x + 3y$ is harmonic. Find a function v such that $f(z) = u + iv$ is analytic. Also express $f(z)$ in terms of z.

12. An electrostatic field in the xy-plane is given by the potential function $\phi = x^2 - y^2$, find the stream function.

13. If $w = \phi + i\psi$ represents the complex potential for an electric field and $\psi = x^2 - y^2 + \dfrac{x}{x^2+y^2}$, determine the function ϕ. (*M.G.U., May 2008*)

14. If the potential function is $\log(x^2 + y^2)$, find the flux function and the complex potential function.

15. In a two dimensional fluid flow, the stream function is $\psi = \tan^{-1}\left(\dfrac{y}{x}\right)$, find the velocity potential ϕ.

16. If $f(z) = u + iv$ is an analytic function, find $f(z)$ if

(*i*) $u - v = e^x(\cos y - \sin y)$ (*ii*) $u + v = \dfrac{x}{x^2+y^2}$, when $f(1) = 1$

(*iii*) $u - v = \dfrac{\cos x + \sin x - e^{-y}}{2\cos x - e^y - e^{-y}}$, when $f\left(\dfrac{\pi}{2}\right) = 0$.

17. If $f(z)$ is an analytic function of z, prove that

(*i*) $\left(\dfrac{\partial^2}{\partial x^2} + \dfrac{\partial^2}{\partial y^2}\right)\log|f'(z)| = 0$ (*ii*) $\left(\dfrac{\partial^2}{\partial x^2} + \dfrac{\partial^2}{\partial y^2}\right)|\text{R} f(z)|^2 = 2|f'(z)|^2$.

18. Show that an analytical function with constant modulus is constant. (*M.G.U., July 2007; M.G.U., Nov. 2008*)

19. Find the analytic function $f(z)$ whose imaginary part is $2\sin 2x/(e^{2y} + e^{-2y} - 2\cos 2x)$. (*M.G.U., July 2007*)

20. Define an analytic function is a domain D. Check whether $f(z) = \dfrac{1}{\sin z}$ is analytic inside a unit circle. (*M.G.U., May 2008*)

21. If u and v are harmonic functions then show that $u_y - v_x + i(u_x + v_y)$ is analytic function (*M.G.U., May 2008*)

22. Show that $f(z) = z^4$ is analytic for positive integral values of n and find $f'(z)$. (*M.G.U., Nov. 2008*)

23. Verify that $u = x^2 - y^2 - y$ is harmonic in the whole complex plane and find the harmonic conjugate v of u. (*M.G.U., Nov. 2008*)

Answers

1. $a = 2, b = -1, c = -1, d = 2$ **2.** $p = -1$

6. (*i*), (*ii*), (*iii*), (*iv*) except when $z = 0$, (*v*) except when $z = 0$

9. (*i*) $z^3 + 3z^2 + 1 + c$ (*ii*) $\log z + c$ (*iii*) $z e^z + c$

(*iv*) $\cos z + c$ (*v*) $ize^{-z} + 6i$ (*vi*) $\cot z + c$

10. (*i*) $\dfrac{1+i}{z} + c$ (*ii*) $\sin x \sinh y + c$ (*iii*) $-\cosh x \sin y + c$

11. $v = x^2 - y^2 + 2xy - 2y - 3x + 6$, $f(z) = (1+i)z^2 - (2+3i)z + i6$

12. $\psi = 2xy + c$	**13.** $-2xy + \dfrac{x}{x^2 + y^2} + c$	**14.** $2\tan^{-1}\left(\dfrac{y}{x}\right), 2\log z + c$
15. $\dfrac{1}{2}\log(x^2 + y^2) + c$	**16.** (*i*) $e^z + c$	(*ii*) $\dfrac{1}{1-i}\left(\dfrac{1}{z} - 1\right)$
(*iii*) $\dfrac{1}{2}\left(1 - \cot\dfrac{z}{2}\right)$	**19.** $i\cot z$	**23.** $2xy + x$.

4.12. COMPLEX INTEGRATION

Let $f(z)$ be a continuous function of the complex variable $z = x + iy$ defined at all points of a curve C having end points A and B. Divide the curve C into n parts at the points

$$A = P_0(z_0), P_1(z_1), \ldots\ldots, P_i(z_i), \ldots\ldots, P_n(z_n) = B.$$

Let $\delta z_i = z_i - z_{i-1}$ and ξ_i be any point on the arc $P_{i-1}P_i$. Then the limit of the sum

$$\sum_{i=1}^{n} f(\xi_i)\,\delta z_i$$

as $n \to \infty$ and each $\delta z_i \to 0$, if it exists, is called the **line integral of f(z)** along the curve C. It is denoted by

$$\int_C f(z)\,dz$$

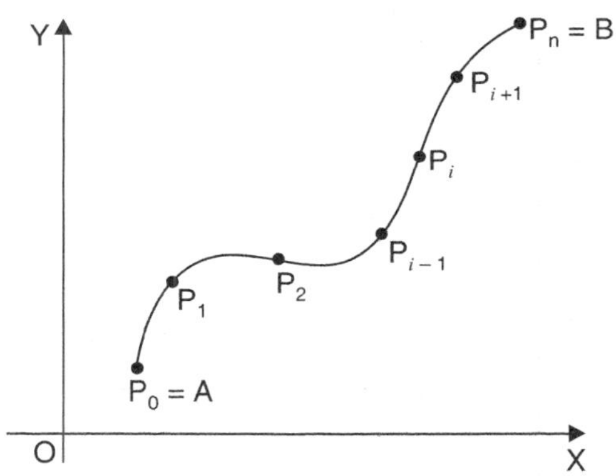

In case the points P_0 and P_n coincide so that C is a closed curve, then this integral is called **contour integral** and is denoted by $\oint_C f(z)\,dz$.

If $f(z) = u(x, y) + iv(x, y)$, then since $dz = dx + idy$, we have

$$\int_C f(z)\,dz = \int_C (u + iv)(dx + idy)$$

$$= \int_C (udx - vdy) + i\int_C (vdx + udy)$$

which shows that the evaluation of the line integral of a complex function can be reduced to the evaluation of two line integrals of real functions.

Moreover, the value of the integral depends on the path of integration unless the integrand is analytic. When the same path of integration is used in each integral, then

$$\int_a^b f(z)\,dz = -\int_b^a f(z)\,dz$$

If C is a point on the arc joining a and b, then

$$\int_a^b f(z)\,dz = \int_a^c f(z)\,d(z) + \int_c^b f(z)\,dz.$$

ILLUSTRATIVE EXAMPLES

Example 1. *Evaluate* $\int_0^{1+i} (x - y + ix^2)\, dz$

(a) along the straight line from z = 0 to z = 1 + i

(b) along the real axis from z = 0 to z = 1 and then along a line parallel to imaginary axis from z = 1 to z = 1 + i.

(c) along the imaginary axis from z = 0 to z = i and then along a line parallel to real axis from z = i to z = 1 + i.

Sol. (*a*) Along the straight line OP joining O($z = 0$) and P($z = 1 + i$), $y = x$, $dy = dx$ and x varies from 0 to 1.

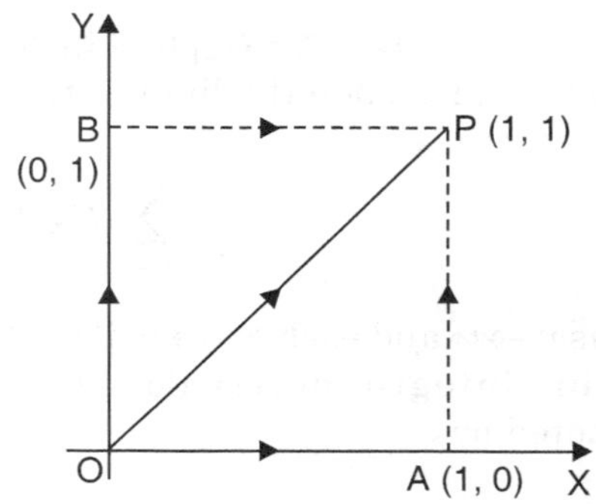

$$\therefore \quad \int_0^{1+i} (x - y + ix^2)\, dz = \int_0^{1+i} (x - y + ix^2)(dx + idy)$$

$$= \int_0^1 (x - x + ix^2)(dx + idx) = \int_0^1 ix^2(1+i)\, dx$$

$$= (-1 + i) \int_0^1 x^2\, dx = (-1+i)\left[\frac{x^3}{3}\right]_0^1$$

$$= (-1 + i)\left(\frac{1}{3}\right) = -\frac{1}{3} + \frac{1}{3} i.$$

(*b*) Along the path OAP where A is $z = 1$

$$\int_0^{1+i} (x - y + ix^2) dz = \int_{OA} (x - y + ix^2) dz + \int_{AP} (x - y + ix^2)\, dz \qquad \ldots(1)$$

Now along OA, $y = 0$, $dz = dx$ and x varies from 0 to 1.

$$\therefore \quad \int_{OA} (x - y + ix^2) dz = \int_0^1 (x + ix^2) dx = \left[\frac{x^2}{2} + i\frac{x^3}{3}\right]_0^1 = \frac{1}{2} + \frac{1}{3} i$$

Also, along AP, $x = 1$, $dz = idy$ and y varies from 0 to 1

$$\therefore \quad \int_{AP} (x - y + ix^2)\, dz = \int_0^1 (1 - y + i)\, idy = \left[(-1 + i)y - i\frac{y^2}{2}\right]_0^1$$

$$= -1 + i - \frac{1}{2} i = -1 + \frac{1}{2} i$$

Hence, from (1),

$$\int_0^{1+i} (x - y + ix^2)\, dz = \left(\frac{1}{2} + \frac{1}{3} i\right) + \left(-1 + \frac{1}{2} i\right) = -\frac{1}{2} + \frac{5}{6} i.$$

(*c*) Along the path OBP where B is $z = i$

$$\int_0^{1+i} (x - y + ix^2)\, dz = \int_{OB} (x - y + ix^2) dz + \int_{BP} (x - y + ix^2)\, dz \qquad \ldots(2)$$

Now along OB, $x = 0$, $dz = idy$ and y varies from 0 to 1

$$\therefore \quad \int_{OB} (x - y + ix^2) dz = \int_0^1 (-y)\, idy = -i\left[\frac{y^2}{2}\right]_0^1 = -\frac{1}{2} i$$

Also, along BP, $y = 1$, $dz = dx$ and x varies from 0 to 1

$$\therefore \qquad \int_{BP} (x - y + ix^2)\,dz = \int_0^1 (x - 1 + ix^2)\,dx = \left[\frac{x^2}{2} - x + i\frac{x^3}{3}\right]_0^1 = -\frac{1}{2} + \frac{1}{3}i$$

Hence, from (2), $\displaystyle\int_0^{1+i} (x - y + ix^2)\,dz = -\frac{1}{2}i + \left(-\frac{1}{2} + \frac{1}{3}i\right) = -\frac{1}{2} - \frac{1}{6}i.$

Note. The values of the integral are different along the three different paths.

Example 2. *Evaluate* $\displaystyle\int_0^{1+i} (x^2 - iy)\,dz$ *along the paths*

(a) $y = x$ *(b)* $y = x^2$.

Sol. (*a*) Along the line $y = x$,

$$dy = dx \quad \text{so that} \quad dz = dx + idx = (1 + i)\,dx$$

$$\therefore \quad \int_0^{1+i} (x^2 - iy)\,dz = \int_0^1 (x^2 - ix)(1 + i)\,dx$$

$$= (1 + i)\left[\frac{x^3}{3} - i\frac{x^2}{2}\right]_0^1 = (1 + i)\left(\frac{1}{3} - \frac{1}{2}i\right)$$

$$= \frac{(1 + i)(2 - 3i)}{6} = \frac{5}{6} - \frac{1}{6}i.$$

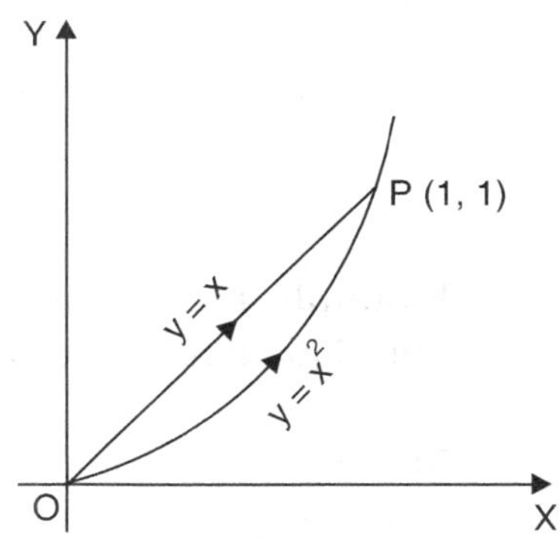

(*b*) Along the parabola $y = x^2$, $dy = 2x\,dx$ so that

$$dz = dx + 2ix\,dx = (1 + 2ix)\,dx$$

and x varies from 0 to 1.

$$\therefore \qquad \int_0^{1+i} (x^2 - iy)\,dz = \int_0^1 (x^2 - ix^2)(1 + 2ix)\,dx$$

$$= (1 - i)\int_0^1 x^2(1 + 2ix)\,dx = (1 - i)\left[\frac{x^3}{3} + i\frac{x^4}{2}\right]_0^1$$

$$= (1 - i)\left(\frac{1}{3} + \frac{1}{2}i\right) = \frac{(1 - i)(2 + 3i)}{6} = \frac{5}{6} + \frac{1}{6}i.$$

Example 3. *Evaluate* $\displaystyle\int_0^{2+i} (\bar{z})^2\,dz$*, along*

(a) the real axis to 2 and then vertically to 2 + i.

(b) along the line 2y = x.

Sol. $(\bar{z})^2 = (x - iy)^2 = (x^2 - y^2) - 2ixy$

(*a*) Along the path OAP where A is (2, 0) and P is (2, 1).

$$\int_0^{2+i} (\bar{z})^2\,dz$$

$$= \int_{OA} (x^2 - y^2 - 2ixy)\,dz + \int_{AP} (x^2 - y^2 - 2ixy)\,dz \qquad \ldots(1)$$

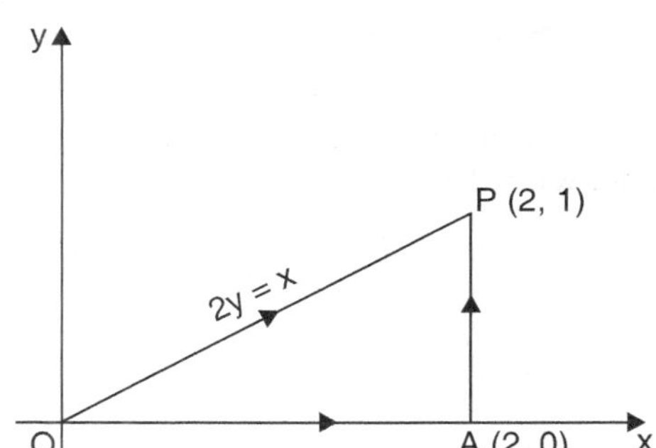

Now, along OA, $y = 0$, $dz = dx$ and x varies from 0 to 2

$$\therefore \quad \int_{OA} (x^2 - y^2 - 2ixy)\, dz = \int_0^2 x^2\, dx = \left[\frac{x^3}{3}\right]_0^2 = \frac{8}{3}$$

Also, along AP, $x = 2$, $dz = idy$ and y varies from 0 to 1

$$\therefore \quad \int_{AP} (x^2 - y^2 - 2ixy)\, dz = \int_0^1 (4 - y^2 - 4iy)\, idy$$

$$= \left[4iy - i\frac{y^3}{3} + 2y^2\right]_0^1 = 4i - \frac{1}{3}i + 2 = 2 + \frac{11}{3}i$$

Hence from (1), we have $\int_0^{2+i} (\bar{z})^2\, dz = \frac{8}{3} + 2 + \frac{11}{3}i = \frac{14}{3} + \frac{11}{3}i.$

(*b*) Along the line OP, $2y = x$, $dx = 2dy$

so that $dz = 2dy + i\, dy = (2 + i)\, dy$

and y varies from 0 to 1.

$$\therefore \quad \int_0^{2+i} (\bar{z})^2\, dz = \int_0^{2+i} (x^2 - y^2 - 2ixy)\, dz = \int_0^1 (4y^2 - y^2 - 4iy^2)(2 + i)\, dy$$

$$= (2 + i)(3 - 4i) \int_0^1 y^2\, dy = (10 - 5i)\left[\frac{y^3}{3}\right]_0^1 = \frac{10}{3} - \frac{5}{3}i.$$

Example 4. *Integrate $f(z) = x^2 + ixy$ from A(1, 1) to B(2, 4) along the curve $x = t$, $y = t^2$.*

Sol. Equations of the path of integration are $x = t$, $y = t^2$

$$\therefore \quad dx = dt, \quad dy = 2t\, dt$$

At A(1, 1), $t = 1$ and at B(2, 4), $t = 2$

$$\therefore \quad \int_A^B f(z)\, dz = \int_A^B (x^2 + ixy)(dx + idy) = \int_1^2 (t^2 + it^3)(dt + 2it\, dt)$$

$$= \int_1^2 (t^2 - 2t^4)\, dt + i\int_1^2 3t^3\, dt = \left[\frac{t^3}{3} - \frac{2t^5}{5}\right]_1^2 + i\left[\frac{3t^4}{4}\right]_1^2$$

$$= \left(\frac{8}{3} - \frac{64}{5}\right) - \left(\frac{1}{3} - \frac{2}{5}\right) + i\left(12 - \frac{3}{4}\right) = -\frac{151}{5} + \frac{45}{4}i.$$

Example 5. *Prove that*

(*i*) $\oint_C \frac{dz}{z - a} = 2\pi i$

(*ii*) $\oint_C (z - a)^n\, dz = 0$ *[n is an integer $\neq -1$] where C is the circle* $|z - a| = r$.

Sol. The equation of the circle C is

$$|z - a| = r \quad \text{or} \quad z - a = re^{i\theta}$$

where θ varies from 0 to 2π as z describes C once in the anti-clockwise direction. $dz = ire^{i\theta}\, d\theta$.

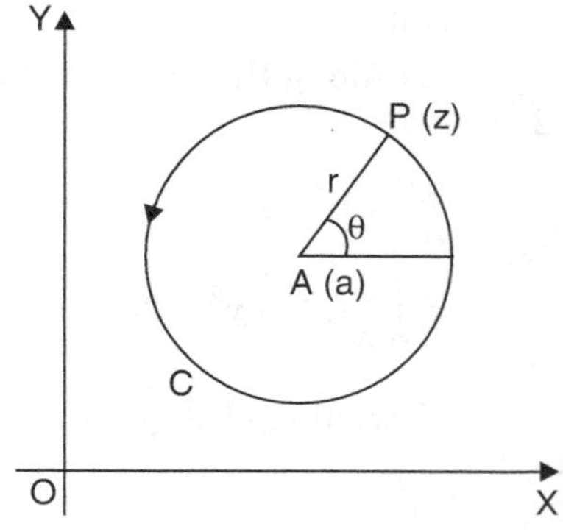

(*i*) $$\oint_C \frac{dz}{z - a} = \int_0^{2\pi} \frac{ire^{i\theta}\, d\theta}{re^{i\theta}} = i\int_0^{2\pi} d\theta = 2\pi i$$

(*ii*) $$\oint_C (z - a)^n\, dz = \int_0^{2\pi} r^n e^{ni\theta} \,.\, ire^{i\theta}\, d\theta$$

$$= ir^{n+1}\int_0^{2\pi} e^{i(n+1)\theta}\, d\theta = ir^{n+1}\left[\frac{e^{i(n+1)\theta}}{i(n+1)}\right]_0^{2\pi} \qquad [\because \; n \neq -1]$$

$$= \frac{r^{n+1}}{n+1}\left[e^{i2(n+1)\pi} - 1\right]$$

$$= 0. \qquad [\because \; e^{i2(n+1)\pi} = \cos 2(n+1)\pi + i \sin 2(n+1)\pi = 1 + i0 = 1]$$

TEST YOUR KNOWLEDGE

1. Evaluate $\int_0^{3+i} z^2\, dz$, along

(a) the line $y = \frac{x}{3}$ (b) the real axis to 3 and then vertically to $3 + i$

(c) the parabola $x = 3y^2$.

2. Evaluate $\int_{1-i}^{2+i} (2x + iy + 1)\, dz$, along *(M.G.U., July 2007)*

(a) the straight line joining $(1 - i)$ to $(2 + i)$. (b) the curve $x = t + 1$, $y = 2t^2 - 1$.

3. Evaluate $\int_0^{4+2i} \bar{z}\, dz$, along the curve given by $z = t^2 + it$.

4. Evaluate $\oint_C |z|^2\, dz$, around the square with vertices at (0, 0), (1, 0), (1, 1) and (0, 1).

5. Show that $\oint_C (z + 1)\, dz = 0$, where C is the boundary of the square whose vertices are at the points $z = 0$, $z = 1$, $z = 1 + i$ and $z = i$.

6. Evaluate $\oint_C (y - x - 3x^2 i)\, dz$, where C is the straight line from $z = 0$ to $z = 1 + i$.

7. Evaluate $\oint_C (z - z^2)\, dz$, where C is the upper half of the circle $|z| = 1$.

8. Prove that $\int_C \frac{1}{z}\, dz = -\pi i$ or πi according as C is the semi-circular arc $|z| = 1$ from $z = -1$ to $z = 1$ above or below the real axis.

9. Evaluate $\oint_C |z|\, dz$, where C is the left half of the unit circle $|z| = 1$ from $z = -i$ to $z = i$.

10. Evaluate $\oint_C \log z\, dz$, where C is the unit circle $|z| = 1$.

11. Evaluate $\int_{1-i}^{2+3i} (z^2 - 2)\, dz$ along the straight line joining the points (1, – 1) and (2, 3).

(M.G.U., Jan. 2007)

12. Evaluate $\int_C z^2\, dz$, where C is given by (i) the line $x = 2y$ from (0, 0) to (2, 1) (ii) the line segment along the real axis from (0, 0) to (2, 0) and then vertically to (2, 1). Can you expect path independancy for the above integrals ? Give reason. *(M.G.U., May 2009)*

[**Hint.** $\frac{(2+i)^3}{3}$, yes, *i.e.*, path independent, due to the analyticity of the function $f(z) = z^2$ is the respective domain.]

Answers

1. (*a*) $6 + \frac{26}{3} i$	(*b*) $6 + \frac{26}{3} i$	(*c*) $6 + \frac{26}{3} i$	
2. (*a*) $4 + 8i$	(*b*) $4 + \frac{25}{3} i$	**3.** $10 - \frac{8}{3} i$	**4.** $-1 + i$
6. $1 - i$	**7.** $\frac{2}{3}$	**9.** $2i$	**10.** 0
11. $\frac{-50 - 86i}{3}$	**12.** $\frac{(2+i)^3}{3}$, yes.		

4.13. SIMPLY AND MULTIPLY CONNECTED REGIONS

A curve is called *simple closed curve* if it does not cross itself (Fig. 1). A curve which crosses itself is called a *multiple curve* (Fig. 2).

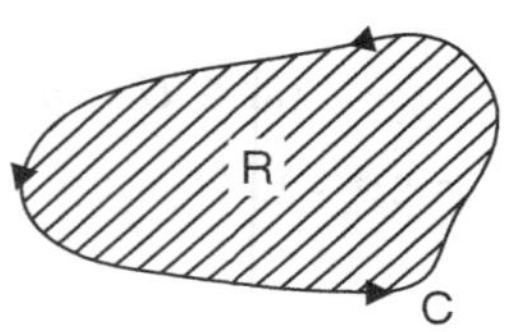

Fig.1

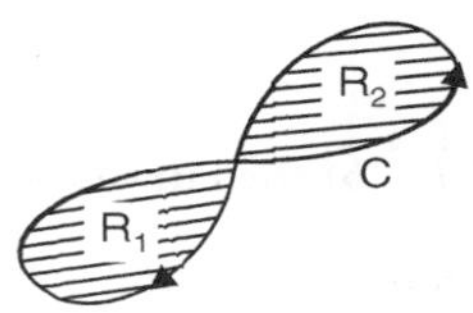

Fig. 2

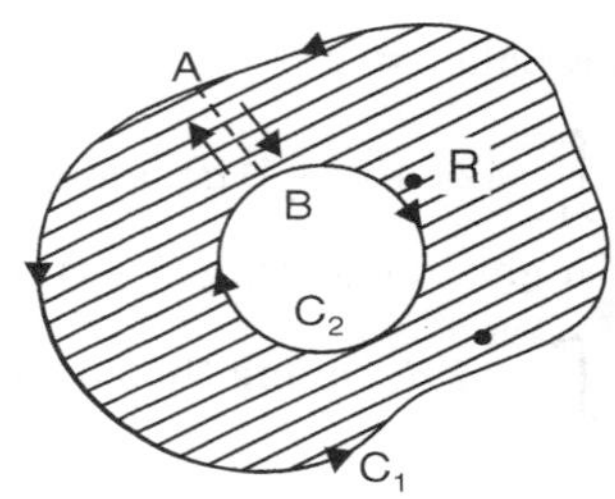

Fig. 3

A region is called *simply connected* if every closed curve in the region encloses points of the region only, *i.e.*, every closed curve lying in it can be contracted indefinitely without passing out of it. A region which is not simply connected is called a *multiply connected* region. In plain terms, a simply connected region is one which has no holes. Figure 3 shows a multiply connected region R enclosed between two separate curves C_1 and C_2. (There can be more than two separate curves). We can convert a multiply connected region into a simply connected one, by giving it one or more cuts (*e.g.*, along the dotted line AB).

4.14. CAUCHY'S INTEGRAL THEOREM

Statement. *If f(z) is an analytic function and f ′(z) is continuous at each point within and on a simple closed curve C, then*

$$\oint_C f(z)\,dz = 0.$$

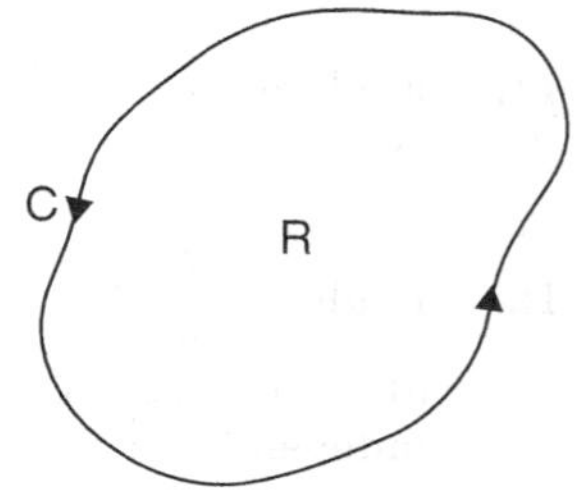

Proof. Let R be the region bounded by the curve C.

Let $f(z) = u(x, y) + iv(x, y)$, then

$$\oint_C f(z)\,dz = \oint_C (u + iv)(dx + idy)$$

$$= \oint_C (udx - vdy) + i \oint_C (vdx + udy) \qquad \ldots(1)$$

Since $f'(z)$ is continuous, the partial derivatives $\frac{\partial u}{\partial x}, \frac{\partial u}{\partial y}, \frac{\partial v}{\partial x}, \frac{\partial v}{\partial y}$ are also continuous in R.

Hence, by Green's Theorem, we have

$$\oint_C f(z)\,dz = \iint_R \left(-\frac{\partial v}{\partial x} - \frac{\partial u}{\partial y}\right) dx\,dy + i \iint_R \left(\frac{\partial u}{\partial x} - \frac{\partial v}{\partial y}\right) dx\,dy \qquad \ldots(2)$$

Now $f(z)$ being analytic at each point of the region R, by Cauchy-Riemann equations, we have

$$\frac{\partial u}{\partial x} = \frac{\partial v}{\partial y} \quad \text{and} \quad \frac{\partial u}{\partial y} = -\frac{\partial v}{\partial x}$$

Thus, the integrals of the two double integrals in (2) vanish.

Hence, $\oint_C f(z)\,dz = 0.$

Cor. 1. *If $f(z)$ is analytic in a region R and P and Q are two points in R, then $\int_P^Q f(z)dz$ is independent of the path joining P and Q and lying entirely in R.*

Let PAQ and PBQ be any two paths joining P and Q.

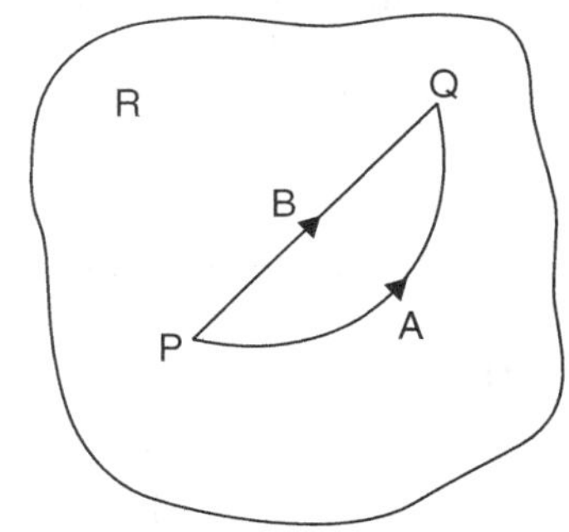

By Cauchy's theorem,

$$\int_{PAQBP} f(z)\,dz = 0$$

$$\Rightarrow \quad \int_{PAQ} f(z)\,dz + \int_{QBP} f(z)\,dz = 0$$

$$\Rightarrow \quad \int_{PAQ} f(z)\,dz - \int_{PBQ} f(z)\,dz = 0$$

Hence $\int_{PAQ} f(z)\,dz = \int_{PBQ} f(z)\,dz.$

Cor. 2. *If $f(z)$ is analytic in the region bounded by two simple closed curves C_1 and C_2, then*

$$\oint_C f(z)\,dz = \oint_{C_1} f(z)\,dz$$

Let AB be a cross-cut joining the curves C and C_1, then the doubly connected region becomes simply connected.

By Cauchy's theorem, $\int_{APQABDEBA} f(z)\;dz = 0$

$$\Rightarrow \quad \int_{APQA} f(z)\,dz + \int_{AB} f(z)\,dz + \int_{BDEB} f(z)\,dz + \int_{BA} f(z)\,dz = 0$$

$$\Rightarrow \quad \oint_C f(z)\,dz + \int_{AB} f(z)\,dz - \int_{BEDB} f(z)\,dz - \int_{AB} f(z)\,dz = 0$$

$$\Rightarrow \quad \oint_C f(z)\,dz - \oint_{C_1} f(z)\,dz = 0$$

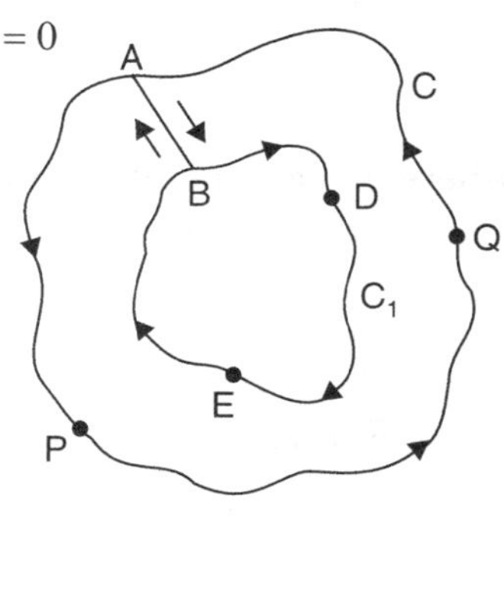

(integrals around a closed curve are taken positive when the curve is traversed in counter-clockwise direction)

Hence, $\oint_C f(z)\,dz = \oint_{C_1} f(z)\,dz$

The theorem can be extended.

If a closed curve C contains non-intersecting closed curves $C_1, C_2, \ldots\ldots, C_n$, then by introducing cross-cuts, it can be shown that

$$\oint_C f(z)\,dz = \oint_{C_1} f(z)\,dz + \oint_{C_2} f(z)\,dz + \ldots\ldots + \oint_{C_n} f(z)\,dz.$$

4.15. CAUCHY'S INTEGRAL FORMULA

Statement. *If f(z) is analytic within and on a closed curve C and a is any point within C, then*

$$f(a) = \frac{1}{2\pi i}\oint_C \frac{f(z)}{z-a}\,dz.$$

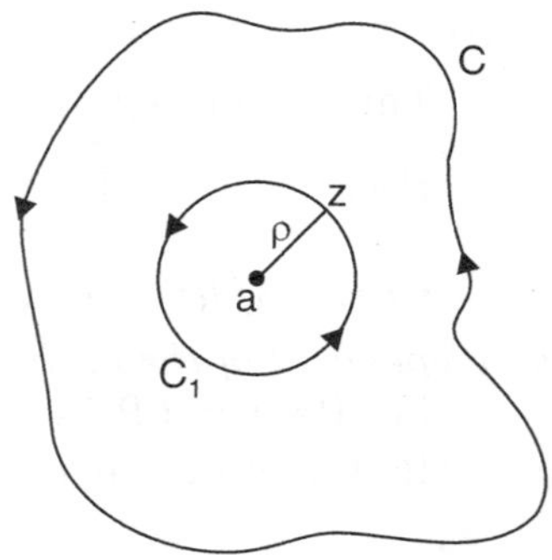

Proof. Consider the function $\frac{f(z)}{z-a}$, which is analytic at every point within C except at $z = a$.

Draw a circle C_1 with a as centre and radius ρ such that C_1 lies entirely inside C.

Thus $\frac{f(z)}{z-a}$ is analytic in the region between C and C_1.

∴ By Cauchy's theorem, we have

$$\oint_C \frac{f(z)}{z-a}\,dz = \oint_{C_1} \frac{f(z)}{z-a}\,dz \qquad \ldots(1)$$

Now, the equation of circle C_1 is

$$|z-a| = \rho \quad \text{or} \quad z - a = \rho e^{i\theta}$$

so that $\qquad dz = i\rho e^{i\theta}\,d\theta$

$$\oint_{C_1} \frac{f(z)}{z-a}\,dz = \int_0^{2\pi} \frac{f(a+\rho e^{i\theta})}{\rho e^{i\theta}}\,.\,i\rho e^{i\theta}\,d\theta = i\int_0^{2\pi} f(a+\rho e^{i\theta})\,d\theta$$

Hence, by (1), we have

$$\oint_C \frac{f(z)}{z-a}\,dz = i\int_0^{2\pi} f(a+\rho e^{i\theta})\,d\theta \qquad \ldots(2)$$

In the limiting form, as the circle C_1 shrinks to the point a, *i.e.*, $\rho \to 0$, then from (2),

$$\oint_C \frac{f(z)}{z-a}\,dz = i\int_0^{2\pi} f(a)\,d\theta = i\,f(a)\int_0^{2\pi} d\theta = 2\pi i\,f(a)$$

Hence, $$f(a) = \frac{1}{2\pi i}\oint_C \frac{f(z)}{z-a}\,dz$$

which is the required Cauchy's integral formula.

Cor. By Cauchy's integral formula, we have

$$f(a) = \frac{1}{2\pi i}\oint_C \frac{f(z)}{z-a} \qquad \ldots(1)$$

where a is any point within C, it may be treated as a parameter.

Differentiating both sides of (1) w.r.t. a,

$$f'(a) = \frac{1}{2\pi i}\oint_C \frac{\partial}{\partial a}\left[\frac{f(z)}{z-a}\right]dz = \frac{1}{2\pi i}\oint_C \frac{f(z)}{(z-a)^2}\,dz$$

Similarly, $$f''(a) = \frac{2\,!}{2\pi i}\oint_C \frac{f(z)}{(z-a)^3}\,dz$$

$$f'''(a) = \frac{3\,!}{2\pi i} \oint_C \frac{f(z)}{(z-a)^4}\, dz$$

and in general, $$f^{\,n}(a) = \frac{n\,!}{2\pi i} \oint_C \frac{f(z)}{(z-a)^{n+1}}\, dz.$$

Thus, *if a function of a complex variable has a first derivative in a simply connected region, all its higher derivatives exist in that region. This property is not exhibited by the functions of real variables.*

ILLUSTRATIVE EXAMPLES

Example 1. *Evaluate* $\oint_C (x^2 - y^2 + 2ixy)\,dz$*, where C is the contour* $|\,z\,| = 1$.

Sol. $f(z) = x^2 - y^2 + 2ixy = (x + iy)^2 = z^2$ is analytic everywhere within and on $|\,z\,| = 1$.

∴ By Cauchy's integral theorem,

$$\oint_C f(z)\,dz = 0.$$

Example 2. *Evaluate* $\oint_C (3z^2 + 4z + 1)\,dz$*, where C is the arc of the cycloid* $x = a(\theta - \sin\theta)$*,* $y = a(1 - \cos\theta)$ *between* $(0, 0)$ *and* $(2\pi a, 0)$.

Sol. Here, $f(z) = 3z^2 + 4z + 1$ is analytic everywhere so that the integral is independent of the path of integration and depends only on the end points $z_1 = 0 + i0$ and $z_2 = 2\pi a + i0$.

$$\therefore \quad \int_C (3z^2 + 4z + 1)\,dz = \int_0^{2\pi a} (3z^2 + 4z + 1)\,dz = \Big[z^3 + 2z^2 + z \Big]_0^{2\pi a}$$

$$= 8\pi^3 a^3 + 8\pi^2 a^2 + 2\pi a$$

$$= 2\pi a\,(4\pi^2 a^2 + 4\pi a + 1).$$

Example 3. *Evaluate* $\oint_C \frac{e^{-z}}{z+1}\,dz$*, where C is the circle*

(*a*) $|\,z\,| = 2$ (*b*) $|\,z\,| = \frac{1}{2}$.

Sol. $f(z) = e^{-z}$ is an analytic function.

(*a*) The point $a = -1$ lies inside the circle $|\,z\,| = 2$.

∴ By Cauchy's integral formula,

$$\frac{1}{2\pi i} \oint_C \frac{f(z)}{z - (-1)}\,dz = f(-1) \quad \Rightarrow \quad \oint_C \frac{e^{-z}}{z+1}\,dz = 2\pi i e.$$

(*b*) The point $a = -1$ lies outside the circle $|\,z\,| = \frac{1}{2}$.

∴ The function $\frac{e^{-z}}{z+1}$ is analytic within and on C.

By Cauchy's integral theorem, we have $\oint_C \frac{e^{-z}}{z+1}\,dz = 0.$

Example 4. *Evaluate* $\oint_C \frac{\cos \pi z^2}{(z-1)(z-2)} dz$, *where C is the circle* $|z| = 3$.

Sol. The integrand has singularities where

$(z-1)(z-2) = 0$ *i.e.*, at $z = 1$ and $z = 2$.

Both these points lie within the circle $|z| = 3$

$f(z) = \cos \pi z^2$ is an analytic function.

Also $$\frac{1}{(z-1)(z-2)} = -\frac{1}{z-1} + \frac{1}{z-2}$$

$$\therefore \quad \oint_C \frac{\cos \pi z^2}{(z-1)(z-2)} dz = -\oint_C \frac{\cos \pi z^2}{z-1} dz + \oint_C \frac{\cos \pi z^2}{z-2} dz \quad \ldots(1)$$

$$= -2\pi i f(1) + 2\pi i f(2) \quad \text{where} \quad f(z) = \cos \pi z^2$$

$$= -2\pi i \cos \pi + 2\pi i \cos 4\pi = 2\pi i + 2\pi i = 4\pi i.$$

Example 5. *Evaluate* $\oint_C \frac{3z^2 + z}{z^2 - 1} dz$, *where C is the circle* $|z - 1| = 1$.

Sol. The integrand has singularities where $z^2 - 1 = 0$ *i.e.*, at $z = 1$ and $z = -1$.

The circle $|z - 1| = 1$ has centre at $z = 1$ and radius 1 and includes the point $z = 1$. $f(z) = 3z^2 + z$ is an analytic function.

Also $$\frac{1}{z^2-1} = \frac{1}{(z-1)(z+1)} = \frac{1}{2}\left(\frac{1}{z-1} - \frac{1}{z+1}\right)$$

$$\therefore \quad \oint_C \frac{3z^2+z}{z^2-1} dz = \frac{1}{2}\oint_C \frac{3z^2+z}{z-1} dz - \frac{1}{2}\oint_C \frac{3z^2+z}{z+1} dz \quad \ldots(1)$$

By Cauchy's integral formula,

$$\oint_C \frac{3z^2+z}{z-1} dz = 2\pi i f(1), \quad \text{where } f(z) = 3z^2 + z$$

$$= 8\pi i$$

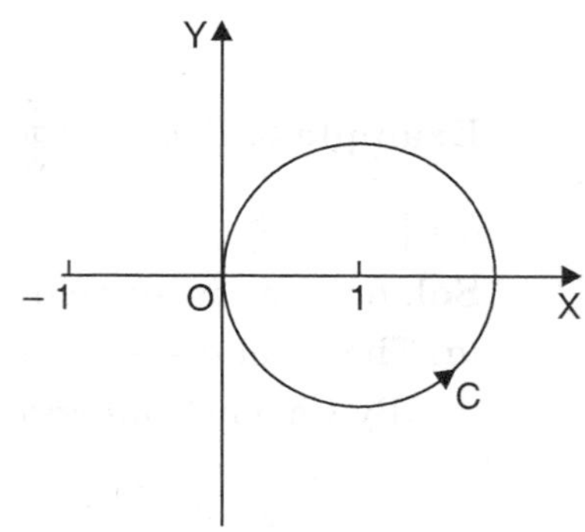

By Cauchy's integral theorem,

$$\oint_C \frac{3z^2+z}{z-1} dz = 0$$

$\therefore$ From (1), we have

$$\oint_C \frac{3z^2+z}{z^2-1} dz = 4\pi i.$$

Example 6. *Use Cauchy's integral formula to evaluate*

$$\oint_C \frac{e^{2z}}{(z+1)^4} dz, \text{ where C is the circle } |z| = 2.$$

Sol. The integrand has a singularity at $z = -1$ which lies within the circle $|z| = 2$.

Now $$f^n(a) = \frac{n!}{2\pi i} \oint_C \frac{f(z)}{(z-a)^{n+1}} dz \quad \ldots(1)$$

Here $a = -1, \quad n + 1 = 4 \quad i.e., \quad n = 3, f(z) = e^{2z}$

$\therefore \quad f^{n}(z) = 2^n e^{2z}, f^{3}(a) = f^{3}(-1) = 2^3 e^{-2}$

From (1), we have $f^{3}(-1) = \dfrac{3!}{2\pi i} \oint_C \dfrac{e^{2z}}{(z+1)^4} dz \quad \Rightarrow \quad 8e^{-2} = \dfrac{3}{\pi i} \oint_C \dfrac{e^{2z}}{(z+1)^4} dz$

Hence $\quad \oint_C \dfrac{e^{2z}}{(z+1)^4} dz = \dfrac{8\pi i}{3e^2}$.

Example 7. *If* $f(\xi) = \int_C \dfrac{3z^2 + 7z + 1}{z - \xi} dz$, *where C is the circle* $x^2 + y^2 = 4$, *find the values of* $f(3)$, $f'(1 - i)$ *and* $f''(1 - i)$. (M.G.U. May 2008)

Sol. The given circle C is $x^2 + y^2 = 4$ or $|z| = 2$.

The point $z = 3$ lies outside the circle $|z| = 2$ while $z = 1 - i$ and $z = 1 + i$ lie inside the circle.

Now $f(3) = \oint_C \dfrac{3z^2 + 7z + 1}{z - 3} dz$ and $\dfrac{3z^2 + 7z + 1}{z - 3}$ is analytic within and on C.

$\therefore$ By Cauchy's integral theorem, we have

$$\oint_C \frac{3z^2 + 7z + 1}{z - 3} dz = 0 \quad \Rightarrow \quad f(3) = 0.$$

Now let $\phi(z) = 3z^2 + 7z + 1$ which is analytic everywhere.

$\therefore$ By Cauchy's integral formula, we have

$$\phi(\xi) = \frac{1}{2\pi i} \oint_C \frac{\phi(z)}{z - \xi} dz, \quad \text{where } \xi \text{ is a point within C.}$$

$$\Rightarrow \quad 2\pi i \phi(\xi) = \oint_C \frac{3z^2 + 7z + 1}{z - \xi} dz = f(\xi)$$

$$\Rightarrow \quad f(\xi) = 2\pi i(3\xi^2 + 7\xi + 1) \quad \Rightarrow \quad f'(\xi) = 2\pi i(6\xi + 7)$$

$$\therefore \quad f'(1 - i) = 2\pi i[6(1 - i) + 7] = 2\pi i(13 - 6i) = 2\pi(6 + 13i)$$

Also $\quad f''(\xi) = 12\pi i$

$\therefore \quad f''(1 - i) = 12\pi i.$

TEST YOUR KNOWLEDGE

1. Evaluate $\oint_C \dfrac{z^2 + 5}{z - 3} dz$, where C is the circle

   (a) $|z| = 4$ (b) $|z| = 1$.

2. Evaluate $\int_C \dfrac{e^z}{z - 2} dz$, where C is the circle

   (a) $|z| = 3$ (b) $|z| = 1$.

3. Evaluate $\oint_C \dfrac{3z^2 + 7z + 1}{z+1}\, dz$, where C is the circle

(*a*) $|z| = 1.5$ (*b*) $|z + i| = 1$.

4. Evaluate $\oint_C \dfrac{\sin 3z}{z + \dfrac{\pi}{2}}\, dz$, where C is the circle $|z| = 5$.

5. Evaluate $\oint_C \dfrac{z^3 + z + 1}{z^2 - 3z + 2}\, dz$, where C is the ellipse $4x^2 + 9y^2 = 1$.

6. Evaluate $\oint_C \dfrac{\cos \pi z}{z^2 - 1}\, dz$ around a rectangle with vertices

(*a*) $2 \pm i, -2 \pm i$ (*b*) $-i, 2-i, 2+i, i$.

7. Evaluate $\oint_C \dfrac{\sin^2 z}{\left(z - \dfrac{\pi}{6}\right)^3}\, dz$, where C is the circle $|z| = 1$.

8. Evaluate $\oint_C \dfrac{z\, dz}{(z-1)(z-3)}$, where C is the circle

(*a*) $|z| = 3$ (*b*) $|z| = 3/2$.

9. Evaluate $\oint_C \dfrac{z+4}{z^2 + 2z + 5}\, dz$, where C is the circle $|z| = 1$.

10. Evaluate $\oint_C \dfrac{\sin \pi z^2 + \cos \pi z^2}{(z-1)(z-2)}\, dz$, where C is the circle $|z| = 3$.

11. Evaluate $\oint_C \dfrac{e^z}{(z-1)(z-4)}\, dz$, where C is the circle $|z| = 2$.

12. Evaluate $\oint_C \dfrac{e^z}{z(z+1)}\, dz$, where C is the circle $|z| = \dfrac{1}{4}$.

13. Evaluate $\oint_C \dfrac{\cos z}{z - \pi}\, dz$, where C is the circle $|z - 1| = 3$.

14. Evaluate $\oint_C \dfrac{e^z}{(z+3)(z+2)}\, dz$, where C is the circle $|z - 1| = \dfrac{1}{2}$.

15. Let $P(z) = a + bz + cz^2$ and $\oint_C \dfrac{P(z)}{z}\, dz = \oint_C \dfrac{P(z)}{z^2}\, dz = \oint_C \dfrac{P(z)}{z^3}\, dz = 2\pi i$ where C is the circle $|z| = 1$. Evaluate $P(z)$.

16. Evaluate $\oint_C \dfrac{e^{-z}}{z^2}\, dz$, where C is the circle $|z| = 1$.

17. Evaluate $\oint_C \dfrac{e^{-2z}\, dz}{(z+1)^3}$, where C is the circle $|z| = 2$.

18. If $f(\xi) = \oint_C \dfrac{4z^2 + z + 5}{z - \xi}\, dz$, where C is the ellipse $\dfrac{x^2}{4} + \dfrac{y^2}{9} = 1$, find $f(1)$, $f(i)$, $f'(-1)$ and $f''(-i)$.

19. Using Cauchy's integral formula, evaluate $\int_C \dfrac{z+1}{z^2 + 2z + 5}\, dz$ where C is the circle $|z + 1 - i| = 2$, integration being taken in the anti-clockwise direction. *(M.G.U. Jan. 2007)*

20. Using Cauchy's integral formula, evaluate $\int_C \frac{2z^2+1}{(z+1)^2(z-2)}\,dz$ where C in the circle $|z| = 3$ integration being taken in the anticlockwise direction. *(M.G.U., July 2007)*

21. Using Cauchy's integral formula, evaluate $\int_C \frac{e^z}{(z+1)^4(z-2)}\,dz$, where C is $|z-1| = 3$. *(M.G.U., June 2006)*

22. Evaluate $\int_C (z - z^2)\,dz$, where C is the upper half of the circle $|z| = 1$. Apply Cauchy's theorem to find the value of the integral along the lower half of the same circle. *(M.G.U., May 2009)*

Answers

1. (*a*) $28\pi i$ (*b*) 0	**2.** (*a*) $2\pi i\, e^2$ (*b*) 0	**3.** (*a*) $-6\pi i$ (*b*) 0	**4.** $2\pi i$
5. 0	**6.** (*a*) 0 (*b*) $-\pi i$	**7.** πi	**8.** (*a*) $2\pi i$ (*b*) $-\pi i$
9. 0	**10.** $4\pi i$	**11.** $-\frac{2}{3}\pi i e$	**12.** $2\pi i$
13. $-2\pi i$	**14.** 0	**15.** $1 + z + z^2$	**16.** $-2\pi i$
17. $4\pi i e^2$	**18.** $20\pi i,\ 2\pi(i-1),\ -14\pi i,\ 16\pi i$		**19.** πi
20. $4\pi i$	**21.** $(e^2 - 13e^{-1})\frac{1}{81}$	**22.** $-\frac{2}{3}, -\frac{2}{3}$.	

4.16. SERIES OF COMPLEX TERMS

A series of the form $(a_1 + ib_1) + (a_2 + ib_2) + \ldots + (a_n + ib_n) + \ldots$
where $a_1, b_1, a_2, b_2, \ldots\ldots$ are real numbers, is called a series of complex terms and can be expressed as

$$\sum_{n=1}^{\infty} a_n + i \sum_{n=1}^{\infty} b_n \qquad \ldots(1)$$

The series (1) is convergent if Σa_n and Σb_n both are convergent.

If the series Σa_n and Σb_n converge to a and b respectively, then the series (1) is said to converge to $a + ib$.

The necessary (not sufficient) condition for convergence of a series (1) is $\underset{n \to \infty}{\text{Lt}} (a_n + ib_n) = 0$.

The series (1) is said to be **absolutely convergent** if the series
$|a_1 + ib_1| + |a_2 + ib_2| + \ldots\ldots + |a_n + ib_n| + \ldots\ldots$ is convergent.

Since $|a_n| \le |a_n + ib_n|$ and $|b_n| \le |a_n + ib_n|$, we conclude that an absolutely convergent series is convergent. The converse is not true.

If the series of functions $u_1(z) + u_2(z) + \ldots\ldots + u_n(z) + \ldots\ldots = \sum_{n=1}^{\infty} u_n(z) \qquad \ldots(2)$

converges to $S(z)$ and $S_n(z)$ is its nth partial sum, then the series (2) is said to be **uniformly convergent** in a region R, if given any positive number ε, there exists a positive number N, depending on ε but not on z, such that for every z in R,

$$|S(z) - S_n(z)| < \varepsilon \text{ for all } n > N.$$

A series of the form

$$a_0 + a_1(z-a) + a_2(z-a)^2 + \dots + a_n(z-a)^n + \dots\dots = \sum_{n=0}^{\infty} a_n (z-a)^n \qquad \dots(3)$$

is called a **power series** in $(z - a)$.

If the series (3) is convergent for all values of z satisfying $|z-a| < \text{R}$, *i.e.*, for all values of z lying inside the circle with centre at $z = a$ and radius R, then this circle is called the **circle of convergence** and R is called the **radius of convergence.**

The power series (3) is uniformly convergent in a region R if there exists a series of positive terms ΣM_n such that $|a_n(z-a)^n| \le \text{M}_n$ for all values of z in the region R.

This is called **Weierstrass M-test** for uniform convergence of a power series.

4.17. TAYLOR'S SERIES

Statement. *If f(z) is analytic inside a circle C with centre at a, then for all z inside C,*

$$f(z) = f(a) + (z-a) f'(a) + \frac{(z-a)^2}{2!} f''(a) + \dots + \frac{(z-a)^n}{n!} f^n(a) + \dots$$

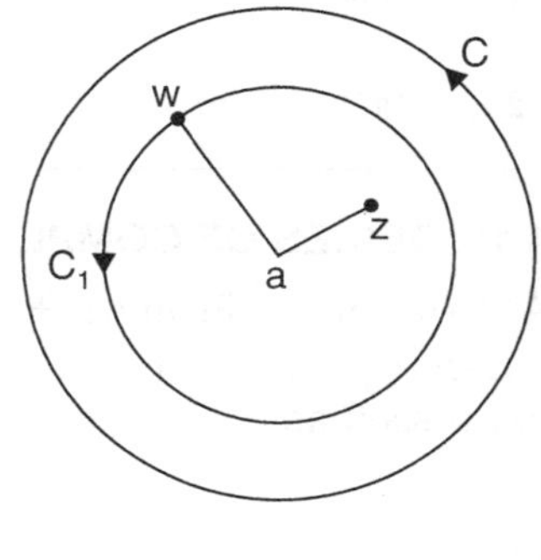

Proof. Let z be any point inside the circle C. Draw a circle C_1 with centre at a and radius smaller than that of C such that z is an interior point of C_1. Let w be any point on C_1, then

$$|z-a| < |z-w| \quad i.e., \left|\frac{z-a}{z-w}\right| < 1$$

Now, $$\frac{1}{w-z} = \frac{1}{(w-a)-(z-a)} = \frac{1}{w-a}\left[1 - \frac{z-a}{w-a}\right]^{-1}$$

Expanding R.H.S. by binomial theorem as $\left|\frac{z-a}{w-a}\right| < 1$, we get

$$\frac{1}{w-z} = \frac{1}{w-a}\left[1 + \frac{z-a}{w-a} + \left(\frac{z-a}{w-a}\right)^2 + \dots + \left(\frac{z-a}{w-a}\right)^n + \dots\right] \qquad \dots(1)$$

This series converges uniformly since $\left|\frac{z-a}{w-a}\right| < 1$. Multiplying both sides of (1) by $\frac{1}{2\pi i} f(w)$ and integrating term by term w.r.t. w, over C_1, we get

$$\frac{1}{2\pi i}\oint_{\text{C}_1} \frac{f(w)}{w-z}\, dw = \frac{1}{2\pi i}\oint_{\text{C}_1} \frac{f(w)}{w-a}\, dw + \frac{z-a}{2\pi i}\oint_{\text{C}_1} \frac{f(w)}{(w-a)^2}\, dw + \frac{(z-a)^2}{2\pi i}\oint_{\text{C}_1} \frac{f(w)}{(w-a)^3}\, dw +$$

$$\dots\dots + \frac{(z-a)^n}{2\pi i}\oint_{\text{C}_1} \frac{f(w)}{(w-a)^{n+1}}\, dw + \dots \qquad \dots(2)$$

Since $f(w)$ is analytic on and inside C_1, by Cauchy's formula,

$$\frac{1}{2\pi i}\oint_{\text{C}_1} \frac{f(w)}{w-z}\, dw = f(z)$$

Also $$f^n(a) = \frac{n!}{2\pi i}\oint_{\text{C}_1} \frac{f(w)}{(w-a)^{n+1}}\, dw \quad i.e., \quad \frac{1}{2\pi i}\oint_{\text{C}_1} \frac{f(w)}{(w-a)^{n+1}}\, dw = \frac{f^n(a)}{n!}$$

$\therefore$ From (2), we have

$$f(z) = f(a) + (z-a)f'(a) + \frac{(z-a)^2}{2!}f''(a) + \dots + \frac{(z-a)^n}{n!}f^n(a) + \dots \qquad \dots(3)$$

which is the required *Taylor's series* for $f(z)$ about $z = a$.

Cor. 1. Putting $z = a + h$ in (3), we get

$$f(a+h) = f(a) + hf'(a) + \frac{h^2}{2!}f''(a) + \dots\dots + \frac{h^n}{n!}f^n(a) + \dots$$

Cor. 2. If $a = 0$, the series (3) becomes

$$f(z) = f(0) + zf'(0) + \frac{z^2}{2!}f''(0) + \dots\dots + \frac{z^n}{n!}f^n(0) + \dots$$

This series is called **Maclaurin's series.**

4.18. LAURENT'S SERIES

If f(z) is analytic inside and on the boundary of the ring shaped region R bounded by two concentric circles C_1 and C_2 of radii r_1 and r_2 ($r_1 > r_2$) respectively having centre at a, then for all z in R,

$$f(z) = a_0 + a_1(z-a) + a_2(z-a)^2 + \dots + a_{-1}(z-a)^{-1} + a_{-2}(z-a)^{-2} + \dots$$

where $$a_n = \frac{1}{2\pi i}\oint_{C_1}\frac{f(w)}{(w-a)^{n+1}}dw \ ; \ n = 0, 1, 2, \dots$$

and $$a_{-n} = \frac{1}{2\pi i}\oint_{C_2}\frac{f(w)}{(w-a)^{-n+1}}dw \ ; \ n = 1, 2, 3, \dots$$

Proof. Let z be any point in the region R, then by Cauchy's integral formula for double connected region, we have

$$f(z) = \frac{1}{2\pi i}\oint_{C_1}\frac{f(w)}{w-z}dw - \frac{1}{2\pi i}\oint_{C_2}\frac{f(w)}{w-z}dw \qquad \dots(1)$$

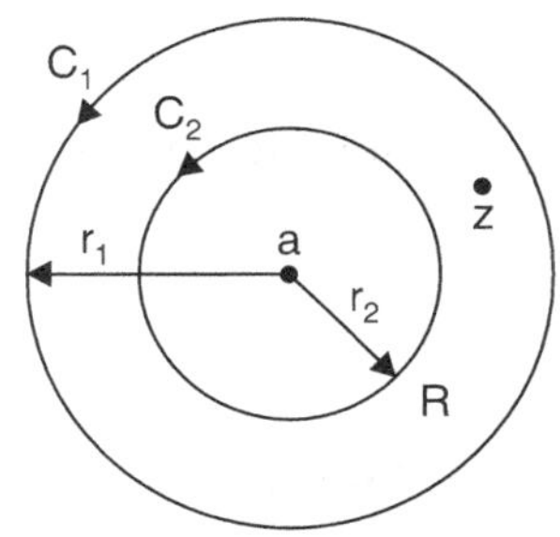

For the first integral in (1), w lies on C_2

$\therefore$ $$|z-a| < |w-a| \quad i.e., \quad \left|\frac{z-a}{w-a}\right| < 1$$

Now $$\frac{1}{w-a} = \frac{1}{(w-a)-(z-a)} = \frac{1}{w-a}\left(1-\frac{z-a}{w-a}\right)^{-1}$$

$$= \frac{1}{w-a}\left[1 + \frac{z-a}{w-a} + \left(\frac{z-a}{w-a}\right)^2 + \dots\dots\right]$$

Multiplying both sides by $\frac{1}{2\pi i}f(w)$ and integrating term by term w.r.t. w, along the circle C_1, we get

$$\frac{1}{2\pi i}\oint_{C_1}\frac{f(w)}{w-z}dw = \frac{1}{2\pi i}\oint_{C_1}\frac{f(w)}{w-a}dw + \frac{z-a}{2\pi i}\oint_{C_1}\frac{f(w)}{(w-a)^2}dw + \frac{(z-a)^2}{2\pi i}\oint_{C_1}\frac{f(w)}{(w-a)^3}dw + \dots\dots$$

$$= a_0 + a_1(z-a) + a_2(z-a)^2 + \dots\dots$$

$$= \sum_{n=0}^{\infty} a_n (z-a)^n \quad \ldots(2) \quad \left[\because \ a_n = \frac{1}{2\pi i} \oint_{C_1} \frac{f(w)}{(w-a)^{n+1}} dw, n = 0, 1, 2, \ldots\ldots \right]$$

For the second integral in (1), w lies on C_2

$$\therefore \qquad |w-a| < |z-a| \quad i.e., \quad \left| \frac{w-a}{z-a} \right| < 1$$

Now $$\frac{1}{w-z} = \frac{1}{(w-a)-(z-a)} = -\frac{1}{z-a}\left(1 - \frac{w-a}{z-a}\right)^{-1}$$

$$= -\frac{1}{z-a}\left[1 + \frac{w-a}{z-a} + \left(\frac{w-a}{z-a}\right)^2 + \ldots\ldots\right]$$

Multiplying both sides by $\frac{1}{2\pi i} f(w)$ and integrating term by term w.r.t. w, along the circle C_2, we get

$$-\frac{1}{2\pi i}\oint_{C_2} \frac{f(w)}{w-z} dw = \frac{1}{z-a} \cdot \frac{1}{2\pi i}\oint_{C_2} f(w)\, dw + \frac{1}{(z-a)^2} \cdot \frac{1}{2\pi i}\oint_{C_2} (w-a) f(w)\, dw$$

$$+ \frac{1}{(z-a)^3} \cdot \frac{1}{2\pi i}\oint_{C_2} (w-a)^2 f(w)\, dw + \ldots\ldots$$

$$= a_{-1}(z-a)^{-1} + a_{-2}(z-a)^{-2} + a_{-3}(z-a)^{-3} + \ldots\ldots$$

$$= \sum_{n=1}^{\infty} a_{-n}(z-a)^{-n} \qquad \ldots(3)$$

$$\left[\because \ a_{-n} = \frac{1}{2\pi i}\oint_{C_2} \frac{f(w)}{(w-a)^{-n+1}} dw, n = 1, 2, 3, \ldots\ldots \right]$$

Substituting from (2) and (3) in (1), we get

$$f(z) = \sum_{n=0}^{\infty} a_n (z-a)^n + \sum_{n=1}^{\infty} a_{-n}(z-a)^{-n}$$

Note 1. In the statement of Laurent's series, $a_n = \frac{1}{2\pi i}\oint_{C_1} \frac{f(w)}{(w-a)^{n+1}} dw \neq \frac{f^n(a)}{n!}$ because $f(z)$ is not given to be analytic inside C_1.

Note 2. In case $f(z)$ is analytic inside C_1, then $a_{-n} = 0$ and $a_n = \frac{1}{2\pi i}\oint_{C_1} \frac{f(w)}{(w-a)^{n+1}} dw = \frac{f^n(a)}{n!}$ and Laurent's series reduces to Taylor's series.

Note 3. If C is any simple closed curve which lies in the ring-shaped region R and encloses the circle C_1, then

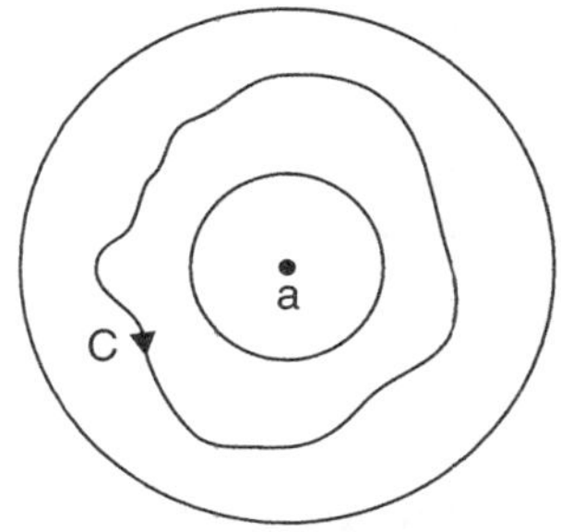

$$\oint_{C_1} \frac{f(w)}{(w-a)^{n+1}}\, dw = \oint_C \frac{f(w)}{(w-a)^{n+1}}\, dw$$

and $$\oint_{C_2} \frac{f(w)}{(w-a)^{-n+1}}\, dw = \oint_C \frac{f(w)}{(w-a)^{-n+1}}\, dw$$

$\therefore$ Laurent's series can be written as

$$f(z) = \sum_{n=-\infty}^{\infty} a_n (z-a)^n, \quad \text{where } a_n = \frac{1}{2\pi i} \oint_C \frac{f(w)}{(w-a)^{n+1}}\, dw.$$

Note 4. The process of finding the co-efficient a_n by complex integration is complicated. In practice, we expand the function $f(z)$ by binomial theorem or by some other method to obtain Taylor's or Laurent's series.

ILLUSTRATIVE EXAMPLES

Example 1. *Expand* $\dfrac{1}{z^2 - 3z + 2}$ *in the region*

(*a*) $|z| < 1$ (*b*) $1 < |z| < 2$

(*c*) $|z| > 2$ (*d*) $0 < |z - 1| < 1.$

Sol. Here $f(z) = \dfrac{1}{z^2 - 3z + 2} = \dfrac{1}{(z-1)(z-2)} = \dfrac{1}{z-2} - \dfrac{1}{z-1}$ (Partial Fractions)

(*a*) If $|z| < 1$, then $\left|\dfrac{z}{2}\right| < 1$

$$\therefore \quad f(z) = \frac{1}{-2\left(1 - \frac{z}{2}\right)} + \frac{1}{1-z}$$

[Arranged suitably to make the binomial expansions valid]

$$= -\frac{1}{2}\left(1 - \frac{z}{2}\right)^{-1} + (1-z)^{-1}$$

$$= -\frac{1}{2}\left(1 + \frac{z}{2} + \frac{z^2}{4} + \frac{z^3}{8} + \ldots\ldots\right) + (1 + z + z^2 + z^3 + \ldots\ldots)$$

(By binomial theorem)

$$= \frac{1}{2} + \frac{3z}{4} + \frac{7}{8}z^2 + \frac{15}{16}z^3 + \ldots\ldots$$

(*b*) If $1 < |z| < 2$, then $\left|\dfrac{1}{z}\right| < 1$ and $\left|\dfrac{z}{2}\right| < 1$

$$\therefore \quad f(z) = \frac{1}{-2\left(1 - \frac{z}{2}\right)} - \frac{1}{z\left(1 - \frac{1}{z}\right)} = -\frac{1}{2}\left(1 - \frac{z}{2}\right)^{-1} - \frac{1}{z}\left(1 - \frac{1}{z}\right)^{-1}$$

$$= -\frac{1}{2}\left(1+\frac{z}{2}+\frac{z^2}{4}+\frac{z^3}{8}+......\right)-\frac{1}{z}\left(1+\frac{1}{z}+\frac{1}{z^2}+\frac{1}{z^3}+......\right)$$

(By binomial theorem)

$$= -\frac{1}{2}\left(1+\frac{z}{2}+\frac{z^2}{4}+......\right) - (z^{-1} + z^{-2} + z^{-3} + ...)$$

(*c*) If $|z| > 2$, then $\left|\frac{2}{z}\right| < 1$ and $\left|\frac{1}{z}\right| < 1$

$$\therefore \quad f(z) = \frac{1}{z\left(1-\frac{2}{z}\right)} - \frac{1}{z\left(1-\frac{1}{z}\right)} = \frac{1}{z}\left(1-\frac{2}{z}\right)^{-1} - \frac{1}{z}\left(1-\frac{1}{z}\right)^{-1}$$

$$= \frac{1}{z}\left(1+\frac{2}{z}+\frac{4}{z^2}+\frac{8}{z^3}+......\right)-\frac{1}{z}\left(1+\frac{1}{z}+\frac{1}{z^2}+\frac{1}{z^3}+......\right)$$

(By binomial theorem)

$$= z^{-2} + 3z^{-3} + 7z^{-4} + ...$$

(*d*) For $0 < |z-1| < 1$, we have

$$f(z) = \frac{1}{(z-1)-1} - \frac{1}{z-1} = -\frac{1}{1-(z-1)} - \frac{1}{z-1} = -(z-1)^{-1} - [1-(z-1)]^{-1}$$

$$= -(z-1)^{-1} - [1 + (z-1) + (z-1)^2 + (z-1)^3 + ...].$$

Example 2. *Show that when* $|z+1| < 1$, $z^{-2} = 1 + \sum_{n=1}^{\infty} (n+1)(z+1)^n$.

Sol. $$f(z) = z^{-2} = \frac{1}{z^2} = \frac{1}{[(z+1)-1]^2} = \frac{1}{[1-(z+1)]^2} = [1-(z+1)]^{-2}$$

$$= 1 + 2(z+1) + 3(z+1)^2 + 4(z+1)^3 + ...$$

[By binomial theorem, since $|z+1| < 1$]

$$= 1 + \sum_{n=1}^{\infty} (n+1)(z+1)^n.$$

Example 3. *Expand* $\cos z$ *in a Taylor's series about* $z = \frac{\pi}{4}$.

Sol. Here $f(z) = \cos z$, $f'(z) = -\sin z$, $f''(z) = -\cos z$, $f'''(z) = \sin z$, ...

$$\therefore \quad f\left(\frac{\pi}{4}\right) = \frac{1}{\sqrt{2}},\quad f'\left(\frac{\pi}{4}\right) = -\frac{1}{\sqrt{2}},\quad f''\left(\frac{\pi}{4}\right) = -\frac{1}{\sqrt{2}},\quad f'''\left(\frac{\pi}{4}\right) = \frac{1}{\sqrt{2}}, ...$$

Hence $\cos z = f(z)$

$$= f\left(\frac{\pi}{4}\right) + \left(z-\frac{\pi}{4}\right) f'\left(\frac{\pi}{4}\right) + \frac{\left(z-\frac{\pi}{4}\right)^2}{2!} f''\left(\frac{\pi}{4}\right) + \frac{\left(z-\frac{\pi}{4}\right)^3}{3!} f'''\left(\frac{\pi}{4}\right) + ...$$

$$= \frac{1}{\sqrt{2}}\left[1-\left(z-\frac{\pi}{4}\right)-\frac{1}{2!}\left(z-\frac{\pi}{4}\right)^2+\frac{1}{3!}\left(z-\frac{\pi}{4}\right)^3+......\right].$$

Example 4. *Expand the function* $\dfrac{\sin z}{z-\pi}$ *about* $z = \pi$.

Sol. Putting $z - \pi = t$, we have

$$\frac{\sin z}{z-\pi} = \frac{\sin(\pi + t)}{t} = \frac{-\sin t}{t}$$

$$= -\frac{1}{t}\left(t - \frac{t^3}{3!} + \frac{t^5}{5!} \ldots\ldots\right) = -1 + \frac{t^2}{3!} - \frac{t^4}{5!} + \ldots\ldots = -1 + \frac{(z-\pi)^2}{3!} - \frac{(z-\pi)^4}{5!} + \ldots\ldots$$

Example 5. *Expand* $f(z) = \dfrac{z}{(z+1)(z+2)}$ *about* $z = -2$.

Sol. To expand $f(z)$ about $z = -2$, *i.e.*, in powers of $z + 2$, we put $z + 2 = t$.

$$\therefore \quad f(z) = \frac{z}{(z+1)(z+2)} = \frac{t-2}{(t-1)t} = \frac{2-t}{t(1-t)} = \frac{2-t}{t}(1-t)^{-1}$$

$$= \frac{2-t}{t}(1 + t + t^2 + t^3 + \ldots\ldots) \qquad \text{for } 0 < |t| < 1$$

$$= \frac{1}{t}(2 + t + t^2 + t^3 + \ldots\ldots) = \frac{2}{t} + 1 + t + t^2 + \ldots\ldots$$

$$= \frac{2}{z+2} + 1 + (z+2) + (z+2)^2 + \ldots\ldots \qquad \text{for } 0 < |z+2| < 1$$

which is the required Laurent's series.

TEST YOUR KNOWLEDGE

Expand the following functions as a Taylor's series:

1. $\log(1 + z)$ about $z = 0$.
2. $\sin z$ about $z = \dfrac{\pi}{4}$.
3. $\dfrac{z}{(z+1)(z+2)}$ about $z = 2$.

Expand the following functions in Laurent's series:

4. $\dfrac{1}{z-2}$, for $|z| > 2$.
5. $\dfrac{1}{z^2 - 4z + 3}$, for $1 < |z| < 3$.
6. $\dfrac{1}{z(z-1)(z-2)}$, for $|z| > 2$.
7. $\dfrac{z^2 - 1}{(z+2)(z+3)}$, for $|z| > 3$.
8. $\dfrac{1 - \cos z}{z^3}$, about $z = 0$.
9. $\dfrac{e^z}{(z-1)^2}$, about $z = 1$.
10. Expand $f(z) = \dfrac{(z-2)(z+2)}{(z+1)(z+4)}$ in the region:

    (*a*) $|z| < 1$ (*b*) $1 < |z| < 4$ (*c*) $|z| > 4$.
11. Obtain the Laurent's series expansion of $f(z) = \dfrac{1}{(z-1)(z-2)}$ valid in the region

    (*a*) $|z - 1| < 1$ (*b*) $1 < |z| < 2$.

Answers

1. $z - \dfrac{z^2}{2} + \dfrac{z^3}{3} - \dfrac{z^4}{4} + \ldots\ldots$
2. $\dfrac{1}{\sqrt{2}}\left[1 + \left(z - \dfrac{\pi}{4}\right) - \dfrac{1}{2!}\left(z - \dfrac{\pi}{4}\right)^2 - \dfrac{1}{3!}\left(z - \dfrac{\pi}{4}\right)^3 + \ldots\ldots\right]$
3. $\left(\dfrac{1}{2} - \dfrac{1}{3}\right) - \left(\dfrac{1}{2^3} - \dfrac{1}{3^2}\right)(z-2) + \left(\dfrac{1}{2^5} - \dfrac{1}{3^3}\right)(z-2)^2 - \ldots\ldots$

4. $\frac{1}{z}+\frac{2}{z^2}+\frac{2^2}{z^3}+\frac{2^3}{z^4}+\ldots\ldots$

5. $-\frac{1}{6}-\frac{1}{6}\sum_{n=1}^{\infty}\frac{z^n}{3^n}-\frac{1}{2}\sum_{n=1}^{\infty}z^{-n}$

6. $z^{-3}+3z^{-4}+7z^{-5}+\ldots\ldots+(2^{n-1}-1)z^{-(n+1)}+\ldots\ldots$

7. $1+\frac{3}{z}\sum_{n=0}^{\infty}\left(-\frac{2}{z}\right)^n-\frac{8}{z}\sum_{n=0}^{\infty}\left(-\frac{3}{z}\right)^n$

8. $-\sum_{n=2}^{\infty}\frac{z^{2n-5}}{(2n-2)\,!}$

9. $e\left[(z-1)^{-2}+(z-1)^{-1}+\frac{1}{2\,!}+\frac{1}{3\,!}(z-1)+\frac{1}{4\,!}(z-1)^2+\ldots\ldots\right]$

10. (a) $-1+\sum_{n=1}^{\infty}(-1)^{n+1}(1+4^{-n})\,z^n$

(b) $\sum_{n=0}^{\infty}\frac{(-1)^{n+1}}{4^n}z^n+\sum_{n=1}^{\infty}(-1)^n z^{-n}$

(c) $1+\sum_{n=1}^{\infty}(-1)^n(1+4^n)\,z^{-n}$

11. (a) $\frac{-1}{z-1}-1-(z-1)-(z-1)^2-\ldots\ldots$

(b) $-\frac{1}{2}-\frac{z}{2^2}-\frac{z^2}{2^3}-\ldots\ldots-\frac{1}{z}-\frac{1}{z^2}-\frac{1}{z^3}\ldots\ldots$

4.19. SINGULAR POINTS, RESIDUES

A point at which a function $f(z)$ ceases to be analytic is called a *singular point* or *singularity* of $f(z)$.

For example, $z = 2$ is a singular point of $f(z)=\frac{1}{z-2}$.

A singular point $z = a$ of a function $f(z)$ is called an *isolated singular point* if there exists a circle with centre a which contains no other singular point of $f(z)$.

For example, $z = -1, 1$ are two isolated singular points of the function $f(z)=\frac{z}{z^2-1}$.

The function $f(z)=\frac{1}{\sin(\pi z)}$ has an infinite number of isolated singular points at $z = \pm 1, \pm 2, \ldots\ldots$

When $z = a$ is an isolated singular point of $f(z)$, we can expand $f(z)$ in a Laurent's series about $z = a$.

Thus,
$$f(z)=\sum_{n=0}^{\infty}a_n(z-a)^n+\sum_{n=1}^{\infty}a_{-n}(z-a)^{-n}$$

$$=\sum_{n=0}^{\infty}a_n(z-a)^n+[a_{-1}(z-a)^{-1}+a_{-2}(z-a)^{-2}+\ldots\ldots+a_{-m}(z-a)^{-m}+\ldots\ldots] \quad \ldots(1)$$

If the series with negative powers has a finite number of terms, say m, so that $a_{-m}\neq 0$; $a_{-m-1}=a_{-m-2}=\ldots\ldots=0$, then $z = a$ is called a *pole of order m*. A pole of order one is called a *simple pole*.

If the series with negative powers does not terminate, *i.e.*, has an infinite number of terms, then $z = a$ is called an *essential singular point* of $f(z)$.

The co-efficient of $(z-a)^{-1}$ in the expansion of $f(z)$ about an isolated singularity $z=a$ is called the *residue* of $f(z)$ at $z=a$. Thus from equation (1), the residue of $f(z)$ at $z=a$ is a_{-1} and may be denoted by

$$a_{-1} = \text{Res}\,\{f(z), a\}$$

Since $$a_{-1} = \frac{1}{2\pi i}\oint_C f(z)\,dz$$

$\therefore$ $$\oint_C f(z)\,dz = 2\pi i a_{-1} = 2\pi i\,\text{Res}\,\{f(z), a\}.$$

4.20. RESIDUE THEOREM

If f (z) is analytic at all points inside and on a simple closed curve C, except at a finite number of isolated singular points within C, then

$$\oint_C f(z)\,dz = 2\pi i \text{ (sum of residues at singular points within C).}$$

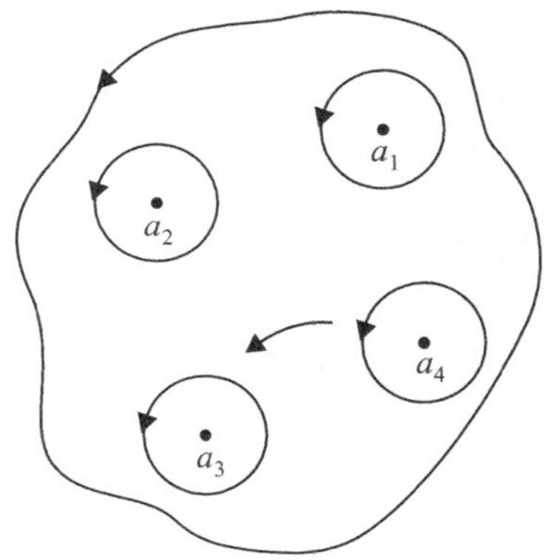

Proof. Around each of the isolated singular points $a_1, a_2, \ldots\ldots, a_n$ draw small non-intersecting circles $C_1, C_2, \ldots\ldots, C_n$ lying wholly inside C, with centres at $z = a_1, a_2, \ldots\ldots, a_n$ respectively.

Since $f(z)$ is analytic in the multiply connected region bounded by C, $C_1, C_2, \ldots\ldots, C_n$, we have by Cauchy's theorem for multiply connected region.

$$\oint_C f(z)\,dz = \oint_{C_1} f(z)\,dz + \oint_{C_2} f(z)\,dz + \ldots\ldots + \oint_{C_n} f(z)\,dz$$
$$= 2\pi i\,[\text{Res}\,\{(z), a_1\} + \text{Res}\,\{f(z), a_2\} + \ldots\ldots + \text{Res}\,\{f(z), a_n\}]$$
$$= 2\pi i \text{ (sum of residues at } a_1, a_2, \ldots\ldots, a_n).$$

4.21. CALCULATION OF RESIDUES

(1) *If $f(z)$ has a simple pole (i.e., pole of order 1) at $z=a$, then* $\text{Res}\,\{f(z), a\} = \underset{z\to a}{\text{Lt}}\,(z-a)\,f(z)$.

Since $z=a$ is a pole of order 1, the Laurent's series becomes

$$f(z) = a_0 + a_1(z-a) + a_2(z-a)^2 + \ldots\ldots + a_{-1}(z-a)^{-1}.$$

Multiplying both sides by $(z-a)$, we get

$$(z-a)\,f(z) = a_0(z-a) + a_1(z-a)^2 + a_2(z-a)^3 + \ldots\ldots + a_{-1}$$

$\therefore$ $$\underset{z\to a}{\text{Lt}}\,(z-a)\,f(z) = a_{-1} = \text{Res}\,\{f(z), a\}$$

(2) *If $f(z)$ has a pole of order m at $z=a$, then*

$$\textbf{Res}\,\{\mathbf{f(z), a}\} = \frac{1}{(m-1)!}\underset{z\to a}{\text{Lt}}\frac{d^{m-1}}{dz^{m-1}}[(z-a)^m f(z)]$$

Since $z=a$ is a pole of order m, the Laurent's series becomes

$$f(z) = a_0 + a_1(z-a) + a_2(z-a)^2 + \ldots\ldots + a_{-1}(z-a)^{-1} + a_{-2}(z-a)^{-2} + \ldots\ldots + a_{-m}(z-a)^{-m}$$

Multiplying both sides by $(z-a)^m$, we get

$$(z-a)^m f(z) = a_0(z-a)^m + a_1(z-a)^{m+1} + a_2(z-a)^{m+2} + \ldots\ldots$$
$$+ a_{-1}(z-a)^{m-1} + a_{-2}(z-a)^{m-2} + \ldots\ldots + a_{-m}$$

Differentiating both sides $(m-1)$ times w.r.t. z and taking the limit as $z \to a$, we get

$$\underset{z \to a}{\text{Lt}} \frac{d^{m-1}}{dz^{m-1}} [(z-a)^m f(z)] = a_{-1} = (m-1)\,!$$

or

$$\frac{1}{(m-1)\,!} \underset{z \to a}{\text{Lt}} \frac{d^{m-1}}{dz^{m-1}} [(z-a)^m f(z)] = a_{-1} = \text{Res}\,\{ f(z), a\}.$$

ILLUSTRATIVE EXAMPLES

Example 1. *Determine the poles of the function* $f(z) = \dfrac{z^2}{(z-1)^2(z+2)}$ *and the residue at each pole.*

Sol. The function $f(z)$ has a pole of order 2 at $z = 1$ and a simple pole at $z = -2$.

Residue of $f(z)$ at $z = 1$ is

$$\underset{z \to 1}{\text{Lt}} \frac{d}{dz} [(z-1)^2 f(z)] = \underset{z \to 1}{\text{Lt}} \frac{d}{dz}\left(\frac{z^2}{z+2}\right)$$

$$= \underset{z \to 1}{\text{Lt}} \frac{(z+2)\,.\,2z - z^2\,.\,1}{(z+2)^2} = \underset{z \to 1}{\text{Lt}} \frac{z^2+4z}{(z+2)^2} = \frac{5}{9}$$

Residue of $f(z)$ at $z = -2$ is

$$= \underset{z \to -2}{\text{Lt}} [(z+2) f(z)] = \underset{z \to -2}{\text{Lt}} \frac{z^2}{(z-1)^2} = \frac{4}{9}.$$

Example 2. *Find the sum of the residues of the function* $f(z) = \dfrac{\sin z}{z \cos z}$ *at its poles inside the circle* $|\, z \,| = 2$.

Sol. The function $f(z)$ has simple poles at $z = 0, \pm \dfrac{\pi}{2}, \pm \dfrac{3\pi}{2}, \ldots\ldots$ Of these, $z = 0, \pm \dfrac{\pi}{2}$ lie inside $|\, z \,| = 2$.

Residue of $f(z)$ at $z = 0$ is $\underset{z \to 0}{\text{Lt}} [z\,.\,f(z)] = \underset{z \to 0}{\text{Lt}} \dfrac{\sin z}{\cos z} = 0$

Residue of $f(z)$ at $z = \dfrac{\pi}{2}$ is

$$\underset{z \to \frac{\pi}{2}}{\text{Lt}} \left(z - \frac{\pi}{2}\right) f(z) = \underset{z \to \frac{\pi}{2}}{\text{Lt}} \frac{\left(z - \frac{\pi}{2}\right)\sin z}{z \cos z} \qquad \left|\; \text{Form } \frac{0}{0} \right.$$

$$= \underset{z \to \frac{\pi}{2}}{\text{Lt}} \frac{\left(z - \frac{\pi}{2}\right)\cos z + \sin z}{\cos z - z \sin z} \qquad \text{[By L' Hospital's Rule]}$$

$$= \frac{1}{-\frac{\pi}{2}} = -\frac{2}{\pi}$$

Similarly, residue of $f(z)$ at $z = -\frac{\pi}{2}$ is $\frac{2}{\pi}$.

$\therefore$ Sum of residues $= 0 - \frac{2}{\pi} + \frac{2}{\pi} = 0$.

Example 3. *Evaluate* $\oint_C \frac{e^z}{(z+1)^2} dz$, *where C is the circle* $| z - 3 | = 3$.

Sol. Here $f(z) = \frac{e^z}{(z+1)^2}$ has only one singular point $z = -1$ which is a pole of order 2 and it lies inside the circle $| z - 1 | = 3$.

Residue of $f(z)$ at $z = -1$ is $\underset{z \to -1}{\text{Lt}} \frac{d}{dz} [(z+1)^2 f(z)] = \underset{z \to -1}{\text{Lt}} \frac{d}{dz}(e^z) = \underset{z \to -1}{\text{Lt}} e^z = e^{-1}$

$\therefore$ By residue theorem, we have $\oint_C \frac{e^z}{(z+1)^2} dz = 2\pi i(e^{-1}) = \frac{2\pi i}{e}$.

Example 4. *Evaluate* $\oint_C \frac{2z-1}{z(z+1)(z-3)} dz$, *where C is the circle* $| z | = 2$.

Sol. Here $f(z) = \frac{2z-1}{z(z+1)(z-3)}$ has three simple poles at $z = 0, -1, 3$ of which only $z = 0, -1$ lie inside the circle $| z | = 2$.

Residue of $f(z)$ at $z = 0$ is $\underset{z \to 0}{\text{Lt}}\, z f(z) = \underset{z \to 0}{\text{Lt}} \frac{2z-1}{(z+1)(z-3)} = \frac{1}{3}$

Residue of $f(z)$ at $z = -1$ is $\underset{z \to -1}{\text{Lt}} (z+1) f(z) = \underset{z \to -1}{\text{Lt}} \frac{2z-1}{z(z-3)} = -\frac{3}{4}$

$\therefore$ By residue theorem,

$$\oint_C \frac{2z-1}{z(z+1)(z-3)} dz = 2\pi i \text{ (sum of residues)}$$

$$= 2\pi i \left(\frac{1}{3} - \frac{3}{4}\right) = -\frac{5\pi i}{6}.$$

Example 5. *Evaluate* $\oint_C \frac{z-3}{z^2+2z+5} dz$, *where C is the circle*

(*i*) $| z | = 1$ (*ii*) $| z + 1 - i | = 2$ (*iii*) $| z + 1 + i | = 2$.

Sol. The poles of $f(z) = \dfrac{z-3}{z^2+2z+5}$ are given by

$$z^2 + 2z + 5 = 0 \quad i.e., \quad z = \frac{-2 \pm \sqrt{4-20}}{2} = -1 \pm 2i$$

(*i*) Both the poles lie outside the circle $|z| = 1$.

$\therefore$ By Cauchy's theorem, we have $\displaystyle\oint_C \frac{z-3}{z^2+2z+5}\,dz = 0$

(*ii*) Only the pole $z = -1 + 2i$ lies inside the circle $|z + 1 - i| = 2$.

Residue of $f(z)$ at $z = -1 + 2i$ is

$$\underset{z \to -1+2i}{\text{Lt}} (z + 1 - 2i)\, f(z) = \underset{z \to \alpha}{\text{Lt}} \frac{(z-\alpha)(z-3)}{z^2+2z+5}, \text{ where } \alpha = -1 + 2i \qquad \Big|\text{ Form } \frac{0}{0}$$

$$= \underset{z \to \alpha}{\text{Lt}} \frac{(z-\alpha)+(z-3)}{2z+2} \qquad |\text{ By L' Hospital's Rule}$$

$$= \frac{\alpha-3}{2\alpha+2} = \frac{-1+2i-3}{-2+4i+2} = \frac{i-2}{2i}$$

$\therefore$ By residue theorem, $\displaystyle\oint_C \frac{z-3}{z^2+2z+5}\,dz = 2\pi i\left(\frac{i-2}{2i}\right) = \pi(i-2).$

(*iii*) Only the pole $z = -1 - 2i$ lies inside the circle $|z + 1 + i| = 2$

Residue of $f(z)$ at $z = -1 - 2i$ is

$$\underset{z \to -1-2i}{\text{Lt}} (z + 1 + 2i)\, f(z) = \underset{z \to \beta}{\text{Lt}} \frac{(z-\beta)(z-3)}{z^2+2z+5}, \text{ where } \beta = -1 - 2i \qquad \Big|\text{ Form } \frac{0}{0}$$

$$= \underset{z \to \beta}{\text{Lt}} \frac{(z-\beta)\,(z-3)}{2z+2} \qquad |\text{ By L' Hospital's Rule}$$

$$= \frac{\beta-3}{2\beta+2} = \frac{-4-2i}{-4i} = \frac{i+2}{2i}$$

$\therefore$ By residue theorem, $\displaystyle\oint_C \frac{z-3}{z^2+2z+5}\,dz = 2\pi i\left(\frac{i+2}{2i}\right) = \pi(i+2).$

Example 6. *Evaluate* $\displaystyle\oint_C \frac{e^z}{\cos \pi z}$, *where C is the unit circle* $|z| = 1$.

Sol. Here $f(z) = \dfrac{e^z}{\cos \pi z}$ has simple poles at $z = \pm\dfrac{1}{2}, \pm\dfrac{3}{2}, \pm\dfrac{5}{2}, \ldots\ldots$, of which only $z = \pm\dfrac{1}{2}$ lie inside the circle $|z| = 1$.

Residue of $f(z)$ at $z = \dfrac{1}{2}$ is

$$\underset{z \to \frac{1}{2}}{\text{Lt}} \left(z - \tfrac{1}{2}\right) f(z) = \underset{z \to \frac{1}{2}}{\text{Lt}} \frac{\left(z-\frac{1}{2}\right)e^z}{\cos \pi z} \qquad \Big|\text{ Form } \frac{0}{0}$$

$$= \underset{z \to \frac{1}{2}}{\text{Lt}} \frac{\left(z - \frac{1}{2}\right) e^z + e^z}{-\pi \sin \pi z} \quad \text{| By L' Hospital's Rule}$$

$$= \frac{e^{1/2}}{-\pi}.$$

Similarly, residue of $f(z)$ at $z = -\frac{1}{2}$ is $\frac{e^{-1/2}}{\pi}$.

$\therefore$ By residue theorem, $\oint_C \frac{e^z}{\cos \pi z} dz = 2\pi i$ (sum of residues)

$$= 2\pi i \left(-\frac{e^{1/2}}{\pi} + \frac{e^{-1/2}}{\pi} \right) = -4i \left(\frac{e^{1/2} - e^{-1/2}}{2} \right) = -4i \sinh \tfrac{1}{2}.$$

TEST YOUR KNOWLEDGE

Determine the poles of the following functions and the residue at each pole:

1. $\frac{2z+1}{z^2 - z - 2}$
2. $\frac{z+1}{z^2(z-2)}$
3. $\frac{z^2}{(z-1)(z-2)^2}$
4. $\frac{1-e^{2z}}{z^4}$
5. $\frac{e^z}{z^2 + \pi^2}$
6. $\frac{z}{\cos z}$
7. $\frac{z^2 - 2z}{(z+1)^2 (z^2+4)}$.

Find the residues at z = 0 of the following functions:

8. $z \cos \frac{1}{z}$
9. $\text{cosec}^2 z$
10. $\frac{1+e^z}{\sin z + z \cos z}$.

Evaluate the following integrals:

11. $\oint_C \frac{z^2 + 2z - 2}{z - 4} dz$, where C is a closed curve containing the point $z = 4$ in its interior.
12. $\oint_C \frac{1 - 2z}{z(z-1)(z-2)} dz$, where C is the circle $|z| = 1.5$.
13. $\oint_C \frac{z}{(z-1)(z-2)^2} dz$, where C is the circle $|z - 2| = \frac{1}{2}$.
14. $\oint_C \frac{12z - 7}{(z-1)^2 (2z+3)} dz$, where C is the circle $|z| = 2$.
15. $\oint_C \frac{\sin \pi z^2 + \cos \pi z^2}{(z-1)^2 (z-2)} dz$, where C is the circle $|z| = 3$.
16. $\oint_C \frac{z \sec z}{(1-z)^2} dz$, where C is the circle $|z| = 2$.
17. $\oint_C \frac{dz}{\sinh z}$, where C is the circle $|z| = 4$.
18. $\oint_C \tan z \, dz$, where C is the circle $|z| = 2$.

Answers

1. $z = -1, 2; \frac{1}{3}, \frac{5}{3}$ **2.** $z = 0, 2; -\frac{3}{4}, \frac{3}{4}$ **3.** $z = 1, 2; 1, 0$ **4.** $z = 0; -\frac{4}{3}$

5. $z = \pm \pi i; \pm \frac{i}{2\pi}$ **6.** $z = (2n+1)\frac{\pi}{2}; (-1)^{n+1}(2n+1)\frac{\pi}{2}$, where n is an integer.

7. $z = -1, \pm 2i; -\frac{14}{25}, \frac{7 \pm i}{25}$ **8.** $-\frac{1}{2}$ **9.** 0

10. 1 **11.** $44\pi i$ **12.** $3\pi i$

13. $-2\pi i$ **14.** 0 **15.** $4\pi i(\pi + 1)$

16. $2\pi i \sec 1(1 + \tan 1)$ **17.** $-2\pi i$ **18.** $-4\pi i$.

4.22. APPLICATION OF RESIDUES TO EVALUATE REAL INTEGRALS

The residue theorem provides a simple and elegant method for evaluating many important definite integrals of real variables. Some of these are illustrated below:

(1) Integrals of the type $\int_0^{2\pi} F(\cos\theta, \sin\theta)\, d\theta$,

where F(cos θ, sin θ) is a rational function of cos θ and sin θ.

Such integrals can be reduced to complex line integrals by the substitution $z = e^{i\theta}$, so that,

$$dz = ie^{i\theta}\, d\theta, \ i.e., \ d\theta = \frac{dz}{iz}.$$

Also,
$$\cos\theta = \frac{e^{i\theta} + e^{-i\theta}}{2} = \frac{1}{2}\left(z + \frac{1}{z}\right)$$
$$\sin\theta = \frac{e^{i\theta} + e^{-i\theta}}{2i} = \frac{1}{2i}\left(z - \frac{1}{z}\right).$$

As θ varies from 0 to 2π, z moves once round the unit circle in the anti-clockwise direction.

$$\therefore \quad \int_0^{2\pi} F(\cos\theta, \sin\theta)\, d\theta = \oint_C F\left(\frac{z+z^{-1}}{2}, \frac{z-z^{-1}}{2i}\right)\frac{dz}{iz}$$

where C is the unit circle $|z| = 1$.

The integral on the right can be evaluated by using the residue theorem.

ILLUSTRATIVE EXAMPLES

Example 1. *Evaluate* $\int_0^{2\pi} \frac{d\theta}{2 + \cos\theta}$.

Sol. Put $z = e^{i\theta}$ so that $\cos\theta = \frac{1}{2}\left(z + \frac{1}{z}\right)$ and $d\theta = \frac{dz}{iz}$

Then
$$\int_0^{2\pi} \frac{d\theta}{2 + \cos\theta} = \oint_C \frac{1}{2 + \frac{1}{2}\left(z + \frac{1}{z}\right)} \frac{dz}{iz} = \frac{2}{i}\oint_C \frac{1}{z^2 + 4z + 1}\, dz$$

where C is the circle $|z| = 1$.

The poles of the integrand are the roots of $z^2 + 4z + 1 = 0$, which are $z = -2 \pm \sqrt{3}$.

Of the two poles, only $z = -2 + \sqrt{3}$ lies inside the circle C.

Residue at $z = -2 + \sqrt{3}$ is

$$= \lim_{z \to \alpha} (z - \alpha) \frac{1}{z^2 + 4z + 1}, \quad \text{where } \alpha = -2 + \sqrt{3} \qquad \left| \text{Form } \frac{0}{0} \right.$$

$$= \lim_{z \to \alpha} \frac{1}{2z + 4} = \frac{1}{2\alpha + 4} = \frac{1}{2\sqrt{3}}$$

$\therefore$ By residue theorem, $\oint_C \frac{dz}{z^2 + 4z + 1} = 2\pi i \left(\frac{1}{2\sqrt{3}} \right) = \frac{\pi i}{\sqrt{3}}$

Hence $$\int_0^{2\pi} \frac{d\theta}{2 + \cos\theta} = \frac{2}{i} \oint_C \frac{dz}{z^2 + 4z + 1} = \frac{2}{i} \left(\frac{\pi i}{\sqrt{3}} \right) = \frac{2\pi}{\sqrt{3}}.$$

Example 2. *Evaluate* $\int_0^{2\pi} \frac{d\theta}{1 - 2a \sin\theta + a^2}$, $0 < a < 1$.

Sol. Put $z = e^{i\theta}$ so that $\sin\theta = \frac{1}{2i}\left(z - \frac{1}{z} \right)$ and $d\theta = \frac{dz}{iz}$.

Then, $$\int_0^{2\pi} \frac{d\theta}{1 - 2a \sin\theta + a^2} = \oint_C \frac{1}{1 - 2a \cdot \frac{1}{2i}\left(z - \frac{1}{z} \right) + a^2} \frac{dz}{iz}$$

$$= -\oint_C \frac{dz}{az^2 - i(a^2 + 1)z - a} = -\oint_C \frac{dz}{(az - i)(z - ia)}$$

where C is the circle $|z| = 1$.

The integrand has simple poles at $z = \frac{i}{a}$ and $z = ia$ of which only $z = ia$ lies inside the circle C. $[\because \ 0 < a < 1]$

Residue at $z = ia$ is $\lim_{z \to ia} (z - ia) \frac{1}{(az - i)(z - ia)} = \lim_{z \to ia} \frac{1}{az - i} = \frac{1}{i(a^2 - 1)}$

$\therefore$ By residue theorem,

$$\oint_C \frac{dz}{(az - i)(z - ia)} = 2\pi i \cdot \frac{1}{i(a^2 - 1)} = \frac{2\pi}{a^2 - 1}$$

Hence $$\int_0^{2\pi} \frac{d\theta}{1 - 2a \sin\theta + a^2} = -\oint_C \frac{dz}{(az - i)(z - ia)} = \frac{2\pi}{1 - a^2}.$$

Example 3. *Prove that* $\int_0^{2\pi} \frac{\sin^2\theta}{a + b\cos\theta} d\theta = \frac{2\pi}{b^2}\left(a - \sqrt{a^2 - b^2}\right)$, *where* $0 < b < a$.

Sol. Let $$I = \int_0^{2\pi} \frac{\sin^2\theta}{a + b\cos\theta} d\theta = \int_0^{2\pi} \frac{1 - \cos 2\theta}{2(a + b\cos\theta)} d\theta$$

$$= \text{Real part of } \int_0^{2\pi} \frac{1 - e^{2i\theta}}{2a + 2b\cos\theta} d\theta$$

Put $z = e^{i\theta}$ so that $\cos\theta = \frac{1}{2}\left(z + \frac{1}{z} \right)$ and $d\theta = \frac{dz}{iz}$

Then $$\int_0^{2\pi} \frac{1-e^{2i\theta}}{2a+2b\cos\theta}\,d\theta = \oint_C \frac{1-z^2}{2a+b\left(z+\dfrac{1}{z}\right)}\frac{dz}{iz} = \oint_C \frac{1-z^2}{i(bz^2+2az+b)}\,dz$$

where C is the circle $|z| = 1$.

The poles of the integrand are the roots of $bz^2 + 2az + b = 0$, *viz.*

$$z = \frac{-2a \pm \sqrt{4a^2-4b^2}}{2b} = \frac{-a \pm \sqrt{a^2-b^2}}{b}$$

Let $$\alpha = \frac{-a+\sqrt{a^2-b^2}}{b} \quad \text{and} \quad \beta = \frac{-a-\sqrt{a^2-b^2}}{b}$$

Clearly $|\beta| > 1$ so that $z = \alpha$ is the only simple pole inside C.

Also $\quad bz^2 + 2az + b = b(z-\alpha)(z-\beta)$

Residue at $z = \alpha$ is

$$\underset{z\to\alpha}{\text{Lt}}\ (z-\alpha)\,.\,\frac{1-z^2}{ib(z-\alpha)(z-\beta)} = \underset{z\to\alpha}{\text{Lt}}\ \frac{1-z^2}{ib(z-\beta)} = \frac{1-\alpha^2}{ib(\alpha-\beta)}$$

$$= \frac{\alpha\left(\dfrac{1}{\alpha}-\alpha\right)}{ib(\alpha-\beta)} = \frac{\alpha(\beta-\alpha)}{ib(\alpha-\beta)} \qquad [\because \ \alpha\beta = 1]$$

$$= -\frac{\alpha}{ib} = \frac{a-\sqrt{a^2-b^2}}{ib^2}$$

$\therefore$ By residue theorem,

$$\oint_C \frac{1-z^2}{i(bz^2+2az+b)}\,dz = 2\pi i\,.\,\frac{a-\sqrt{a^2-b^2}}{ib^2} = \frac{2\pi}{b^2}\left(a-\sqrt{a^2-b^2}\right)$$

Hence I = Real part of $\displaystyle\oint_C \frac{1-z^2}{i(bz^2+2az+b)}\,dz = \frac{2\pi}{b^2}\left(a-\sqrt{a^2-b^2}\right)$.

Example 4. *Evaluate* $\displaystyle\int_0^{\pi} \frac{d\theta}{a+b\cos\theta}$, *where* $a > |b|$.

Sol. Since $$\int_0^{2a} f(x)\,dx = 2\int_0^{a} f(x)\,dx, \text{ if } f(2a-x) = f(x)$$

$$\therefore \quad \int_0^{2\pi} \frac{d\theta}{a+b\cos\theta} = 2\int_0^{\pi} \frac{d\theta}{a+b\cos\theta} \qquad [\because \ \cos(2\pi-\theta) = \cos\theta]$$

or $$\int_0^{\pi} \frac{d\theta}{a+b\cos\theta} = \frac{1}{2}\int_0^{2\pi} \frac{d\theta}{a+b\cos\theta} \qquad \ldots(1)$$

Putting $z = e^{i\theta}$, so that $\cos\theta = \dfrac{1}{2}\left(z+\dfrac{1}{z}\right)$ and $d\theta = \dfrac{dz}{iz}$, we have

$$\int_0^{2\pi} \frac{d\theta}{a+b\cos\theta} = \oint_C \frac{1}{a+\dfrac{b}{2}\left(z+\dfrac{1}{z}\right)}\frac{dz}{iz} = \oint_C \frac{2dz}{i(bz^2+2az+b)}$$

where C is the circle $|z| = 1$.

Proceeding as in example 3, residue at $z = \alpha$ is

$$= \underset{z \to \alpha}{\text{Lt}} (z - \alpha) \cdot \frac{2}{ib(z-\alpha)(z-\beta)} = \underset{z \to \alpha}{\text{Lt}} \frac{2}{ib(z-\beta)} = \frac{2}{ib(\alpha - \beta)}$$

$$= \frac{2}{ib} \cdot \frac{b}{2\sqrt{a^2 - b^2}} = \frac{1}{i\sqrt{a^2 - b^2}}$$

$\therefore$ By residue theorem,

$$\oint_C \frac{2dz}{i(bz^2 + 2az + b)} = 2\pi i \cdot \frac{1}{i\sqrt{a^2 - b^2}} = \frac{2\pi}{\sqrt{a^2 - b^2}}$$

Hence from (1), $\displaystyle\int_0^\pi \frac{d\theta}{a + b\cos\theta} = \frac{\pi}{\sqrt{a^2 - b^2}}$.

(2) Integrals of the type $\int_{-\infty}^{\infty} \frac{f(x)}{F(x)} dx$, where f(x) and F(x) are polynomials in x such that $\frac{x f(x)}{F(x)} \to 0$ as $x \to \infty$ and F(x) has no zeros on the real axis.

Consider the integral $\oint_C \frac{f(z)}{F(z)} dz$ over the closed contour C consisting of the real axis from – R to R and the semi-circle C_1 of radius R in the upper half plane.

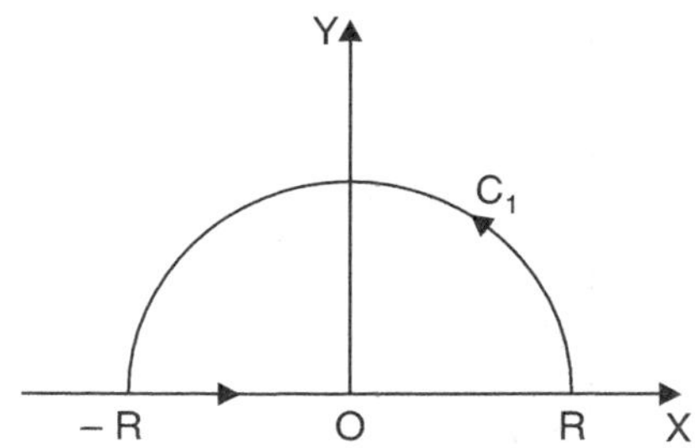

We take R large enough so that all the poles of $\frac{f(z)}{F(z)}$ in the upper half plane lie within C.

By residue theorem, we have

$$\oint_C \frac{f(z)}{F(z)} dz = 2\pi i \left[\text{sum of the residues of } \frac{f(z)}{F(z)} \text{ in the upper half plane}\right]$$

or $$\oint_{C_1} \frac{f(z)}{F(z)} dz + \int_{-R}^{R} \frac{f(x)}{F(x)} dx = 2\pi i \left[\text{sum of the residues of } \frac{f(z)}{F(z)} \text{ in the upper half plane}\right] \quad ...(1)$$

($\because$ on the real axis, $z = x$)

If we put $z = Re^{i\theta}$ in the first integral on the left side, then R is constant on C_1 and as z moves along C_1, θ varies from 0 to π.

$$\therefore \quad \int_{C_1} \frac{f(z)}{F(z)} dz = \int_0^\pi \frac{f(Re^{i\theta})}{F(Re^{i\theta})} Re^{i\theta} \, i\, d\theta$$

For large R, $\displaystyle\left|\int_0^\pi \frac{f(Re^{i\theta})}{F(Re^{i\theta})} Re^{i\theta}\, i d\theta\right| \to 0$ $\quad\Big|$ is of the order $\frac{Rf(R)}{F(R)}$

$$\therefore \quad \int_0^\pi \frac{f(Re^{i\theta})}{F(Re^{i\theta})} Re^{i\theta}\, i d\theta \to 0 \text{ when } R \to \infty$$

Hence from (1), we have $\displaystyle\int_{-\infty}^{\infty} \frac{f(x)}{F(x)} dx = 2\pi i$

$$\left[\text{Sum of the residues of } \frac{f(z)}{F(z)} \text{ in the upper half plane}\right].$$

Example 5. *Evaluate* $\int_{-\infty}^{\infty} \frac{x^2}{(x^2+a^2)(x^2+b^2)}\, dx\ (a > 0,\ b > 0)$.

Sol. The poles of $\phi(z) = \frac{z^2}{(z^2+a^2)(z^2+b^2)}$ are $z = \pm\, ia, \pm\, ib$.

Of these, $z = ia$ and $z = ib$ lie in the upper half of the z-plane.

Residue of $\phi(z)$ at $z = ia$ is

$$\underset{z\to ia}{\text{Lt}}\ (z-ia)\,.\frac{z^2}{(z^2+a^2)(z^2+b^2)} = \underset{z\to ia}{\text{Lt}}\ \frac{z^2}{(z+ia)(z^2+b^2)} = \frac{-a^2}{2ia(-a^2+b^2)} = \frac{a}{2i(a^2-b^2)}$$

Residue of $\phi(z)$ at $z = ib$ is

$$\underset{z\to ib}{\text{Lt}}\ (z-ib)\,.\frac{z^2}{(z^2+a^2)(z^2+b^2)} = \underset{z\to ib}{\text{Lt}}\ \frac{z^2}{(z^2+a^2)(z+ib)} = \frac{-b^2}{(-b^2+a^2)(2ib)} = \frac{-b}{2i(a^2-b^2)}$$

$$\therefore \quad \int_{-\infty}^{\infty} \frac{x^2\, dx}{(x^2+a^2)(x^2+b^2)} = 2\pi i\ [\text{sum of residues of } \phi(z) \text{ in the upper half of } z\text{-plane}]$$

$$= 2\pi i\left[\frac{a}{2i(a^2-b^2)} - \frac{b}{2i(a^2-b^2)}\right] = \pi\left[\frac{a-b}{a^2-b^2}\right] = \frac{\pi}{a+b}.$$

Example 6. *Evaluate* $\int_0^{\infty} \frac{dx}{x^4+1}$.

Sol. The poles of $\phi(z) = \frac{1}{z^4+1}$ are obtained by solving $z^4 + 1 = 0$.

Now $\quad z^4 + 1 = 0.$

$$\Rightarrow \quad z = (-1)^{1/4} = (\cos \pi + i \sin \pi)^{1/4} = [\cos (2n\pi + \pi) + i \sin (2n\pi + \pi)]^{1/4}$$

$$= \cos \frac{(2n+1)\pi}{4} + i \sin \frac{(2n+1)\pi}{4} \qquad \text{(By De Moivre's theorem)}$$

where $n = 0, 1, 2, 3$.

When $n = 0$, $\quad z = \cos \frac{\pi}{4} + i \sin \frac{\pi}{4} = \frac{1}{\sqrt{2}} + i\frac{1}{\sqrt{2}}$

When $n = 1$, $\quad z = \cos \frac{3\pi}{4} + i \sin \frac{3\pi}{4} = -\frac{1}{\sqrt{2}} + i\frac{1}{\sqrt{2}}$

When $n = 2$, $\quad z = \cos \frac{5\pi}{4} + i \sin \frac{5\pi}{4} = -\frac{1}{\sqrt{2}} - i\frac{1}{\sqrt{2}}$

When $n = 3$, $\quad z = \cos \frac{7\pi}{4} + i \sin \frac{7\pi}{4} = \frac{1}{\sqrt{2}} - i\frac{1}{\sqrt{2}}$

Of these, only the poles corresponding to $n = 0, 1$, *viz*, $z = e^{i\frac{\pi}{4}}$ and $z = e^{3i\frac{\pi}{4}}$ lie in the upper half of z-plane.

Residue of $\phi(z)$ at $z = e^{i\frac{\pi}{4}}$ is $\underset{z \to e^{i\frac{\pi}{4}}}{\text{Lt}} \dfrac{z - e^{i\frac{\pi}{4}}}{z^4 + 1}$ | Form $\dfrac{0}{0}$

$$= \underset{z \to e^{i\frac{\pi}{4}}}{\text{Lt}} \frac{1}{4z^3} \quad \text{| By L' Hospital's rule}$$

$$= \frac{1}{4e^{3i\frac{\pi}{4}}} = \frac{1}{4} e^{-3i\frac{\pi}{4}}$$

Similarly, residue of $\phi(z)$ at $z = e^{3i\frac{\pi}{4}}$ is $\frac{1}{4} e^{-9i\frac{\pi}{4}}$

$$\therefore \int_0^\infty \frac{dx}{x^4 + 1} = \frac{1}{2} \int_{-\infty}^\infty \frac{dx}{x^4 + 1}$$

$$= \frac{1}{2} \,.\, 2\pi i \text{ [sum of residues of } \phi(z) \text{ in the upper half of } z\text{-plane]}$$

$$= \pi i \left[\frac{1}{4} e^{-3i\frac{\pi}{4}} + \frac{1}{4} e^{-9i\frac{\pi}{4}}\right] = \frac{1}{4} \pi i \left[\left(\cos\frac{3\pi}{4} - i \sin\frac{3\pi}{4}\right) + \left(\cos\frac{9\pi}{4} - i \sin\frac{9\pi}{4}\right)\right]$$

$$= \frac{1}{4} \pi i \left[-\frac{1}{\sqrt{2}} - \frac{i}{\sqrt{2}} + \frac{1}{\sqrt{2}} - \frac{i}{\sqrt{2}}\right] = \frac{1}{4} \pi i(-i\sqrt{2}) = \frac{\pi\sqrt{2}}{4}.$$

Note. The above method can also be applied to some cases where $f(x)$ contains trigonometric functions also.

Example 7. *Evaluate* $\displaystyle\int_0^\infty \frac{\cos ax}{x^2 + 1} dx, a \geq 0.$ (M.G.U., May 2008)

Sol. Since cos ax is the real part of e^{iax}, we consider the function $\phi(z) = \dfrac{e^{iaz}}{z^2 + 1}$

This has poles at $z = \pm i$, of which only $z = i$ lies in the upper half of z-plane.

Residue of $\phi(z)$ at $z = i$ is $\underset{z \to i}{\text{Lt}} \dfrac{(z - i)e^{iaz}}{z^2 + 1} = \underset{z \to i}{\text{Lt}} \dfrac{(z - i)e^{iaz}}{(z + i)(z - i)} = \underset{z \to i}{\text{Lt}} \dfrac{e^{iaz}}{z + i} = \dfrac{e^{-a}}{2i}$

$$\therefore \quad \oint_C \frac{e^{iaz}}{z^2 + i} dz = 2\pi i \,.\, \frac{e^{-a}}{2i} = \pi e^{-a} \quad \text{...(1)}$$

where C is the contour.

On the semi-circle C_1, $z = Re^{i\theta}$.

$$\therefore \quad z \,.\, \frac{e^{iaz}}{z^2 + 1} = Re^{i\theta} \,.\, \frac{e^{ia R(\cos\theta + i \sin\theta)}}{R^2 e^{2i\theta} + 1} = \frac{(e^{ia R\cos\theta} e^{i\theta})\, e^{-a R \sin\theta}\, R^{-1}}{e^{2i\theta} + R^{-2}}$$

which $\to 0$ as $R \to \infty$, since

$$| e^{iaR\cos\theta} . e^{i\theta} | = | \cos(\theta + aR\cos\theta) + i\sin(\theta + aR\cos\theta) | \le 1,$$
$$| e^{-aR\sin\theta} | \le 1, \; | e^{2i\theta} + R^{-2} | \ne 0 \quad \text{and} \quad R^{-1} \to 0$$

$\therefore$ The integral over C_1 vanishes and (1) gives $\int_{-\infty}^{\infty} \frac{e^{iax}}{x^2+1} dx = \pi e^{-a}$

Equating real parts, we get $\int_{-\infty}^{\infty} \frac{\cos ax}{x^2+1} dx = \pi e^{-a}$

Hence $\int_0^{\infty} \frac{\cos ax}{x^2+1} dx = \frac{1}{2}\int_{-\infty}^{\infty} \frac{\cos ax}{x^2+1} dx = \frac{\pi e^{-a}}{2}$.

(3) Integrals of the type $\int_{-\infty}^{\infty} \frac{f(x)}{F(x)} dx$, when F(x) has zeros on the real axis.

In such cases we proceed in a manner similar to above, axcept that the singularities on the real axis are enclosed in small semi-circles to avoid their inclusion in C, *i.e.*, the contour C is indented at these singularities.

Example 8. *Evaluate* $\int_0^{\infty} \frac{\sin mx}{x} dx, m > 0.$

Sol. Since $\sin mx$ is the imaginary part of e^{imx}, we consider the function

$$\phi(z) = \frac{e^{imz}}{z}.$$

This has a simple pole at $z = 0$, which lies on the real axis. Enclose this singularity by a small semi-circle $C_2 : | z | = r$. Evaluate the function $\phi(z)$ over the contour C shown in the figure consisting of parts of the real axis from $-R$ to $-r$ and r to R, the small semi-circle C_2 and the large semi-circle C_1. Since the function has no singularity within this contour, by Cauchy's theorem, we have

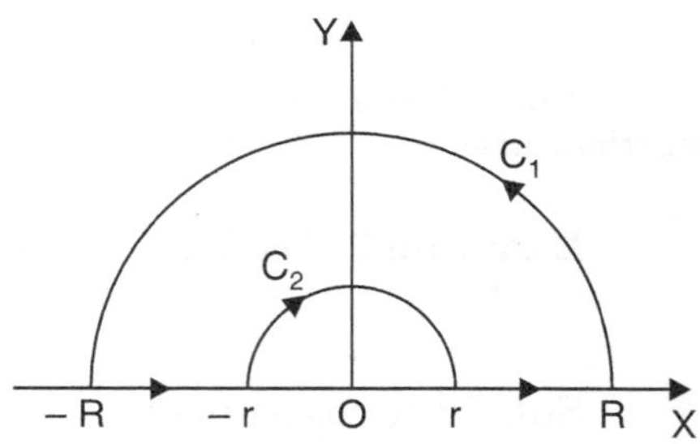

$$\oint_C \phi(z)\, dz = 0$$

$$\Rightarrow \quad \int_{-R}^{-r} \phi(x)\,dx + \int_{C_2} \phi(z)\,dz + \int_r^R \phi(x)\,dx + \int_{C_1} \phi(z)\,dz = 0$$

$$\Rightarrow \quad \int_{-R}^{-r} \frac{e^{imx}}{x} dx + \int_{C_2} \frac{e^{imz}}{z} dz + \int_r^R \frac{e^{imx}}{x} dx + \int_{C_1} \frac{e^{imz}}{z} dz = 0 \qquad \text{...(1)}$$

Substituting $-x$ for x in the first integral and combining it with the third integral, we get

$$\int_r^R \frac{e^{imx} - e^{-imx}}{x} dx + \int_{C_2} \frac{e^{imz}}{z} dz + \int_{C_1} \frac{e^{imz}}{z} dz = 0$$

or

$$2i\int_r^R \frac{\sin mx}{x} dx + \int_{C_2} \frac{e^{imz}}{z} dz + \int_{C_1} \frac{e^{imz}}{z} dz = 0 \qquad \text{...(2)}$$

Now $$\int_{C_2} \frac{e^{imz}}{z} dz = \int_{C_2} \frac{1}{z} dz + \int_{C_2} \frac{e^{imz} - 1}{z} dz \qquad ...(3)$$

On C_2, $z = re^{i\theta}$

$$\therefore \quad \int_{C_2} \frac{1}{z} dz = \int_{\pi}^{0} \frac{re^{i\theta} i\, d\theta}{re^{i\theta}} = - \int_{0}^{\pi} i d\theta = - i\pi$$

Also $$\left| \int_{C_2} \frac{e^{imz} - 1}{z} dz \right| \le M \int_{C_2} \frac{|dz|}{|z|} = \pi M$$

where M is the maximum value on C_2 of $| e^{imz} - 1 | = | e^{imr(\cos\theta + i \sin\theta)} - 1 |$

Clearly, $M \to 0$ as $r \to 0$

$$\therefore \text{ From (3), } \int_{C_2} \frac{e^{imz}}{z} dz = - i\pi \qquad ...(4)$$

Putting $z = Re^{i\theta}$ in the integral over C_1, we get

$$\int_{C_1} \frac{e^{imz}}{z} dz = \int_0^{\pi} \frac{e^{imR(\cos\theta + i\sin\theta)}}{Re^{i\theta}} Re^{i\theta}\, i\, d\theta = i \int_0^{\pi} e^{imR\cos\theta} . e^{-mR\sin\theta}\, d\theta$$

Since $$| e^{imR\cos\theta} | \le 1$$

$$\therefore \quad \left| \int_{C_1} \frac{e^{imz}}{z} dz \right| \le \int_0^{\pi} e^{-mR\sin\theta}\, d\theta = 2\int_0^{\pi/2} e^{-mR\sin\theta}\, d\theta$$

Also $\dfrac{\sin\theta}{\theta}$ continually decreases from 1 to $\dfrac{2}{\pi}$ as θ increases from 0 to $\dfrac{\pi}{2}$.

$$\therefore \quad \text{For } 0 \le \theta \le \frac{\pi}{2}, \frac{\sin\theta}{\theta} \ge \frac{2}{\pi} \quad \text{or} \quad \sin\theta \ge \frac{2\theta}{\pi}$$

$$\therefore \quad \left| \int \frac{e^{imz}}{z} dz \right| \le 2 \int_0^{\pi/2} e^{-2mR\theta/\pi} d\theta = \left[- \frac{\pi}{mR} e^{-2mR\theta/\pi} \right]_0^{\pi/2} = \frac{\pi}{mR}(1 - e^{-mR})$$

As $R \to \infty$, $\dfrac{\pi}{mR}(1 - e^{-mR}) \to 0$

$$\therefore \quad \int_{C_1} \frac{e^{imz}}{z} dz = 0$$

Hence from (2), on taking the limit as $r \to 0$ and $R \to \infty$, we get

$$2i \int_0^{\infty} \frac{\sin mx}{x} dx - i\pi = 0 \quad \text{or} \quad \int_0^{\infty} \frac{\sin mx}{x} dx = \frac{\pi}{2}.$$

TEST YOUR KNOWLEDGE

Evaluate the following integrals by contour integration:

1. $\int_0^{2\pi} \frac{d\theta}{5 - 3\cos\theta}$ (*M.G.U. May 2009*)
2. $\int_0^{2\pi} \frac{d\theta}{a + b\sin\theta}$, where $a > |b|$
3. $\int_0^{\pi} \frac{\cos 3\theta}{5 - 4\cos\theta}\, d\theta$
4. $\int_0^{2\pi} \frac{\cos 2\theta}{5 + 4\cos\theta}\, d\theta$
5. $\int_0^{2\pi} \frac{d\theta}{1 - 2p\cos\theta + p^2}$, $0 < p < 1$
6. $\int_0^{2\pi} \frac{\cos 2\theta\, d\theta}{1 - 2p\cos\theta + p^2}$, $0 < p < 1$
7. $\int_0^{\pi} \frac{a\, d\theta}{a^2 + \sin^2\theta}$
8. $\int_0^{\infty} \frac{dx}{(x^2 + 1)^2}$
9. $\int_{-\infty}^{\infty} \frac{dx}{x^4 + 1}$
10. $\int_0^{\infty} \frac{dx}{x^6 + 1}$
11. $\int_{-\infty}^{\infty} \frac{dx}{(x^2 + a^2)(x^2 + b^2)}$
12. $\int_{-\infty}^{\infty} \frac{x^2 - x + 2}{x^4 + 10x^2 + 9}\, dx$
13. $\int_0^{\infty} \frac{x^2\, dx}{(x^2 + 9)(x^2 + 4)^2}$
14. $\int_0^{\infty} \frac{x\sin x}{x^2 + a^2}\, dx, a > 0$
15. $\int_{-\infty}^{\infty} \frac{\cos x}{(x^2 + a^2)(x^2 + b^2)}\, dx, a > b > 0$
16. $\int_0^{\infty} \frac{\sin mx}{x(x^2 + a^2)}\, dx, m > 0, a > 0$
17. $\int_0^{2\pi} \frac{d\theta}{(5 - 3\cos\theta)^2}$
18. $\int_{-\infty}^{\infty} \frac{x^2}{(x^2 + 1)(x^2 + 4)}\, dx$
19. $\int_0^{\infty} \frac{\cos x}{x}\, dx$
20. $\int_{-\infty}^{\infty} \frac{\sin x}{x^2 + 4x + 5}\, dx.$
21. Using contour integration evaluate $\int_{-\infty}^{\infty} \frac{dx}{(x^2 + a^2)^2}, a > 0.$

Answers

1. $\frac{\pi}{2}$
2. $\frac{2\pi}{\sqrt{a^2 - b^2}}$
3. $\frac{\pi}{24}$
4. $\frac{\pi}{6}$
5. $\frac{2\pi}{1 - p^2}$
6. $\frac{2\pi p^2}{1 - p^2}$
7. $\frac{\pi}{\sqrt{1 + a^2}}$
8. $\frac{\pi}{4}$
9. $\frac{\pi}{\sqrt{2}}$
10. $\frac{\pi}{3}$
11. $\frac{\pi}{ab(a + b)}$
12. $\frac{5\pi}{12}$
13. $\frac{\pi}{200}$
14. $\frac{1}{2}\pi e^{-a}$
15. $\frac{\pi}{a^2 - b^2}\left(\frac{e^{-b}}{b} - \frac{e^{-a}}{a}\right)$
16. $\frac{\pi}{2a^2}(1 - e^{-ma})$
17. $\frac{5\pi}{32}$
18. $\frac{\pi}{3}$
19. 0
20. $\frac{-\pi\sin 2}{e}$
21. $\frac{\pi}{2}\frac{e^{-a}}{a^3}(1 + a).$

MODULE 5
Queuing Theory

5.1. INTRODUCTION

A group of customers/items waiting at some place to receive attention/service including those receiving the service is known as queue. Queuing models are based on the concept of queues where number of customers is waiting for processing. Some examples of queuing models are Railway reservation system, Telephone lines, Bank, Post offices, Petrol pumps, Hospitals etc.

Waiting line problems are generated because there is too much demand, which leads to excess waiting time or large amount of idle time.

Components of Queuing Model: There are various components of queuing model:

(*i*) *Customer:* The main component of queuing model is customer who is utilizing the service. We consider two facilities with the reference of customers, arrival of customers and service of customers.

(*ii*) *Queue:* We maintain arrival of customers in a queue. In a queue there are two conditions: queue under flow and queue overflow.

(*iii*) *Service Channel:* A system which is performing the services of customer is service channel. It may be single channel or it may be multi channel.

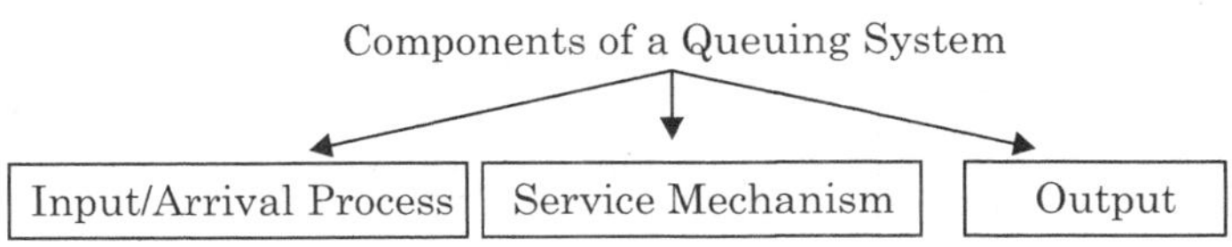

5.2. CHARACTERISTIC OF QUEUING MODEL

(*i*) Input Distribution or Arrival Distribution
(*ii*) Output Distribution or Service Distribution
(*iii*) Service Channel
(*iv*) Queue Discipline
(*v*) Queue Size
(*vi*) Population of Source

Input Process: Input is the mode of arrivals of customers at the service facility. The number of customers emanate from finite or infinite sources. Typically customers arrive at the system randomly single or in batches. The input process is characterized by the nature of the arrivals, capacity of the system and the behaviour of the customer.

Customer Behaviour:

(*i*) **Balking:** A customer may not like to join the queue seeing it very long and he may not like to wait.

(*ii*) **Reneging:** He may leave the queue due to impatience after joining it.

(*iii*) **Collusion:** Several customers may collaborate and only one of them may stand in the queue.

(*iv*) **Jockeying:** If there are number of queues then one may leave the queue to join another.

Service Mechanism/Facility:

- Single channel single phase queue

Input → Queue → Service → Output → Departure

- Single channel k-phase queue

Input → Queue → Service I → Service II →......→ Service K → Output → Departure

- Multi channel single phase queue:

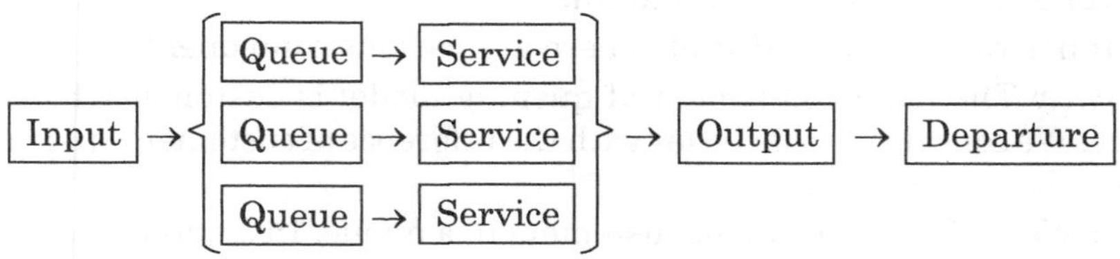

- Multi channel multi phase queue:

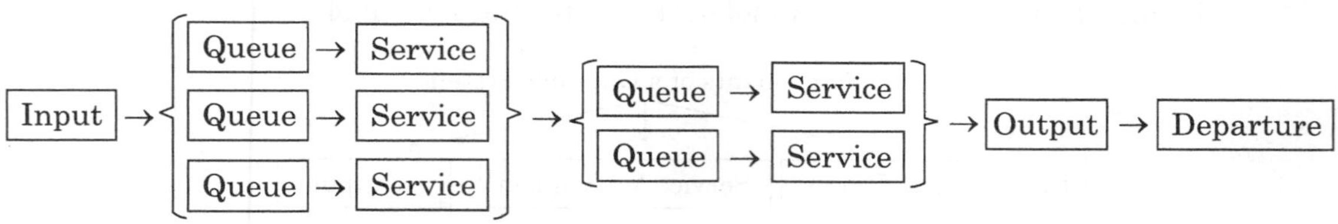

Queue Discipline: Queue discipline is the order in which customers get service. We can consider two types of queue discipline:

- Static queue discipline
- Dynamic queue discipline.

1. ***Static queue discipline:*** In this discipline the customers are served in static manner. Some of these are:

FCFS/FIFO: First Come First Serve/ First In First Out: In this discipline, a customer who is arrived first will serve first in the queue.

LCFS/LIFO: Last Come First Serve/ Last In First Out: In this a customer who is arrived recently (last), will get service first.

2. ***Dynamic queue discipline:*** In this discipline some attributes of customer dynamically change. Some of these are:

Random Order Service: In this customers get service randomly. Any customer can get service at any time.

Priority Based Service: We assign a priority to each customer from 1 to n. If priority '1' is highest priority then a customer who has the highest priority will get service first.

Priority based service is of 2 types:

1. **Non-pre-emptive priority:** If the entering customer's priority is high as compare to the customer who is getting service then new customer has to wait until the service completion of that existing customer.

2. **Pre-emptive priority:** If the priority of new entered customer is high then the lower priority customer's service is interrupted and the high priority customer's get service immediately.

5.3. TRANSIENT AND STEADY STATE OF THE SYSTEM

The analysis of queuing model is based on the behaviour of the system. There exist two types of states in the system: one state that varies with the time, *i.e.,* depend upon the time and the other state that is independent of time. The state in which the behaviour of the system depends upon time is said as 'transient state'. In most systems the transient state occurs during the initial stages of operation where the system behaviour depends upon the initial conditions.

The other state in which the behaviour of system does not depend on time is termed as 'steady state'.

If the average arrival rate is greater than the average service rate then there will be number of customers that will wait in the queue. If the average arrival rate is less than the average service rate then system will remain idle for a long time, when the arrival and service rates are constant. The system settles down to a steady state and finding the probability of the length of queue will same at any time.

5.4. WAITING TIME AND IDLE TIME

Waiting time is the time that a process waits for, like resource allocation, setup time etc. Idle time is that the processor is idle, there is no process to execute. With the reference of these times, we can calculate the cost.

Let C_w = Expected waiting cost/unit/unit time

L_s = Expected average number of units in the system/unit time

C_f = Cost of servicing one unit

So the expected waiting cost/unit time $= C_w \cdot L_s = C_w \cdot \dfrac{\lambda}{\mu - \lambda}$

Expected service cost/unit time $= C_f \cdot \mu$

Therefore total cost $C = C_w \cdot \dfrac{\lambda}{\mu - \lambda} + C_f \cdot \mu$

This optimum cost will be minimum if $\dfrac{d}{d\mu}(C) = 0$.

i.e., $\mu = \lambda \pm \sqrt{\dfrac{C_w}{C_f} \cdot \lambda}$. Negative value of μ is not considerable.

5.5. KENDALL'S NOTATION FOR QUEUING MODELS

D.G. Kendall and later A. Lee represented queuing models by various notations. These notations are as follows:

$$(a/b/c) : (d/e/f)$$

where a – arrival distribution
b – departure distribution
c – number of parallel service channels
d – service discipline
e – maximum number of customers in the system
f – population (source)

Arrival and departure distribution can be represented as:

E_k – Erlang or gamma inter arrival/service time distribution with parameter K.
M – Markov or Poisson arrival/departure distribution or exponential inter arrival/ service time distribution
GI – General independent arrival distribution
G – General departure distribution
D – Deterministic inter arrival/service time.

The service discipline may be considered as:

FCFS/FIFO – First Come First Serve/First In First Out
LCFS/LIFO – Last Come First Serve/Last In First Out
SIRO – Service In Random Order
GD – General Service Discipline.

Maximum number of customers in the system and population of source may be finite (N) or infinite (∞).

Variables used in Queuing Formulae:

$\lambda \rightarrow$ Mean number of arrivals per time (Arrival rate)
$\mu \rightarrow$ Mean number of customers served (Service rate)
$\frac{1}{\lambda} \rightarrow$ Mean time between arrivals
$\frac{1}{\mu} \rightarrow$ Mean time per customer served
$\rho \rightarrow \frac{\lambda}{\mu}$ [traffic intensity] or [utilization factor]
$L_s \rightarrow$ Average number of customers in the system
$L_q \rightarrow$ Average number of customers in the waiting line or queue
$W_s \rightarrow$ Time spent in line and the time spent being served
$W_q \rightarrow$ Average time a customer spends waiting in the queue
$n \rightarrow$ Number of customers in the service system
$P_n \rightarrow$ Probability that there are n customers in the system.

5.6. MODEL 1. {(M/M/1): (∞/FCFS)}

Exponential service unlimited queue.

This model is based on certain assumptions about the queuing system:

(*i*) Arrivals are described by Poisson probability distribution and come from an infinite population.

(*ii*) Single waiting line and each arrival waits to be served regardless of the length of queue and no balking.

(*iii*) Queue discipline is 'first-come, first served'.

(*iv*) Single server and service times follow exponential distribution.

(*v*) Customers arrival is independent but the arrival rate does not change from time to time.

(*vi*) The average service rate is more than the average arrival rate ($\mu > \lambda$).

5.7. MODEL 2. {(M/M/1): (N/FCFS)}

Exponential service–Finite queue:

This model is different from model 1 in respect of capacity of the system. Here N customers can be accommodated at anytime in the system.

Assumptions of this model are same as that of model 1 except that the length of queue is limited. Here the service rate does not have to exceed arrival rate ($\mu > \lambda$) in order to obtain steady state conditions.

Problem. *Consider a hotel in which the mean arrival rate is one customer every 5 minutes and mean service time is 3 minutes. If the waiting cost is ₹ 5 per unit per minute and the cost of servicing one unit is ₹ 4. Find the minimum cost service rate?*

Sol. Mean arrival rate $\lambda = \frac{1}{5} = 0.2$

Waiting cost $C_w =$ ₹ 5 per unit per minute

Service cost $C_f =$ ₹ 4

Minimum cost service rate $\mu = \lambda \pm \sqrt{\frac{C_w}{C_f} \cdot \lambda}$

$\mu = 0.2 \pm \sqrt{\frac{5}{4} \times 0.2} = 0.2 \pm \frac{1}{2} = 0.70$ units/minutes (by taking positive quantity).

5.8. QUEUING FORMULA

Some queuing formula are given below that are used in queuing model to calculate the different parameters.

Let λ be the mean arrival rate and μ be the mean service rate, then:

(*i*) Traffic intensity (utilization factor)

$$\rho = \frac{\lambda}{\mu}.$$

(*ii*) Probability of an empty/ideal system

$$= P_0 = 1 - \rho = 1 - \frac{\lambda}{\mu}.$$

(*iii*) Probability of server being busy/the arriving customer has to wait

$$= 1 - P_0 = \frac{\lambda}{\mu} = \rho.$$

(*iv*) Probability of 'n' units in the system

$$= P_n = P_0\rho^n = \rho^n(1 - \rho) = \left(\frac{\lambda}{\mu}\right)^n \left(1 - \frac{\lambda}{\mu}\right).$$

(*v*) Average number of units in the system

$$L_s = \sum_{n=0}^{\infty} n \, . \, P_n = \sum_{n=0}^{\infty} n \, . \, P_0 \left(\frac{\lambda}{\mu}\right)^n = \frac{\lambda}{\mu - \lambda}.$$

or $$L_s = \frac{\rho}{1-\rho}.$$

(*vi*) Average length of the queue L_q = (Expected number in the system–Expected number in service).

$$L_q = \frac{\lambda}{\mu - \lambda} - \frac{\lambda}{\mu} = \frac{\lambda^2}{\mu(\mu - \lambda)} \quad \text{or} \quad \frac{\rho^2}{1-\rho}.$$

(*vii*) Average length of non-empty queue/ The average length of queue that form from time to time = $L_b = \dfrac{\mu}{\mu - \lambda}$ (or) $\dfrac{1}{1-\rho}$.

(*viii*) Probability that the number of customers in the system exceeds K/Probability that at least K customers in the system = $P(N > K) = \left(\dfrac{\lambda}{\mu}\right)^{K+1}$.

(*ix*) Average waiting time of an arrival (Queue)

$$W_q = \frac{\text{Expected number in the queue}}{\text{Expected rate of arrival}}$$

$$W_q = \frac{\dfrac{\lambda^2}{\mu}(\mu - \lambda)}{\lambda} = \frac{\lambda}{\mu(\mu - \lambda)}.$$

(*x*) Average waiting time of an arrival who waits (System)

$$W_s = \frac{\text{Expected number in the system}}{\text{Expected rate of arrival}} = \frac{\dfrac{\lambda}{\mu} - \lambda}{\lambda}$$

$$W_s = \frac{1}{\mu - \lambda}.$$

(*xi*) Average time an arrival spends in system = $\dfrac{1}{\mu - \lambda}$.

(*xii*) Probability that the waiting time of a customer in the system exceeds t.

$$P(W_s > t) = e^{-(\mu - \lambda)t}.$$

(*xiii*) Probability that the queue size is greater than or equal to k.

$$P(n \geq k) = \sum_{n=0}^{\infty} P_n - (P_0 + P_1 + \cdots + P_{k-1}) = \left\{P_0 + \frac{\lambda}{\mu} P_0 + \cdots + \left(\frac{\lambda}{\mu}\right)^{k-1} P_0\right\}$$

$$P(n \geq k) = 1 - P_0 \frac{\left\{1 - \left(\dfrac{\lambda}{\mu}\right)^k\right\}}{\left\{1 - \left(\dfrac{\lambda}{\mu}\right)\right\}} = \left(\frac{\lambda}{\mu}\right)^k . \text{(or) } \rho^k \text{; and } P(n > k) = \left(\frac{\lambda}{\mu}\right)^{k+1} = \rho^{k+1}$$

(*xiv*) Average length of the queue/queue is always available $= \dfrac{\mu}{\mu - \lambda}$.

(*xv*) Probability that at least n customers in the system $= \rho^{n+1}$.

(*xvi*) The variance (fluctuation) of queue length is

$$\text{Var}(n) = \frac{\rho}{(1-\rho)^2} = \frac{\lambda\mu}{(\mu-\lambda)^2}.$$

(*xvii*) Probability that waiting time is more than t

$$P(x > t) = \begin{cases} (\mu-\lambda)e^{-(\mu-\lambda)t} & \text{(System)} \\ \dfrac{\lambda}{\mu}(\mu-\lambda)\, e^{-(\mu-\lambda)t} & \text{(Queue)} \end{cases}$$

5.9. LITTLE'S FORMULA

Let us find the relationship between L_s, L_q, W_s and W_q.

From the above formulae it is seen that

$$L_s = \lambda \cdot W_s \qquad L_q = \lambda \cdot W_q$$

$$W_s = W_q + \frac{1}{\mu} \qquad L_s = L_q + \frac{\lambda}{\mu}.$$

ILLUSTRATIVE EXAMPLES

Example 1. *A television repair man finds that the time spent on his jobs has an exponential distribution with a mean of 30 minutes. If he repairs sets in the order in which they came in, and if the arrival of sets follows a Poisson distribution approximately with an average rate of 10 per 8 hour day, what is the repairman's expected idle time each day? How many jobs are ahead of the average set just brought in?*

Sol. Arrival rate $\lambda = \dfrac{10}{8} = \dfrac{5}{4}$ sets/hr.

Service rate $\mu = \dfrac{1}{30} \times 60 = 2$ sets/hr.

(*a*) $\rho = \dfrac{\lambda}{\mu} = \dfrac{5}{8}$.

Expected idle time in an 8 hr day

$$= 8P_0 = 8 \times (1-\rho) = 8 \times \left(1 - \frac{5}{8}\right) = 3 \text{ hrs.}$$

(*b*) Expected number of TV sets in the system

$$= L_s = \frac{\lambda}{\mu - \lambda} = \frac{\frac{5}{4}}{2 - \frac{5}{4}} = \frac{5}{3} \approx 2 \text{ sets.}$$

Example 2. *On an average 96 patients per 24 hour day require the service of an emergency clinic. Also on an average, a patient requires 10 minutes of active attention. Assume that the facility can handle only one emergency at a time. Suppose that it costs the clinic ₹ 100 per patient treated to obtain an average servicing time of 10 minutes, and that each minute of decrease in this average time would cost ₹ 10 per patient treated. How much would have to be budgeted by the clinic to decrease the average size of the queue from one and one-third patient to half a patient?*

Sol. Arrival rate $\lambda = \dfrac{96}{24 \times 60} = \dfrac{1}{15}$

Service rate $\mu = \dfrac{1}{10}$ patients/minutes.

$$\rho = \frac{\lambda}{\mu} = \frac{10}{15} = \frac{2}{3}.$$

(*a*) Average number of patients in the queue

$$= L_q = \frac{\rho^2}{1-\rho} = \frac{\left(\frac{2}{3}\right)^2}{1-\frac{2}{3}} = \frac{4}{3} = 1\frac{1}{3}.$$

(*b*) P(idle system) $= P_0 = 1 - \rho = 1 - \dfrac{2}{3} = \dfrac{1}{3}.$

(*c*) When L_q is decreased from $1\frac{1}{3}$ to $\frac{1}{2}$, new $\mu = \mu'$.

$$L_q = \frac{\lambda^2}{\mu(\mu-\lambda)} \Rightarrow \frac{1}{2} = \frac{\left(\frac{1}{15}\right)^2}{\mu'\left(\mu' - \frac{1}{15}\right)}. \quad \therefore \quad \mu = \frac{2}{15} \text{ patients/ minutes.}$$

Therefore average rate of treatment required is $\dfrac{1}{\mu} = \dfrac{15}{2} = 7.5$ minutes/patients.

Therefore decrease in the average rate of treatment = 10 – 7.5 = 2.5 minutes.

Budget/patient = ₹ 100 + ₹ 10 × 2.5 = 100 + 25 = 125

Hence in order to decrease the average size of the queue, the budget should be increased from ₹ 100 to ₹ 125 per patient.

Example 3. *Customers arrive at a one window drive according to a Poisson distribution with mean of 10 minutes and service time per customer is exponential with mean of 6 minutes. The space in front of the window can accommodate only three vehicles including the serviced one. Other vehicles have to wait outside this space. Calculate.*

(*a*) *Probability that an arriving customer can drive directly to the space in front of the window.*

(*b*) *Probability that an arriving customer will have to wait outside the directed space.*

(*c*) *How long an arriving customer is expected to wait before getting the service?*

Sol. Arrival rate λ = 6 customers/hr.

Service rate μ = 10 customers/hr.

$$\rho = \frac{\lambda}{\mu} = \frac{6}{10} = \frac{3}{5} = 0.6.$$

(*a*) P[an arriving customer can drive directly to the space in front of the window]

$$= P_0 + P_1 + P_2 = (1 - \rho) + \rho(1 - \rho) + \rho^2(1 - \rho) = 0.784.$$

(*b*) P[an arriving customer will have to wait outside the directed space]

$$= 1 - (P_0 + P_1 + P_2) = 1 - 0.784 = 0.216.$$

(*c*) Expected waiting time of customer before getting the service

$$W_q = \frac{l}{\mu(\mu - \lambda)} = \frac{6}{10(10 - 6)} = \frac{3}{20} \text{ hr} = 9 \text{ min}.$$

Example 4. *In a railway marshalling yard, goods trains arrive at a rate of 30 trains per day. Assuming that the inter-arrival time follows an exponential distribution and the service time (the time taken to hump a train) distribution is also exponential with an average of 36 minutes. Calculate:*

(*a*) *Expected queue size (line length)*

(*b*) *Probability that the queue size exceeds 10.*

If the input of trains increases to an average of 33 trains per day, what will be the change in (a) and (b)?

Sol. Arrival rate $\lambda = \frac{30}{60 \times 24} = \frac{1}{48}$

Service rate $\mu = \frac{1}{36}$ train/minute.

$$\rho = \frac{\lambda}{\mu} = \frac{36}{48} = 0.75.$$

(*a*) Expected queue size $L_q = \frac{\rho^2}{1 - \rho}$ $\quad \therefore \quad L_q = \frac{\rho^2}{1 - \rho} = 2.25 \approx 3$ trains

(*b*) P(queue size ≥ 10) $\quad \rho^{10} = (0.75)^{10} = 0.06.$

If input increases to 33 trains/day,

$$\lambda = \frac{33}{60 \times 24} \qquad \mu = \frac{1}{36} \qquad \rho = \frac{\lambda}{\mu} = 0.83.$$

Then (*a*) $\quad L_q = \frac{\rho^2}{1 - \rho} = \frac{0.83^2}{1 - 0.83} \approx 5$ trains

(*b*) P(queue size ≥ 10) = $\rho^{10} = (0.83)^{10} \approx 0.2.$

Example 5. *Arrivals at telephone booth are considered to be Poisson with an average time of 10 minutes between one arrival and the next. The length of phone call is assumed to be distributed exponentially, with mean 3 minutes.*

(*a*) *What is the probability that a person arriving at the booth will have to wait?*

(*b*) *The telephone department will install a second booth when convinced that an arrival would expect waiting for at least 3 minutes for a phone call. By how much should the flow of arrivals increases in order to justify a second booth?*

(*c*) *What is the average length of the queue that forms from time to time?*

(*d*) *Find the average number of customers in the system.*

(*e*) *What is the probability that it will take him more than 10 minutes altogether to wait for the phone and complete his call?*

Sol. Arrival rate $\lambda = \dfrac{1}{10}$

Service rate $\mu = \dfrac{1}{3}$ $\rho = \dfrac{\lambda}{\mu} = \dfrac{3}{10} = 0.3.$

(*a*) P[a person has to wait at the booth] $= 1 - P_0 = \rho = 0.3$

(*b*) The installation of second booth will be justified only if the arrival rate is more than the waiting time. Let λ' be the increased arrival rate. Then expected waiting time in the queue will be:

$$W_q = \frac{\lambda'}{\mu(\mu - \lambda')} \Rightarrow 3 = \frac{\lambda'}{\frac{1}{3}\left(\frac{1}{3} - \lambda'\right)} \Rightarrow \lambda' = 0.16$$

Hence increase in the arrival rate is = 0.16 – 0.10 = 0.06/min.

(*c*) Average length of non empty queue

$$L_b = \frac{\mu}{\mu - \lambda} \approx 2 \text{ customers.}$$

(*d*) Average number of customers in the system

$$L_s = \frac{\lambda}{\mu - \lambda} = \frac{0.10}{0.33 - 0.10} \approx 1.$$

(*e*) P(waiting for 10 minutes or more)

$$P(t \geq 10) = \int_{10}^{\infty} \frac{\lambda}{\mu}(\mu - \lambda)\, e^{-(\mu - \lambda)t}\, dt = 0.069 \left[\frac{e^{-0.23t}}{-0.23}\right]_{10}^{\infty} = 0.03.$$

$\Rightarrow$ 3% of arrivals will have to wait for more than 10 minutes.

Example 6. *A hospital employs one person at its registration counter. Nine patients arrive on an average every 4 minutes while the person can serve (register) 10 patients in 4 minutes. Assuming Poisson Distribution for arrival rate and Exponential distribution for service rate, find:*

(*i*) Average number of patients in the system.

(*ii*) Average number of patients in queue.

(*iii*) Average time a patient spends in the system.

(*iv*) Average time a patient waits before being registered.

Sol. Arrival rate $\lambda = \dfrac{9}{4} = 2.25$ patients/minutes.

Service rate $\mu = \dfrac{10}{4} = 2.50$ patients/minutes.

(*i*) Average number of patients in the system

$$L_s = \frac{\lambda}{\mu - \lambda} = \frac{2.25}{2.50 - 2.25} = 8.$$

(*ii*) Average number of patients in queue

$$L_q = \frac{\lambda}{\mu}\frac{\lambda}{\mu-\lambda} = \frac{2.25^2}{2.50(2.50-2.25)} = 8.1.$$

(*iii*) Average time a patient spends in the system

$$W_s = \frac{1}{\mu-\lambda} = \frac{1}{2.50-2.25} = 4.$$

(*iv*) Average time a patient waits before being registered

$$W_q = \frac{1}{\mu}\frac{\lambda}{\mu-\lambda} = \frac{\lambda}{\mu(\mu-\lambda)} = \frac{2.25}{2.50(2.50-2.25)} = 3.6 \text{ minutes.}$$

Example 7. *A branch of Punjab National Bank has only one typist. Since the typing work varies in length (number of pages to be typed), the typing rate is randomly distributed approximating a Poisson distribution with mean service rate of 8 letters per hour. The letters arrive at a rate of 5 per hour during the entire 8 hour work day. If the type writer is valued at ₹ 1.50 per hour, determine:*

(*i*) *Equipment utilization*

(*ii*) *The % time that an arriving letter has to wait*

(*iii*) *Average system time*

(*iv*) *Average cost due to waiting on the part of type writer.*

Sol. Arrival rate $\lambda = 5$/hour

Service rate $\mu = 8$/hour.

(*i*) Equipment utilization $\rho = \frac{\lambda}{\mu} = \frac{5}{8} = 0.625.$

(*ii*) The % time that an arriving letter has to wait = % time the type writer remains busy = 62.5%.

(*iii*) Average system time = $W_s = \frac{1}{\mu-\lambda} = \frac{1}{8-5} = \frac{1}{3}$ hr = 20 min.

(*iv*) Average cost due to waiting on the part of type writer per day

$$= 8 \times \left(1 - \frac{5}{8}\right) \times 1.50 = ₹\ 4.50.$$

Example 8. *A person repairing watches finds that the time spent on the watches has been exponential distribution with mean 20 min. If the watches are repaired in order in which they come in and their arrival is Poisson with an average rate of 10 for 5 hour day. What is the repairman's expected idle time each day? How many jobs are ahead of the average set just brought in?*

Sol. Arrival rate $\lambda = \frac{10}{5} = 2\text{hr} = \frac{2}{60} = \frac{1}{30}$ units/min.

Service rate $\mu = \frac{1}{20}$ units/min.

Number of jobs ahead to the set brought in = Average number of jobs in the system

$$= L_s = \frac{\lambda}{\mu-\lambda} = \frac{1/30}{1/20 - 1/30} = \frac{60}{30} = 2.$$

Number of hours for which the repairman remains busy in an 5 hour day

$$= 5 \times \rho = 5 \times \frac{\lambda}{\mu} = 5 \times \frac{1/30}{1/20} = 3.3 \text{ hours.}$$

Therefore time for which the repairman remains idle in a 5 hour day

$$= 5 - 3.3 = 1.7 \text{ hours.}$$

Example 9. *Arrival rate of telephone calls at a telephone booth are according to Poisson distribution, with an average time of 9 minutes between two consecutive arrivals. The length of telephone call is assumed to be exponentially distributed with mean 3 minutes.*

(*a*) *Determine the probability that a person arriving at the booth will have to wait.*

(*b*) *Find the average queue length that is formed from time to time.*

(*c*) *The telephone company will install a second booth when convinced that an arrival would expect to have to wait at least 4 minutes for the phone. Find the increase in flow of arrivals which will justify a second booth.*

(*d*) *What is the probability that an arrival will have to wait for more than 10 minutes before the phone is free?*

(*e*) *What is the probability that he will have to wait for more than 10 minutes before the phone is available and the call is also complete?*

(*f*) *Find the fraction of a day that the phone will be in use?*

Sol. Arrival rate $\lambda = \frac{1}{9}$ per min

Service rate $\mu = \frac{1}{3}$ per min

(*a*) Probability that a person will have to wait

$$= \rho = \frac{\lambda}{\mu} = \frac{1/9}{1/3} = \frac{1}{3} = 0.33.$$

(*b*) Average queue length

$$= \frac{\mu}{\mu - \lambda} = \frac{1/3}{1/3 - 1/9} = \frac{1/3}{2/9} = 1.5 \text{ persons.}$$

(*c*) Average waiting time in the queue = 4 (given)

$$\therefore \qquad 4 = \frac{\lambda_1}{\mu} \cdot \frac{1}{(\mu - \lambda_1)} = \frac{\lambda_1}{1/3} \cdot \frac{1}{(1/3 - \lambda_1)}$$

$$\frac{1}{9} - \frac{\lambda_1}{3} = \frac{\lambda_1}{4} \text{ or } \lambda_1 \times \frac{7}{12} = \frac{1}{9}$$

$$\lambda_1 = \frac{4}{21} \text{ arrivals/ minutes.}$$

Therefore increase in flow of arrivals $= \frac{4}{21} - \frac{1}{9} = \frac{5}{63}$ per minutes.

(*d*) Here waiting time ≥ 10.

So the probability $= \int_{10}^{\infty} \left(1 - \frac{\lambda}{\mu}\right). \lambda. e^{(\lambda - \mu)t} . dt = \left(1 - \frac{\lambda}{\mu}\right)\lambda \left[\frac{e^{(\lambda - \mu)t}}{\lambda - \mu}\right]_{10}^{\infty}.$

$$= \frac{\lambda}{\mu} e^{(\lambda - \mu)^{10}} = \frac{1}{3} . e^{-20/9} = \frac{1}{30}.$$

(*e*) Probability (when time in system ≥ 10) $= \int_{10}^{\infty} (\mu - \lambda) . e^{(\lambda - \mu)t} . dt.$

$$= e^{(\lambda - \mu)10} = e^{-20/9} = 0.1$$

(*f*) The expected fraction of a day that the phone will be in use $= \rho = \frac{\lambda}{\mu} = \frac{1}{3} = 0.33.$

Example 10. *Workers come to tool store room to receive special tools (required by them) for accomplishing a particular project assigned to them. The average time between 2 arrivals in 60 seconds and the arrivals are assumed to be in Poisson distribution. The average service time (of the tool room attendant) is 40 seconds. Determine:*

(*a*) *Average queue length.*

(*b*) *Average length of non-empty queues.*

(*c*) *Average number of workers in system including the worker being attended*

(*d*) *Mean waiting time of an arrival*

(*e*) *Average waiting time of an arrival (worker) who waits and*

(*f*) *The type of policy to be established. In other words, determine whether to go in for an additional tool store room attendant which will minimize the combined cost for attendants 'idle time and the cost of workers' waiting time. Assume the charges of a skilled worker ₹ 4 per hour and that of tool store room attendant ₹ 0.75 per hour.*

Sol. Arrival rate $\lambda = \frac{1}{60}$ per sec = 1 per min

Service rate $\mu = \frac{1}{40}$ per sec = 1.5 per min.

(*a*) Average queue length

$$= L_q = \frac{\lambda}{\mu} \frac{\lambda}{\mu - \lambda} = \frac{1}{1.5\,(1.5 - 1)} = \frac{1}{0.75} = \frac{4}{3} \text{ workers.}$$

(*b*) Average length of non-empty queue

$$= L_n = \frac{\mu}{\mu - \lambda} = \frac{1.5}{(1.5 - 1)} = \frac{1.5}{0.50} = 3 \text{ workers.}$$

(*c*) Average number of workers in system

$$L_s = \frac{\lambda}{\mu - \lambda} = \frac{1}{1.5 - 1} = 2 \text{ workers.}$$

(*d*) Mean waiting time of an arrival

$$= W_q = \frac{1}{\mu} \frac{\lambda}{\mu - \lambda} = \frac{1}{1.5(1.5 - 1)} = \frac{4}{3} \text{ minutes.}$$

(*e*) Average waiting time of an arrival who waits

$$= W_n = \frac{1}{\mu - \lambda} = \frac{1}{(1.5 - 1)} = 2 \text{ minutes.}$$

(*f*) Probability that the tool room attendant remains idle

$$= P_0 = 1 - \frac{\lambda}{\mu} = 1 - \frac{1}{1.5} = \frac{1}{3}.$$

Therefore idle time cost of one attendant $= \frac{1}{3} \times 8 \times 0.75 =$ ₹ 2/day.

Waiting time cost of workers = W_q × no. of workers arriving/day × cost of worker

$$= \left(\frac{4}{3} \times \frac{1}{60}\right) \times (8 \times 60) \times 4 = \frac{128}{3} = \text{₹ } 42.67/\text{day}.$$

As the waiting time cost is much higher than the idle time cost, it is justified to employ an additional tool room attendant.

Example 11. *At a public telephone booth in a Post office, arrivals are considered to be Poisson with an average inter arrival time of 12 minutes. The length of a phone call may be assumed to be distributed exponentially with an average of 4 minutes. Calculate the following:*

(*a*) *What is the probability that a fresh arrival will not have to wait for the phone?*

(*b*) *What is the probability that an arrival will have to wait more than 10 minutes before the phone is free?*

(*c*) *What is the average length of queue that form from time to time?*

Sol. Arrival rate $\lambda = \frac{1}{12} = 0.085/\text{min}$

Service rate $\mu = \frac{1}{4} = 0.25/\text{min}$ $\rho = \frac{\lambda}{\mu} = \frac{4}{12} = 0.33.$

(*a*) P(arrival will not have to wait) $= P_0 = 1 - \rho = 1 - 0.33 = 0.67$

(*b*) P(an arrival have to wait for a least 10 minutes)

$$= P(t \geq 10) = \int_{10}^{\infty} \frac{\lambda}{\mu} (\mu - \lambda)\, e^{-(\mu - \lambda)t}\, dt = 0.054 \left[\frac{e^{-0.165t}}{-0.165}\right]_{10}^{\infty} = 0.063.$$

⇒ 6.3 % of the arrivals on an average will have to wait of more than 10 minutes before they can use the phone.

(*c*) The average length of queue that form from time to time

$$= L_b = \frac{\mu}{\mu - \lambda} = \frac{0.25}{0.25 - 0.085} \approx 2 \text{ customers.}$$

Example 12. *A foreign bank is considering opening a drive in window for customer service. Management estimates that customers will arrive for service at the rate of 12 per hour. The teller, whom it is considering to staff the window, can serve customers at the rate of one every 3 minutes. Assuming Poisson arrivals and exponential service, find:*

(*a*) *Utilization of teller.*

(*b*) *Average number in the system*

(*c*) *Average waiting time in the line, and*

(*d*) *Average waiting time in the system?*

Sol. Arrival rate $\lambda = 12$ customer/hr.

Service rate $\mu = \frac{1}{3} \times 60 = 20$ customer/hr $\quad \rho = \frac{\lambda}{\mu} = \frac{12}{20} = 0.60$

(*a*) Utilization of the teller $= \rho = 0.60 = 60\%$.

(*b*) Average number in the system $= L_s$

$$L_s = \frac{\rho}{1-\rho} = \frac{0.60}{1-0.60} = 1.5.$$

(*c*) Average waiting time in the line

$$= W_q = \frac{\lambda}{\mu(\mu-\lambda)} = \frac{12}{20 \times 8} = 0.075 \text{ hr}$$

(*d*) Average waiting time in the system

$$= W_s = \frac{1}{(\mu-\lambda)} = \frac{1}{20-12} = 0.125 \text{ hr}.$$

5.10. MODEL 3. {(M/M/1): (N/FCFS)}: SINGLE SERVER, FINITE (OR LIMITED) QUEUE MODEL

$$P_0 = \frac{1-\rho}{1-\rho^{N+1}}; \rho \neq 1 \text{ and } \rho < 1; \rho = \frac{\lambda}{\mu}.$$

$$P_n = \begin{cases} \left(\dfrac{1-\rho}{1-\rho^{N+1}}\right)\rho^n; 0 \le n \le N; \rho \neq 1. \\ \dfrac{1}{N+1}; \rho = 1 (\lambda = \mu) \end{cases}$$

(*i*) Expected number of customers in the system

$$L_s = \sum_{n=1}^{N} nP_n = \sum_{n=1}^{N} n\left(\frac{1-\rho}{1-\rho^{N+1}}\right)\rho^n = \begin{cases} \dfrac{\rho}{1-\rho} - \dfrac{(N+1)\rho^{N+1}}{1-\rho^{N+1}}; \rho \neq 1 \\ \dfrac{N}{2}; \rho = 1 (\lambda = \mu) \end{cases}$$

(*ii*) Expected queue length or expected number of customers waiting in the system

$$L_q = L_s - \frac{\lambda}{\mu}.$$

(*iii*) Expected waiting time of a customer in the system (waiting + service)

$$W_s = \frac{L_s}{\lambda(1-P_N)} \quad \text{where} \quad P_N = P_0\left(\frac{\lambda}{\mu}\right)^N$$

(*iv*) Expected waiting time of a customer in the queue is:

$$W_q = W_s - \frac{1}{\mu} = \frac{L_q}{\lambda(1-P_N)}.$$

Example 13. *At a one man barber shop, the customers arrive according to Poisson process at the average rate of 5 per hour and they are served according to exponential distribution with an average source rate of 10 mts. There are only 5 seats available for the waiting of customers and the customers do not wait if they find no seat available. Find the average number of customers in the system, average queue length and the average time a customer spends in the barber shop. Also find the ideal time of the barber.*

Sol. Given N = 5.

$\lambda = 5$ per hour. $\mu = 10$ mts/person.

(*i*) Probability of system is idle

$$= P_0 = \frac{1 - \frac{\lambda}{\mu}}{1 - \left(\frac{\lambda}{\mu}\right)^{N+1}} = \frac{\left(1 - \frac{5}{6}\right)}{1 - \left(\frac{5}{6}\right)^{5+1}} = 0.2505 = 25.05\%.$$

(*ii*) Average number of customers in the system

$$= L_s = \frac{\rho}{1-\rho} - \frac{(N+1)\rho^{N+1}}{1-\rho^{N+1}} = \frac{5/6}{1-(5/6)} - \frac{(5+1)(5/6)^{5+1}}{1-(5/6)^{5+1}}$$

$$= 5 - \frac{6 \times 5^6}{6^6 - 5^6} = 5 - \frac{93750}{46656 - 15625} = 5 - \frac{93750}{31031} = 5 - 3.021 = 1.979.$$

or
$$L_s = \sum_{n=1}^{N} nP_n = \sum_{n=1}^{N} nP_0\rho^n = P_0 \sum_{n=1}^{N} n\rho^n = (0.2505) \sum_{n=1}^{5} n\frac{5^n}{6} = 1.979.$$

(*iii*) Average queue length

$$= L_q = L_s - \frac{\lambda}{\mu} = 1.979 - \frac{5}{6} = 1.146.$$

(*iv*) Average waiting time in the queue

$$= W_s = \frac{L_s}{\lambda(1 - P_N)}$$

For that
$$P_N = P_0 \times \left(\frac{\lambda}{\mu}\right)^N = (0.2505) \times \left(\frac{5}{6}\right)^5 = 0.1006.$$

Now
$$W_s = \frac{L_s}{\lambda(1-P_N)} = \frac{1.979}{5(1-0.1006)} = \frac{1.979}{4.497} = 0.44.$$

Example 14. *In a godown, materials arrive at the door every 20 minutes in a period of 2 hours (i.e., 10.00 am to 12.00 pm.). but the service rate continues to remain 36 minutes.*

(*a*) *Find the probability that the godown is empty.*

(*b*) *Average number of materials in the system. (Assume that the capacity is only 4 rooms).*

Sol. Given N = 4, $\lambda = \frac{1}{20}$ per min $\mu = \frac{1}{36}$ per min.

(*a*) Probability that the godown is empty

$$= P_0 = \frac{1-\rho}{1-\rho^{N+1}} = \frac{1-\frac{36}{20}}{1-\frac{36^{4+1}}{20}} = \frac{1-1.8}{1-1.8^5} = 0.045.$$

(*b*) Average number of materials in the system

$$= L_s = P_0 \sum_{n=1}^{4} n\rho^n = P_0(\rho + 2\rho^2 + 3\rho^3 + 4\rho^4) = 0.045(67.77) = 3.049 \approx 3.$$

Example 15. *In a railway marshalling yard, goods trains arrive at the rate of 30 trains per day. Assume that the inter arrival time follows an exponential distribution and the service time is also to be assumed as exponential with mean of 36 minutes. Calculate:*

(*a*) *The probability that the yard is empty.*

(*b*) *The average queue length assuming that the line capacity of the yard is 9 trains.*

Sol. Given N = 9 $\quad \lambda = \frac{30}{60 \times 24} = \frac{1}{48} \quad \mu = \frac{1}{36} \quad \rho = \frac{\lambda}{\mu} = \frac{36}{48} = 0.75.$

(*a*) P[the yard is empty] $= P_0 = \frac{1-\rho}{1-\rho^{N+1}} = \frac{1-0.75}{1-(0.75)^{10}} = 0.28.$

(*b*) Average queue length $= L_s = P_0 \sum_{n=1}^{9} n\rho^n = 0.28 \times \sum_{n=1}^{9} n(0.75)^n \approx 3$ trains.

Example 16. *Assuming for a period of 2 hrs (8 – 10 a.m) trains arrive at the yard every 20 minutes, but the service time countinues to remain 36 minutes. Then calculate for this period:*

(*a*) *the probability that the yard is empty.*

(*b*) *average queue length assuming that the capacity of the yard is 4 trains only.*

Sol. Given N = 4 $\quad \lambda = \frac{1}{20} \quad \mu = \frac{1}{36} \quad \rho = \frac{\lambda}{\mu} = \frac{36}{20} = 1.8 > 1.$

(*a*) $P_0 = \frac{1-\rho}{1-\rho^{N+1}} = \frac{\rho-1}{\rho^{N+1}-1} = \frac{1.8-1}{(1.8)^5-1} = 0.04.$

(*b*) Average queue size $= L_s = P_0 \sum_{n=1}^{4} n\rho^n = 0.04 \times \sum_{n=1}^{4} n(1.8)^n = 2.71 \approx 3$ trains.

Example 17. *Consider a single server queuing system with Poisson input, exponential service times. Suppose the mean arrival rate is 3 calling units per hour, the expected service time is 0.25 hr and the maximum permissible calling units in the system is two. Derive the steady-state probability distribution of the number of calling units in the system, and then calculate the expected number in the system?*

Sol. Given N = 2 $\quad \lambda = 3$ units/hr $\quad \mu = 0.25$ hr $= 4$ units/hr

$$\rho = \frac{\lambda}{\mu} = \frac{3}{4} = 0.75.$$

The steady-state probability distribution of the number of 'n' customers (calling units) in the system is P_n.

$$P_n = P_0\rho^n$$

$$P_0 = \frac{1-\rho}{1-\rho^{N+1}} = \frac{1-0.75}{1-(0.75)^3} = 0.43$$

$\therefore$ $$P_n = P_0\rho^n = (0.43)\,(0.75)^n.,\ n = 0,\ 1,\ 2.$$

The expected number of calling units in the system

$$= L_s = P_0 \sum_{n=1}^{2} n\rho^n = 0.43 \times \sum_{n=1}^{2} n(0.75)^n = 0.80625$$

Example 18. *At a railway station, only one train is handled at a time. The railway yard is sufficient only for two trains to wait while other is given singal to leave the station. Trains arrive at the station on an average rate of 6 per hour and the railway station can handle them on an average of 12 per hour. Assuming Poisson arrivals and exponential service distribution, find the steady state probabilities for the various number of trains in the system. Also find the average waiting time of a new train coming into the yard?*

Sol. Given N = 3 (Max queue length = 2. Therefore N = 2 + 1)

$$\lambda = 6 \qquad \mu = 12 \qquad \rho = \frac{\lambda}{\mu} = \frac{1}{2} = 0.5$$

(*a*) $$P_0 = \frac{1-\rho}{1-\rho^{N+1}} = \frac{1-0.5}{1(0.5)^4} = 0.53$$

$$P_n = P_0\rho^n$$

$$P_1 = P_0\rho = 0.53 \times \frac{1}{2} = 0.265$$

$$P_2 = P_0\rho^2 = 0.53 \times \left(\frac{1}{2}\right)^2 = 0.1325$$

$$P_3 = P_0\rho^3 = 0.53 \times \left(\frac{1}{2}\right)^3 = 0.0663$$

(*b*) $$L_s = P_0 \sum_{n=1}^{3} n\rho^n = 0.53 \times \sum_{n=1}^{3} n\left(\frac{1}{2}\right)^n = 0.72875 \approx 1 \text{ train.}$$

Average waiting time of a new train

$$W_s = \frac{L_s}{\lambda} = \frac{0.72875}{6}\text{ hr} = \frac{0.72875}{6} \times 60 = 7.2875 \text{ min.}$$

Example 19. *A petrol station has a single pump and space for not more than 3 cars (2 waiting, 1 being served). A car arriving when the space is filled to capacity goes elsewhere for petrol. Cars arrive according to a Poisson distribution at a mean rate of one every 8 minutes. Their service time has an exponential distribution with a mean for 4 minutes. The owner has the opportunity of renting and adjacent piece of land, which would provide space for an additional car to wait. The rent would be ₹ 100 per week. The expected net profit from each customer is ₹ 5 and the station is open 10 hours everyday. Would it be profitable to rent the additional space?*

Sol. Given N = 3 $\lambda = \frac{1}{8}$ per minute $\mu = \frac{1}{4}$ per minute

$$\rho = \frac{\lambda}{\mu} = \frac{4}{8} = 0.5$$

$$P_0 = \frac{1-\rho}{1-\rho^{N+1}} = \frac{1-0.5}{1-(0.5)^4} = 0.53.$$

P_3 = P(the system is full) = $P_0\rho^3 = 0.53(0.5)^3 = 0.067$.

If maximum number of car in the system is increased to four, *i.e.* N = 4 , then

$$P_0 = \frac{1-\rho}{1-\rho^{N+1}} = \frac{1-0.5}{1-(0.5)^5} = 0.516.$$

P_4 = P(the system is full) = $P_0\rho^4 = 0.516(0.5)^4 = 0.032$.

The increase in cars served per hour

$$= \lambda\,[0.067 - 0.032] = \frac{1}{8} \times 0.035 = 0.0043 \text{ cars/min.}$$

$$= 0.0043 \times 60 = 0.262 \text{ car/hr.}$$

Increase in cars served per week = 0.262 × 10 × 7 = 18.34. (approx. 19 cars.)

Thus increase in profit per week = 18.34 × 5 = ₹ 91.7

Rent for additional space would be ₹ 100 per week, therefore it is not economical to increase the existing space.

Example 20. *A barber shop has space to accommodate only 10 customers. He can serve only one person at a time. If a customer comes to his shop and finds it full he goes to the next shop. Customers randomly arrive at an average rate λ = 10 per hour and the barber service time is negative exponential with an average of* $\frac{1}{\mu} = 5$ *minutes per customer. Find* P_0, P_n?

Sol. Given N = 10

$$\lambda = \frac{10}{60} = \frac{1}{6} \qquad \frac{1}{\mu} = 5 \; i.e., \mu = \frac{1}{5} \qquad \rho = \frac{\lambda}{\mu} = \frac{5}{6}.$$

$$P_0 = \frac{1-\rho}{1-\rho^{N+1}} = \frac{1-\frac{5}{6}}{1-\left(\frac{5}{6}\right)^{11}} = 0.1926.$$

$$P_n = P_0\rho^n = (0.1926)\left(\frac{5}{6}\right)^n ; n = 0, 1, \ldots, 10.$$

TEST YOUR KNOWLEDGE

1. Write a note on characteristics of queuing system.
2. What are single and multiple channel facilities?
3. What are transient and steady states of queuing systems?
4. Describe $M/M/1/\infty$. queue.
5. Customers arrive at a booking office window, being manned by a single individual at the rate of 25 per hour. Time requires to serve a customer has exponential distribution with a mean of 120 seconds. Find the average waiting time of customers.
6. In bank with every 15 minutes, one customer arrives for cashing the cheque. The staff in payment counter caters 10 minutes for serving a customer on an average. State suitable assumptions and find:
   (*a*) the average queue length.
   (*b*) increase in the arrival rate in order to justify a second counter (when the waiting time of a customer is at least 15 minutes, the management will increase one more counter).
7. A petrol station has a single pump and space for not more than 3 cars (two waiting and one being served). A car arriving, when the space is filled to capacity, goes elsewhere for petrol. Cars arrive according to a Poisson distribution at a mean rate of one every 8 minutes. Their service time has an exponential distribution with a mean of 4 minutes. The proprietor has the opportunity of renting an adjacent piece of land, which would provide space for an additional car to wait. The rent would be ₹ 0.50 and the station is open 10 hrs every day. Would it be projetable to rent the additional space?